Four Problems
   in Teaching English:
   A Critique of Research

Four Problems
in Teaching English:
A Critique of Research

J. STEPHEN SHERWIN

Professor of English
State University of New York
College at Buffalo

Published for the

NATIONAL COUNCIL OF TEACHERS OF ENGLISH

by

INTERNATIONAL TEXTBOOK COMPANY

Scranton, Pennsylvania

LIBRARY
The University of Texas
At San Antonio

Library of Congress Catalog Card Number: 78-76405

Standard Book Number 7002 2214 6

Preface

This book assumes that education is both art and science. Without depreciating the role of artistic creativity, one can say that education could be improved by generous injections of whatever rigorous, objective inquiry can provide.

The profession needs to push back its frontiers. But first it must know where its frontiers are. More carefully than ever, the profession must attend to the job of informing its practitioners of the results of past researches. To interpret what is known about a few selected topics is the purpose of this book.

The key word is *interpretation.* Techniques and conditions of whole clusters of studies must be interpreted. After fragmentary results, partial answers, and suggestive findings from different studies and different types of studies have been weighed against one another, the total body of findings must be assessed. The process is interpretive; it requires the exercise of judgment. There are no hard and fast rules, no convenient formulas to assure a uniform outcome. Admittedly, individual studies may sometimes be judged with fair precision. These are the extreme cases, extremely good or extremely bad. In general, however, studies are like people—a complex of interacting strengths and weaknesses. The sum is not mathematically exact but is, rather, a matter of interpretation.

By using the third person, I have, perhaps, created an illusion of objectivity. Possibly I should have followed Thoreau's precedent and sprinkled *I* liberally about to emphasize the inescapable personal ingredient in what I have written. I cannot claim to have purged myself of all biases, but I have, at least, tried to evaluate the research on its merits and to draw conclusions from the evidence. If I have been completely successful, I shall be surprised.

Rather than undertake the impossible task of presenting all the research on every aspect of the English teacher's job, I selected four subjects dealing with language instruction which seemed to me to be particularly troublesome. In choosing these four subjects I relied mostly upon my experiences as a teacher of methods courses and as a supervisor of practice teachers. At first, I tried to find some objective evidence for including a topic. I surveyed methods textbooks to discover conflicting recommendations. I looked through journals to see what people were arguing about. These preliminaries were somewhat helpful and, coupled with my own experience, enabled me to select topics which seemed capable of starting debates in the teachers' cafeteria. Some people will surely think my selections are resurrections of matters long laid to rest. I can only reply that the issues seem to me to be alive in the schools, at PTA meetings, and at teachers' conferences.

The studies I have discussed were selected for a variety of reasons. Some I selected because they appear in well-known reference works. Some I selected because they are cited in methods textbooks or in widely distributed journal summaries of research. Still another set of considerations concerned whether a study represents a type of approach to a problem. Some studies appear in these pages because they are good or because they are bad. If it is possible to speak of an overall guiding purpose, it is to give a reasonably wide-angled and representative picture of the professional literature.

The people I have chosen to address are English teachers and supervisors of instruction in secondary schools, first-year graduate students in research seminars, and upperclassmen in English methods courses. People with advanced preparation in English education may, I hope, find value in some aspect of the book, but I did not have them primarily in mind.

I have tried to avoid statistics as much as possible because a large portion of my intended audience is not trained in statistics. If it is possible to distinguish statistics from research design, I should say that the studies I examined had more flaws in design than in statistics. For this reason I had less trouble than I anticipated in describing and assessing the studies. Nevertheless, some readers will probably have to acquaint or reacquaint themselves with a few basic statistical concepts, such as what it means to say that a result is statistically significant. Any standard textbook on elementary statistics should serve this purpose.

I have found few precedents. The book most similar to this one is R. L. Lyman's *Summary of Investigations Relating to Grammar, Language, and Composition* (1929). However, Lyman's book and mine frequently deal with different topics and are dissimilar in emphasis. Lyman's is mainly (but not exclusively) occupied with presenting research findings, whereas this book is intended to present the findings along with descriptions and evaluations of the methods by which the findings were reached. Lyman based his book upon a bibliography which he hoped would be exhaustive. But this book is selective, not exhaustive. I should hasten to add, however, that I think this book errs on the side of inclusiveness. The chapters on diagraming and on Latin and English probably come close to achieving a full presentation of the relevant studies.

Lyman's book is a monument to scholarship and patience. The flood of studies since 1929 has made it virtually impossible for anyone single-handedly to produce a comparable work. Detailed descriptions and critiques of whole bodies of research should, in the future, be cooperative enterprises involving teams of specialists.

Sooner or later, anyone surveying research should confess his obligation to the *Encyclopedia of Educational Research,* to the periodic summaries of research in the professional journals, to a few individual compilations of research, and to the *Education Index*. The *Index* is an indispensable source of biblio-graphic clues; it is a cumulative record of titles and authors organized by general categories. Users must find out for themselves what is wheat and what is chaff. Somewhat more editorial in nature are the journal summaries, which typically report in a sentence or two what the studies published during a specified time have found. They do not, usually, provide more than an occasional indication of the summarizer's estimate of the quality of the studies.

Chief among the works upon which I have depended for bibliographic infor-mation is the *Encyclopedia of Educational Research*. That it is encyclopedic is its strength and its weakness. It does not, it can not, encompass everything. Sometimes, perhaps for the sake of brevity, it relies upon other summaries rather than upon the research itself. I know how seductive this practice is because I have succumbed to it myself, but only once and not completely. As one might expect, the *Encyclopedia* emphasizes conclusions drawn from research. It does not interpret the research in the light of the research techniques employed. To a degree, then, reading the *Encyclopedia* is an act of faith—faith in the judicious manner by which studies have been weighed against each other. That the *Ency-clopedia* gives an extraordinary amount of good advice is certainly true, but the advice is at least secondhand and does not expose the underlying considerations which determine it. A valuable companion piece to the *Encyclopedia* is H. C. Meckel's "Research on Teaching Composition and Literature" (in N. L. Gage, ed., *Handbook of Research on Teaching*).

Ingrid Strom's "Research in Grammar and Usage and Its Implications for Teaching Writing" (*Bulletin of the School of Education of Indiana University*, September 1960) devotes approximately a paragraph to each study. Her ap-proach is largely descriptive, but she makes clear what she thinks the studies add up to. Hunnicutt and Iverson's *Research in the Three R's* offers careful abstracts of studies which the authors consider significant. Their introductions to the studies are slight. The methodological features of the studies are left to the reader to interpret. More detailed in every respect is Braddock's (and others') *Research in Written Composition*. At this time of growing awareness of the need to become better informed about research, it is important not to overlook such summaries and compilations as the ones I have mentioned.

Although I consulted secondary sources for bibliographic leads and read great numbers of reviews and summaries of research (such as those in the *English Journal, Elementary English*, and the *Review of Educational Research*), I based my discussions upon the research itself. This greatly prolonged my work, but I expect it will save me from the embarrassment of discovering that a study I accepted on someone else's authority does not actually exist. Precisely such a misfortune befell the *Encyclopedia of Educational Research*, which reported findings for a study that was never completed. Only after an alumni association enabled me to reach the supposed author was I able to discover why no library could supply the study.

Except as I shall record shortly, I can say that I have seen firsthand what I have talked about. Occasionally I relied upon published abstracts prepared by the researcher when I felt that the abstract told me what I needed to know. Sometimes I relied upon articles written by the researcher and based upon his original study, usually a dissertation. In either case, it was the researcher's own report which I examined, though not his first report. I do not believe I compromised my announced practice. I merely accepted Tennyson's dictum that even a good custom too long and rigorously adhered to can corrupt the world.

This book is no three-ring circus. Initially, at least, it is a book to be sampled and perused as the questions foremost in one's mind dictate. One might read the introductory section of a chapter and then read selected sections in order of interest. The chapter summaries may be used as previews or as reminders, but they are certainly not digests for those who lack stomach for the main text. The conclusions express whatever meaning I was able to extract after sifting and winnowing the evidence at hand.

In 1960 I compiled the basic bibliography for this work. Although I continued to make alterations in the bibliography through early 1968, I stopped making large bibliographic efforts in 1966. I supply these dates to remind readers that this book, like a dictionary, should be read as though it were a benchmark in time.

I have received more assistance than I can hope to acknowledge. I am grateful to the Research Foundation of the State University of New York for a fellowship which enabled me to do much of the spadework. The staff of Butler Library of the State University of New York, College at Buffalo, provided help beyond the limits of duty. For a meticulous reading of portions of the manuscript and for his sensible suggestions, I am in debt to Hans Gottschalk, the former executive secretary of the New York State English Council and now chairman of the English Department at the State University College at Geneseo. My colleague, George R. Sherrie, director of institutional research, never ducked a question or refused to lend me a book. Frances S. Sherwin, who has notable academic as well as wifely credentials, served as a sounding board and did her best to free my mind and time. My young sons were downright sporting and far better behaved than any parent shackled to his desk has a right to expect.

J. Stephen Sherwin

Buffalo, New York
March, 1969

Contents

*Four Problems
in Teaching English:*
A Critique of Research

Chapter I

Is There a Via Latina *to English Mastery?*

On Sunday, March 5, 1961, the *New York Times* reported that Mason W. Gross, president of Rutgers University, had declared at a conference of private school teachers and administrators that a revival of Latin would provide students with a better sense of values as well as a more thorough grounding in English. No precise figures are available as to how many teachers and others agree with Dr. Gross, but it is quite clear that similar claims for Latin have often been vigorously proposed and vigorously denied.

1. THE HISTORICAL CONTEXT: LATIN AND THE DEVELOPMENT OF ENGLISH

English has been influenced in varying degrees by French, Germanic languages, Greek, Scandinavian, Celtic, Dutch, Spanish, Hebrew, and many other languages. However, the principal ingredients of Modern English are Old English (Anglo-Saxon), French, Latin, and Greek, and of these only Old English, Latin, and, to a lesser extent, French are of concern here.

The earliest known inhabitants of Britain were the Celts. About Celtic language and culture we know tantalizingly little, and Celtic influence upon English was slight. The Roman invasion of Britain, begun in 54 B.C. according to Caesar's *Commentaries,* introduced Latin. But when the Romans abandoned their British outpost early in the fifth century A.D., they left only a small verbal legacy which, however, was somewhat augmented during the period of vigorous missionary activity following the arrival in 597 A.D. of the Roman Benedictine monk St. Augustine, the first Archbishop of Canterbury. That Latin infusions into English were not more numerous during the Old English Period (449-1066) may be explained, at least in part, by the hostility of native speakers to foreign influences. After the Norman Conquest (1066) and through the Middle English Period (1066-1500), the traditional hostility to foreignisms declined. By the time of Chaucer's death (1400) an educated man was expected to know French and Latin in addition to his native language. Gradually, and for reasons that are largely speculative, the status of English rose to the point where it supplanted French as the language of literature and polite society and supplemented Latin as the language of scholarship. Nevertheless, it was during the Middle English

Period that French, itself markedly influenced by Latin, became a primary ingredient of the English vocabulary. Latin influences, though important at this time, did not flood into English until the sixteenth century when a renewal of classical learning swept western Europe.

Modern English (1500 to the present), especially the English of the nineteenth and twentieth centuries, has borrowed heavily from French but more heavily from Latin. It is not, therefore, surprising that the total Modern English vocabulary is Latinate. However, it would be incorrect to assume either that the workaday language is Latinate or that the structure of English had been shaped by Latin. An analysis of the 1,000 most frequently used words in English showed that 61.7 percent are of Old English origin, 30.9 percent are of French origin, 2.9 percent are of Latin origin, 1.7 percent are of Scandinavian origin, and 2.9 percent are of other origins.[1]

Furthermore, results of research into historical and contemporary usage reveal that English structure differs considerably from the structure of Latin. The difference is that Latin is a highly inflected language with loose word order, whereas English has developed from the highly inflected and loose word order of Old English to a much less inflected language with a much more rigid word order. The word order in "The cat ate the bird" distinguishes the eater from the eaten, but in Latin one can arrange the words any way one pleases without altering the meaning, although there are stylistic considerations. *Feles avem edit* and *Avem feles edit* are stylistically acceptable and identical in meaning.

In addition to this conclusion that the structure of Modern English differs markedly from the structure of Latin, the study of the history of the English language shows that English vocabulary is heavily in debt to Latin. However, the most commonly used words in speech and writing are Anglo-Saxon rather than Latin in origin.

Some further information on the question of whether there is a Latin road to English mastery may be obtained by examining certain social, economic, theological, and pedagogical events in eighteenth century England. By the middle 1700's, the emergence of a large middle class, a generation newly arrived at economic respectability, created an unprecedented demand for instruction in "correct" English. One of the purposes of Samuel Johnson's *Dictionary of the English Language* (1755), the first English dictionary, was to establish once and for all the correct meanings of words. Prefixed to the dictionary was a grammar in which Johnson formulated many now familiar rules for the first time.

William Lyly's *Latin Grammar* (possibly 1513) was the first Latin grammar written in English. The significance of it and of the several which followed during the next century is that it suggested through its pairing of declined Latin words with English translations that English and Latin grammar were similar and that similar grammatical terms could be applied to both. Ben Jonson's *English*

---

[1] Edward L. Thorndike, *The Teacher's Word Book*; Lawrence Faucett and Itsu Maki, *A Study of English Word Values*. Cited in Stuart Robertson and Frederic G. Cassidy, *The Development of Modern English* (New York: Prentice-Hall, Inc., 1954), p. 155.

Grammar, which appeared in 1640, was heavily influenced by the grammars of Latin and Greek. The grammatical analogy between Latin and English was, therefore, established by the beginning of the eighteenth century. The earlier grammars differed from the eighteenth century grammars in that they were intended primarily to assist in the study of Latin or were designed to help foreigners learn English. Their eighteenth century successors, however, were intended to teach "correct" English to native Englishmen.[2] The difference between modern claims for Latin, such as Dr. Gross's, and eighteenth century uses of Latin is that the eighteenth century writers tried to "rectify" English by making it conform to Latin, whereas modern claimants assert that the study of Latin as a foreign language will, if properly taught, significantly increase the English mastery of native users of English. The modern claim is, thus, even more extreme in that it assumes a transfer of training from the study of Latin as Latin, whereas the eighteenth century writers tried to improve English by directly altering English grammar to conform to a Latin model.

The analogy between Latin and English gained strength during the eighteenth century because, among other things, it fit the theological opinions of grammarians, some of whom were ministers. Language, on scriptural evidence, was held to be the gift of God, and God was held to be a supremely rational being in whose image rational man was made. All things before the Fall of Man were considered to have been in a state of rational order and perfection, but, thereafter, all things lapsed into a state of imperfection and deterioration. Grammarians, according to the eighteenth century theory, should seek to improve the language by restoring as much as possible of the orderliness and rationality which had been lost when Adam's sin destroyed the Golden Age. Latin becomes the standard against which English was measured because, for one thing, it most closely approximated the eighteenth century idea of what language must have been like before corruption came into the world.

By the beginning of the nineteenth century, the study of Latin grammar in English and American schools had largely given way to the study of English grammar. But English grammar had already been shaped in a Latin mold and was taught by the rote-rule method that had been worked out when Latin, not English, was the language being taught.

It is easy to overstate the linguistic influence of the eighteenth century and to charge it with more than is its due. The eighteenth century emphasis upon logic in language tended to encourage the development of English as an effective, disciplined instrument of communication and to discourage rhetorical excesses. On the other hand, the emphasis upon logic tended to postpone the day when the psychological structure of language would be recognized and studied. To its credit, the century succeeded in establishing a popular respect for the art of using language; but, to its discredit, it sacrificed idiomatic flavor in order to achieve what it believed to be the virtues of purity, propriety, and consistency.

[2] C. C. Fries, *The Teaching of the English Language* (New York: Thomas Nelson and Sons, 1927), p. 10.

In one respect, contemporary English has inherited very little from the eighteenth century. Leonard, our greatest historian of eighteenth century doctrines about language, pointed out that the activities of eighteenth century grammarians "appear in perspective to have been a prodigious raising of issues already laid, and of points irrelevant and insignificant. . . . The glossary in Appendix I lists eighteenth-century opinion on over three hundred grammatical and logical issues. Of this total of prescriptions, in spite of the violence of censure. . ., less than a dozen condemned types of constructions. . .are actually regarded as illiterate or popular usage today."[3]

In another respect, contemporary English has inherited a great deal from the eighteenth century. Of great importance to one interested in the teaching of language is the fact that contemporary English has inherited a grammatical vocabulary and a way of looking at English syntax which are derived from Latin. Equally important is the fact that the eighteenth century analogy with Latin and the dependence upon rules derived from Latin established a prescriptive philosophy of language which survives to the present day in classrooms, in textbooks, and in the popular mind. Between the established prescriptivism of the past and the rising descriptivism of the present stand large transitional figures such as Rasmus Rask, Jacob Grimm, Henry Sweet, Karl Verner, and (closer to the present) Otto Jespersen. Such people as these created the foundation upon which recent scholarship was to build. It is the linguistic scholarship of the present century which has challenged the substance of eighteenth century grammar and begun to replace it with grammatical systems that more closely report— describe—the way English actually works. That none of the newer grammars has yet gained wide and unqualified support merely testifies to the strength of eighteenth century tradition and to the complexity of the task to which the earlier grammar, in spite of its superficial plausibility, was so unequal.

The historical evidence indicates that English syntax and Latin syntax have developed along quite different lines. Therefore, the claim that Latin will greatly help the student to master English syntax does not seem tenable from the historical point of view. This is not to say that Latin style and syntax have not had some influence upon English. The efforts of classical grammarians during the eighteenth and nineteenth centuries and during part of the twentieth century have ended in the creation of, for example, a popular uneasiness about ending sentences with prepositions, a reluctance to use *that* in place of *who* and *which,* an arbitrary preference for the nominative case after the verb *to be,* and confusion in the use of the apostrophe with possessive pronouns. None of these inheritances from Latin can fairly be said to have benefited or enriched Modern English, but they do qualify as influences.

However, the historical evidence does admit the possibility that a knowledge of Latin may assist a student to increase his vocabulary. It would be imprudent

[3] S. A. Leonard, *The Doctrine of Correctness in English Usage, 1700-1800.* University of Wisconsin Studies in Language and Literature, No. 25 (Madison, Wis.: University of Wisconsin, 1929), p. 237.

to express this possibility in stronger terms because of the fact that words change their forms and their meanings. As a result, a Modern English word of Latin origin, or any other origin, may not resemble its ancestor in either meaning or appearance.

Expert opinion may be found on either side of the issue. A. M. Withers has argued vigorously that the study of Latin will enable a person "to walk with confidence and friendship among the big and little families of English words related and interrelated through Latin stock."[4] On the other hand, according to Otto Jespersen, "we shall be nearer the truth if we recognize in the latest influences from the classical languages 'something between a hindrance and a help'."[5] After exploring opinions and reviewing history, what is left in the form of investigative evidence to guide our thinking?

2. LATIN IN NEWSPAPERS, PERIODICALS, AND LITERATURE

Does the language used in newspapers, magazines, and books on lists of school readings contain a significant number of classical allusions, Latin words and phrases, and "naturalized" (adopted into English) Latin words? Three studies by Louisa V. Walker,[6] R. B. King,[7] and M. F. Bunyan[8] purport to show that there is a large Latin element in popular publications in English. These studies imply that their identification of a large Latin element in contemporary English writing makes it desirable for students to study Latin for general cultural enrichment and as a ready aid to mastery of their native tongue.

Now in retrospect, these studies are interesting primarily because they illustrate the hazard in accepting results without examining the methods by which the results were obtained.

Walker's finding that Latin students received better scores on a translation test (of words, phrases, and abbreviations) than did non-Latin students is not conclusive because all scores were low and because the method of pairing students of like ability was not clearly explained. Walker did find 1,615 different Latin items in periodicals and newspapers which occurred 17,149 times, but since she did not say how many words she had to examine to cull that number, it is impossible to judge whether her find is large or small. King found 2,738 references to classical subjects in 24 newspapers and magazines, but he, too, did not provide a basis for estimating the size of his find. The same criticism can be made of Bunyan's study. Indeed, information about quantity may be less important than information about whether Latin elements are central to the meaning of the passage in which they appear. Neither Walker, King, nor Bunyan dealt

[4] A. M. Withers, "What It Takes To Get English," *Word Study*, 26 (October 1959), 3.

[5] Otto Jespersen, *Growth and Structure of the English Language* (9th ed.; Oxford: Basil Blackwell, 1938), p. 139.

[6] Louisa V. Walker, "Latin in Current Periodicals and Newspapers" (Ph.D. dissertation, University of Wisconsin, 1923).

[7] R. B. King, "Classical Allusions in Certain Newspapers and Magazines" (Master's thesis, University of Wisconsin, 1922).

[8] M. F. Bunyan, "Classical Allusions in the English Reading of High School Pupils" (Master's thesis, University of Wisconsin, 1922).

with this possibility. However, all three showed that to some extent Latin words and classical references are to be found in publications designed for mass distribution. In sum, these three studies do not supply convincing evidence that there is enough Latin or enough important Latin embodied in ways central to meaning to justify modifying the Latin course or to justify urging non-Latin students to study Latin as a valuable aid to English mastery.

Unlike Walker, King, and Bunyan, Grace W. Clark started from the assumption that "Literature is crowded" with classical elements and that "Without a knowledge of the traditions of the Greeks and Romans the reading of great authors loses half its charm." Clark devised a classical reference test which she gave to "over three thousand high school pupils of all grades."[9] The test covered the following topics: Religion and Mythology, Trojan War, Literature, History, Roman Life and Ideas, Geography and Topography. After comparing the test scores of students of Latin (including some students of Greek) with the scores of students who had not studied Latin or Greek, Clark concluded that "without Latin or Greek there is not the gain in this cultural knowledge that should be...."[10] The study convincingly demonstrates that students of classical languages recognize more classical references than those who have not studied classical languages. But how should this be interpreted?

To put it another way, Clark urged the study of classical languages on the grounds that it enriches English vocabulary and, hence, enriches one's literary experience. However, if a knowledge of classical references is truly important and enriching cultural information (which is an issue outside present concerns), it is at least possible that the knowledge can be obtained more economically through classical studies in translation. In short, it is possible to accept the results of this study without reservation and still find in it no compelling argument for the study of classical languages as an enrichment of the English vocabulary.

3. THE TRANSLATION OF LATIN AND THE IMPROVEMENT OF ENGLISH COMPOSITION

George R. Miller, Jr., and Thomas H. Briggs attempted to test the common claim that Latin study improves pupils' English, that "the intense scrutiny given to the writing of classic authors develops powers of original expression." They secured 300 student translations from 14 public high schools and one private preparatory school. "Cicero was chosen so that pupils would have had at least two and one-half years of Latin and one and one-half years of continuous practice in the translation of prose. Three-fourths of those who had begun the study of Latin had probably abandoned it; at any rate, it may be assumed that the pupils...represented the survival of the fittest."[11]

After discussing the use of "trots" and the curious unwillingness of students

---

[9]Grace W. Clark, "The Relative Ability of Latin and Non-Latin Pupils To Explain Classical References" (Master's thesis, State University of Iowa, 1923), p. 2.

[10]*Ibid.,* p. 52.

[11]George R. Miller, Jr. and Thomas H. Briggs, "The Effect of Latin Translations on English," *School Review,* 31 (December 1923), 756.

to use the editorial helps in the texts, the investigators presented different sorts of translations, all but 26 percent being very poor as English composition. They concluded that they think better teaching methods would give better results but that "the evidence is overwhelming that [present] translations are likely to do more harm than good to English." [12]

M. N. Woodring found confirming evidence in a somewhat more elaborate study. In addition to examining the English used in Latin translations, Woodring examined the English in English compositions. Woodring obtained 150 College Entrance Examination books in Latin; these included the 50 highest grades, the 50 rated 60 percent and above, and the 50 rated lowest. Also, Woodring obtained the English examination book for each of the 150 students whose Latin examination had been included in the study. Of Woodring's many conclusions, the following are especially relevant: (1) Only one third of the translations were found to be written in acceptable English and (2) English used in translating Latin was decidedly inferior to the language used in English compositions. [13]

Woodring's study provides strong experimental support for the observation of many teachers that students who function competently in one subject do not necessarily apply this competence when they are working in another area. Apparently, the students' "mental set" crucially influences their performance level. Apparently, also, Woodring's Latin students were not thinking about English even though they were translating from Latin into English, but the same students wrote far better English when they were faced with the task of writing a composition as part of their College Entrance Examination.

What Woodring and Miller and Briggs have shown is that (under the teaching conditions prevalent at the time) Latin courses were not realizing any potential they might have for improving English. As Woodring pointed out in a final comment, it is essential that Latin instruction achieve its ultimate objectives, among which is the improvement of English, and if "this cannot be done then Latin cannot justify the time it is consuming in the high school program."[14]

4. THE STUDY OF A FOREIGN LANGUAGE AND THE IMPROVEMENT OF ENGLISH

In a statistically elaborate and apparently well-controlled study, Roy B. Hackman and Henry W. Duel obtained some curious results. First, "there is association between foreign language studied and gain in English Usage, but no association between foreign language studied and gain or loss in either Vocabulary or Spelling."[15] Second, those students "who studied French and Spanish

[12] *Ibid.,* p. 762.

[13] Maxie Nave Woodring, *A Study of the Quality of English in Latin Translations* (New York: Bureau of Publications, Teachers College, Columbia University, 1925), pp. 69, 72.

[14] *Ibid.,* p. 76.

[15] Roy B. Hackman and Henry W. Duel, "Do High School Students Who Study a Foreign Language Acquire Larger Vocabularies, Spell Their Words More Correctly and Use Better English than High School Students Who Study No Foreign Language?" *Journal of the American Association of Collegiate Registrars,* 16 (January 1941), 160.

gained more than those who studied German and Latin."[16] It is impossible to explain these findings in terms of what we know about the sources of the present English vocabulary or the numbers of cognate words in English and in each of the foreign languages included in the study. One might merely speculate that foreign languages in which the structure is less dissimilar to English structure (for example, French and Spanish) have a greater influence upon English usage than do foreign languages in which the structure is more dissimilar (for example, German and Latin). Speculation aside, the results of this study should be small comfort to those who would espouse the teaching of Latin on the grounds that it increases skill in English; admittedly, the study found an "association" of Latin study and increased English mastery, but both French and Spanish, according to the study, did the job better.

L. E. Cole found a "positive relationship between the amount of Latin studied in high school" and performance in French and Spanish.[17] Cole's study contains nothing to indicate that the benefits are the result of something inherent in Latin. The best claim one can make is that the study shows that Latin students who study another foreign language have some advantage over those students who study a foreign language without ever having studied Latin. Such a conclusion is not really astonishing because Romance languages do have their similarities which might be expected to assist the student to some extent as he turns from the study of one language to the study of another. Cole's study would be more interesting if it had included information on whether there is an even more "positive relationship" between the study of French and the study of Spanish. There are decent theoretical grounds for hypothesizing, for example, that the student seeking to master Spanish would be helped more by the prior study of French than by the prior study of Latin; also, the Hackman-Duel study would encourage one to predict such an outcome. In any case, Cole's study provides no reason to suppose that Latin has any intrinsic properties which make it especially valuable as an introduction to the study of French or Spanish.

Like Cole, Thomas J. Kirby investigated Latin as preparation for French. Kirby found a "positive correspondence between the number of years students have pursued Latin in high school and the marks they make in first- and second-semester French in the university." However, "This correlation is so low [Latin and first-semester French: +.23 ± .04; Latin and second-semester French: +.25 ± .04] as to indicate that the study of Latin. . .has only a slight relationship to the probable future success in first- and second-semester French in the university."[18] Again, the case for Latin as preparation for learning something else cannot be said to be well supported.

Harry N. Rivlin approached the problem in a reverse way. He sought to

[16] *Ibid.,* p. 161.
[17] L. E. Cole, "Latin as a Preparation for French and Spanish," *School and Society,* 19 (May 24, 1924), 621-622.
[18] Thomas J. Kirby, "Latin as Preparation for French," *School and Society,* 17 (November 10, 1923), 569.

discover whether a knowledge of English grammar is valuable preparation for a study of a foreign language. After examining the opinions of 240 foreign language teachers and 227 English teachers, he found that "half the items desired by foreign-language teachers are not essential so far as the teaching of English is concerned."[19] Rivlin observed that even "when an item is considered important by both English teacher and foreign-language teacher, the fundamental difference in their respective aims may necessitate two distinct presentations. . . ."[20] Rivlin's work is relevant here to the extent that it raises this question: If English grammar is not especially valuable as preparation for learning a foreign language, is it not reasonable to suppose (in the absence of convincing contrary evidence) that a knowledge of the grammar of a foreign language (Latin or another) is not especially valuable to students of English? Since Rivlin did not actually test the supposed connection between a knowledge of English grammar and an increased facility to learn a foreign language, it is best to say only that his work is indicative and does no more than buttress somewhat such doubts as one might have about the wisdom of approaching one language through the grammar of another.

5. LATIN AND IMPROVEMENT IN ENGLISH VOCABULARY

Prominent among claims for the study of Latin is the assertion that Latin will directly and/or indirectly increase one's English word knowledge. Two often cited dissertations by Raymond I. Haskell and A. A. Hamblin undertook to explore this claim.

Haskell investigated whether greater vocabulary improvement occurred when derivations were studied in English classes or in Latin classes. Haskell set up 4 groups. The first contained beginning Latin pupils who did not study derivations; the second contained beginning Latin pupils who studied derivations regularly; the third contained non-Latin pupils who did not study derivations; and the fourth contained non-Latin pupils who studied derivations regularly. At the start, the study involved 800 ninth grade pupils, but by the time the experiment was completed two semesters later, this number was reduced to 525, owing to dropouts and other causes "not within the control of the experimenter."[21]

Haskell found, first, that the regular ninth grade English course taken by non-Latin students "produces a very small contribution" to the pupil's English vocabulary and, second, that the inclusion of derivation (etymology) in the English (non-Latin) course resulted in only a slight further vocabulary gain. Also, Haskell found that the regular ninth grade Latin course which contained "little if any" study of derivation produced only slightly better vocabulary scores than

[19] Harry N. Rivlin, "English Grammar as Preparation for the Study of a Modern Foreign Language," *English Journal,* 23 (March 1934), 205.

[20] *Loc. cit.*

[21] Raymond I. Haskell, "A Statistical Study of the Comparative Results Produced by Teaching Derivation in the Ninth-Grade Latin Classes and in the Ninth-Grade English Classes of Non-Latin Pupils in Four Philadelphia High Schools" (Ph.D dissertation, University of Pennsylvania, 1923), p. 13.

did the English (non-Latin) course which stressed derivations. Finally, Haskell found that the regular ninth grade Latin course in which there was "conscious effort in the study of etymology" produced "a large and significant contribution to the range of the English vocabulary. . . ." [22]

The conclusions which Haskell reached are interesting and provocative, but it would be prudent not to regard them as facts. For one thing, it is hard to see why derivations taught in the Latin class should lead to significantly larger vocabulary gains than derivations taught in the English class. It seems best to add the study to the list of those which provide less than conclusive answers while raising questions as difficult as the ones they seek to resolve.

Two years after the publication of Haskell's study, A. A. Hamblin completed a companion study using the same data. [23] Whereas Haskell's chief aim was to compare the effectiveness of derivation study in Latin classes and English classes, Hamblin's objectives were to (1) learn how much, if any, English vocabulary improvement takes place when English derivations are deliberately taught in connection with Latin and (2) identify instructional methods and materials which most readily facilitate learning English vocabulary through derivation study in Latin classes. In short, both men were concerned with English vocabulary improvement, but Haskell was interested primarily in comparing the effectiveness of Latin and English courses whereas Hamblin was interested primarily in examining the effectiveness of different Latin courses.

According to Hamblin, students completing one year of Latin with "little or no attention to derivation" increase their Latin-derived English vocabulary slightly, but as Hamblin pointed out, he was unable to tell whether the gain resulted from automatic transfer or was simply the result of normal vocabulary growth during the year. Hamblin's second finding was that Latin students whose course included derivation study showed "superior gains" in their Latin-derived English vocabulary (the experimental group making approximately twice the gain of the control group). A third finding was that a satisfactory textbook treatment of derivations and the use of student notebooks and the teacher's derivative list "are important aids in the teaching of derivatives." [24]

What Hamblin concluded was that one type of Latin course (Latin plus derivation study) did a better job of improving students' Latin-derived English vocabulary than did another type of Latin course (Latin without derivation study). Also, certain instructional arrangements led to improved gains. Unfortunately, it is easy to jump to the conclusion that, since one sort of Latin instruction improved students' English vocabulary, therefore Latin instruction is desirable if the English vocabulary is to be improved. Actually, the study did not say

[22] *Ibid.*, pp. 111-112.
[23] A. A. Hamblin, "An Investigation To Determine the Extent to Which the Effect of the Study of Latin upon a Knowledge of English Derivatives Can Be Increased by Conscious Adaptation of Content and Method to the Attainment of This Objective" (Ph.D. dissertation, University of Pennsylvania, 1925), p. 12.
[24] *Ibid.*, pp. 48-51.

anything directly or by implication—was not designed to say anything—about whether Latin study is more effective than English study in improving vocabulary.

In their review of Haskell's and Hamblin's studies, two other researchers, Percival M. Symonds and Edith M. Penney, observed that Haskell's and Hamblin's figures "must be taken at face value. In both monographs the results are inadequately reported. In no case is the number of cases or reliability reported. Glaring errors in arithmetic are to be found." [25]

Like Hamblin, W. L. Carr found that Latin was a "definite aid" in increasing students' vocabulary and that this effectiveness of Latin "depends largely upon definite instruction and training in the techniques of derivation." [26] Carr gave a vocabulary test to both Latin and non-Latin students in order to compare the vocabulary growth of the Latin students with the "normal" growth of the non-Latin students. Although in each of the 7 schools participating in the study the Latin students' vocabulary growth significantly exceeded the non-Latin students' vocabulary growth, Carr did not claim that Latin (plus derivation work) was more effective than English (with or without derivation work) in improving students' vocabulary. Apparently the reason was that the study did not systematically examine or control the content of English courses so that it is entirely possible that some English classes received work in derivation whereas others received little or none. In sum, although this study did involve groups of Latin students and non-Latin students, it cannot be said to show anything about the relative merits of Latin and English as instruments of vocabulary enrichment.

A teacher of Latin, Alvah Talbot Otis, who said he became "tired of hearing that his pupils might better be studying how to sell ribbons or drive automobiles," [27] embarked upon an investigation of whether "Latin study pursued for two years by the care-free youths of an American City actually fulfills the hopes of its defenders by adding materially to English vocabulary. . . ." [28]

At first, Otis tried to match 50 Latin and 50 non-Latin students by using their school averages, but he said he soon discovered that the Latin group surpassed the non-Latins by 16.6 percent on scores obtained on the Terman Mental Ability Test. Consequently, Otis had to exclude the most able students in his Latin group and "scour the school" for non-Latins to match with the Latins who remained. This demonstration of the risks in using grades for matching purposes was regarded by Otis as one of the valuable by-products of his study, as indeed it seems to be. However, Otis' belief that Latin students are, in general, overwhelmingly superior to non-Latin students is probably wrong in view of evidence

[25] Percival M. Symonds and Edith M. Penney, "The Increasing of English Vocabulary in the English Class," *Journal of Educational Research,* 15 (February 1927), 99.

[26] W. L. Carr, "First-year Latin and Growth in English Vocabulary," *School and Society,* 14 (September 17, 1921), 198.

[27] Alvah Talbot Otis, "The Relation of Latin Study to Ability in English Vocabulary and Composition," *School Review,* 30 (January 1922), 45.

[28] *Loc. cit.*

supplied by Newcomb (in a study to be discussed later) who found, among other things, that the characteristics of groups vary greatly from school to school.

After obtaining two groups satisfactorily matched in intelligence scores, Otis administered a vocabulary test and a composition test. The 50 words comprising the vocabulary test were obtained by taking the first Latin-derived word on every eighteenth page of a "certain school dictionary." Otis omitted obsolete and technical words and words which he considered too simple to provide a genuine test of vocabulary. The composition test consisted of asking students to write about 150 words on one of 3 topics which Otis believed had general appeal. The compositions were rated according to a standard scale and were read by experienced teachers who did not know the students.

The findings were dramatic: The Latin group scored 6.5 percent above the non-Latin group in composition and 33.0 percent above the non-Latin group in vocabulary. Otis concluded that his study, conducted with "utmost care," "seems to have proved something," namely, that "there is some tangible value in Latin study." [29]

It is difficult to share Otis' confidence in his conclusions. First, the non-Latin group consisted of "commercial" students and the Latin group of "college-preparatory" students. Although the intelligence scores for both groups are approximately equal, it would have been merely cautious to equate the groups in terms of prelanguage study, vocabulary skill, verbal aptitude, and socioeconomic background. It is not really sufficient to assume, as Otis did, that the groups are equal in these additional respects because there is a "high correlation"[30] between general intelligence and language ability. There may very well be social and other factors which operate to cause commercial students to be linguistically deprived in comparison with their college-preparatory coevals, and such factors, unless carefully controlled, could effectively tilt the study in favor of the Latin group.

Second, the vocabulary test contained such words as *sumptuary, pomegranate, quaternary, nonpareil, herculean,* and *druidism* which, though decipherable from their Latin components, are also more likely to be known by college-preparatory students than by other students either because of a possible difference in socioeconomic background or because the college-preparatory (Latin) group took a more academic English course.

Third, the composition test required the students to choose one of these 3 topics: "Why a Citizen Ought to Vote," "The Advantages of *Any* Labor-saving Device," and "The Description of a Person." These topics do not seem to have been selected with the presumed interests of the non-Latin, commercial group in mind, and the first and third seem especially weak in this respect. Less a matter of opinion, however, is the point that it is impossible to tell from the information Otis supplied whether both groups had equal experience and instruction in

[29] *Ibid.,* p. 50.
[30] *Ibid.,* p. 48.

the writing of compositions, especially impromptu compositions. Indeed, this study leaves so many variables uncontrolled and is silent on matters of such pertinence that it seems best to discount its findings.

Another study by E. L. Thorndike and G. J. Ruger found that first-year Latin students learned more Latin-derived words (by a ratio of 5 to 2) than did non-Latin students but that Latin and non-Latin students made approximately equal gains in the mastery of words of non-Latin origin.[31] The study is marred by the failure to allow for the possible superior intelligence of the Latin group. However, if one accepts the study, its significance is in pointing out to Latin teachers that they have the means to contribute to their students' Latin-related English vocabulary. But the study neither supports nor denies the contention that the improvement of the Latin-related English vocabulary is best done by way of the study of Latin.

Harl R. Douglass and Clifford Kittleson set out to answer the question: "Are Latin pupils, as they are taught in the typical secondary school of today, significantly superior to non-Latin pupils of equal mental ability in English vocabulary, spelling, and grammar?"[32] The strength of this study lies in its painstaking pairing of Latin and non-Latin students according to "sex, chronological age, intelligence, economic status of family, the number of years spent in the study of modern foreign languages, and the first year English mark."[33] The authors noted that the Latin students made slightly greater gains over the non-Latin students in spelling, vocabulary, and grammar. But they concluded that the advantage of the Latin students was "so small as to invite suspicion" concerning the ability of Latin as presently taught to improve English spelling, vocabulary, and grammar.[34]

The Douglass-Kittleson study is supported by Frederick L. Pond's study which found that intelligence is of "maximum importance in the acquisition of vocabulary knowledge" and that "little, if any, difference in vocabulary knowledge on the part of Latin and non-Latin pupils" was revealed when pupils were matched on the basis of intelligence, sex, age, semesters in school, and school achievement.[35]

Further support comes from J. B. Carroll, who sought in a carefully controlled study to "determine the relative influence of Latin study upon morpheme knowledge and vocabulary."[36] To explain the object of the study in

[31] E. L. Thorndike and G. J. Ruger, "The Effect of First-year Latin upon Knowledge of English Words of Latin Derivation," *School and Society*, 18 (September 1, 1923), 260-261.
[32] Harl R. Douglass and Clifford Kittleson, "The Transfer of Training in High School Latin to English Grammar, Spelling, and Vocabulary," *Journal of Experimental Education*, 4 (September 1935), 28.
[33] *Ibid.*, p. 29.
[34] *Ibid.*, p. 33.
[35] Frederick L. Pond, "Influence of the Study of Latin on Word Knowledge," *School Review*, 46 (October 1938), 618.
[36] J. B. Carroll, "Knowledge of English Roots and Affixes as Related to Vocabulary and Latin Study," *Journal of Educational Research*, 34 (October 1940), 102.

another way, there are those who "assume that the mere knowledge of English roots and affixes derived from Latin—a knowledge presumably automatically obtained from the study of Latin—will automatically aid in enlarging an individual's English vocabulary. The present study is in part an attempt to test this assumption."[37] Carroll devised a Morpheme Recognition Test which he described as a "fairly reliable instrument for testing knowledge of English roots, prefixes, and suffixes."[38] In order to identify other variables, Carroll administered the Revised Army Alpha Examination, Form D, and the English Recognition Test, Form 1, by Robert H. Seashore and Lois D. Eckerson; and Carroll also noted the number of years of secondary school and college Latin. Complete data were obtained for 76 students. These data were analyzed statistically in order to determine whether morpheme scores and vocabulary scores could be predicted from other variables. The conclusion, which Carroll characterized as paradoxical, was that "whereas Latin definitely influences the ability to recognize morphemes and the knowledge of their meanings, it has no necessary effect on English vocabulary. This is true in spite of the fact that morpheme recognition ability is partly related to vocabulary."[39]

Carroll's interpretation of his findings affords an interesting illustration of how one can be betrayed by one's personal commitments. After granting that teaching derivations *per se* in Latin classes does not help to enlarge students' English vocabulary, he goes on to suggest that derivation study (to include, of course, the study of affixes and roots) may be more effective if specific attention were given to unfamiliar words. Thus, presumably, derivation study of a familiar word like *semicircle* does not improve vocabulary, but derivation study of an unfamiliar word like *hemidemisemiquaver* does improve vocabulary. What then, one may ask in rebuttal, is the value of derivation study if it is not the learning of word components, such as *semi*, but the introduction to students of unfamiliar whole words which makes the difference? Having been encouraged by finding no fatal flaw in Carroll's experimental method, although one might wish that the study were based on more than 76 cases, it is distressing to detect the author in an attempt to explain away his own study.

In seeking to discover whether the teaching of prefixes and the word roots in English classes is effective, Lois M. Otterman found 440 seventh grade students whom she divided into experimental and control groups of 220 students each. Experimental and control groups were matched for sex, chronological age, mental age, average reading score, vocabulary, and spelling. Each teacher cooperating in the study taught one experimental class and one matching control class. "The only difference in the work of the two groups for the six weeks' duration of the study was that the experimental group was to have. . .ten-minute lessons each day in addition to the regular English class work."[40] Each

[37]*Ibid.,* p. 103.
[38]*Ibid,,* p. 104.
[39]*Ibid.,* pp. 109-110.
[40]Lois M. Otterman, "The Value of Teaching Prefixes and Word-Roots," *Journal of Educational Research,* 48 (April 1955), 611-612.

lesson dealt with only one prefix or root, and familiar words—not "new words"—were used to illustrate the prefix or root being taught.

Otterman gave tests before and after the experimental teaching in order to detect any changes "in ability to interpret new words containing the studied elements, in incidental learning of spelling, in speed of visual and auditory perception, in general vocabulary, in reading comprehension, and in speed reading. A delayed recall test was given six weeks after the close of the experimental teaching to determine if the meanings of the studied prefixes and word-roots were still remembered."[41]

The Otterman study found that (1) students' general vocabulary, reading comprehension, and speed of reading showed no significant improvement attributable to the study of prefixes and roots; (2) students of low mental age significantly improved in speed of visual perception, but the experimental group as a whole showed no significant gain in either visual or auditory perception; (3) students in the experimental group were clearly superior in their ability to recall prefix and root meanings after a lapse of 6 weeks; (4) students in the experimental group improved significantly in spelling; and (5) students of high mental age were the only ones who significantly increased their ability to interpret new words.

These findings invite some comment. First, it should be noted that students' success on the delayed recall test tells us only that the students remembered for a specific length of time the meanings of prefixes and roots which they had been drilled on. Students' success in recall tells us nothing about their ability to convert what they have recalled into useful linguistic knowledge. Second, the finding that the high-ability students were better able to interpret new words supports the findings of Douglass and Kittleson and the findings of Pond (both previously cited). In the light of these studies it would appear that the significant factor is intelligence rather than the study of prefixes or roots. Third, that low-ability students improved in visual perception whereas abler students did not, confirms the informal observation of teachers that subject matter and method successful with one sort of student are not necessarily successful with another and that (abstract reason to the contrary) what works with slow students is not necessarily what works with quick students. Finally, students' increased ability to spell, as Otterman recognized, is probably owing to the attention to word parts inherent in any instruction in prefixes and roots. If this is true, then it is possible that the study of the meanings of prefixes and roots is really unrelated to improvement in spelling, and improvement in spelling, then, might be achieved by any structurally sound, word-segmenting scheme.

The study by Jacob S. Orleans challenged the theory that Latin study increases one's English vocabulary because English contains a preponderance of words derived from Latin. Orleans pointed out correctly that the part of a student's vocabulary which is Latin-derived is one matter and the part Latin plays in developing a student's English vocabulary is quite another matter. The Latin

[41]*Ibid.,* p. 112.

element in one's English vocabulary may be determined by a word count with the help of an etymological dictionary. But the degree of influence of Latin-derived words upon the English vocabulary is "limited not only by the percent-age of English words derived from Latin but also by the possibility of transfer from the Latin to the English as determined by such elements as similarity of form, similarity of meaning, and perhaps number of derivatives."[42] It is, there-fore, hasty to assume that because Latin derivatives bulk large in the total En-glish vocabulary, Latin study will benefit the English vocabulary.

By sampling the lists in Thorndike's *The Teacher's Word Book,* Orleans ob-tained a list of words together with Thorndike's frequency-of-occurrence rating for each word. Orleans then asked 9 judges to estimate "the extent to which transfer might occur, from a knowledge of the meaning of the Latin original to an understanding of the meaning of the derivative."[43] The judges were asked to consider only "similarity in form and meaning." Another panel of 3 judges, in-cluding 2 of the original 9, were asked to consider "transfer as limited by con-ditions in the classroom."[44] Orleans found that his judges were considerably less confident about the possibilities for transfer under classroom conditions. He found, also, that his judges saw greater transfer possibilities for the less common words and smaller transfer possibilities for the more common words.

Admittedly, there is an obvious limit beyond which one cannot push a study based on judges' opinions, no matter how qualified those judges may be. Never-theless, Orleans' findings cannot be brushed aside and, thus, add yet another slender thread to the fabric of doubt about the validity of the argument that Latin study helps to increase one's English vocabulary because English contains a preponderance of Latinate words.

One experiment already mentioned, conducted by Percival M. Symonds and Edith M. Penney, was designed "to determine the possibilities of building a pu-pil's English vocabulary in the English class."[45]   Thirty ninth–graders in the Horace Mann School for Girls at Teachers College, Columbia University, were divided into equal control and experimental groups. All the students were given a 750-word test of word knowledge (The Thorndike Test of Word Knowledge, Forms A to H, slightly modified). This test provided, in the researchers' opinion, a reliable gauge of the students' knowledge of words of different degrees of dif-ficulty. Since this test measured recognition only, the researchers devised a test of recall, consisting of 100 completion sentences. Both tests were given to all students before and after the four-month experimental period.

All but 3 of the 30 girls were, at the time of the experiment, studying Latin, and therefore any increases in vocabulary must be regarded as being "in

---

[42] Jacob S. Orleans, "Possible Transfer Value of the Study of Latin to English Vocabu-lary," *School and Society,* 16 (November 11, 1922), 559.
[43] *Ibid.,* p. 560.
[44] *Loc. cit.*
[45] Symonds and Penney, "The Increasing of English Vocabulary," *Journal of Educa-tional Research,* p. 93.

addition to the gains due to the Latin instruction."[46] The girls were described, at one point, as being "superior,"[47] which is probably an accurate description considering where they were going to school; but, aside from this one curiosity-whetting observation and the fact that the control and experimental groups at the start scored about equally on both word tests, the researchers do not explicitly make clear whether or how they matched the control and experimental groups.

Symonds and Penney compared their control group's gains with the gains made by Thorndike's half-year Latin students[48] and concluded, after allowing for differences in test difficulty and the girls' "superiority," that probably the gains made by their control group and the gains made by Thorndike's Latin students "may be considered approximately equal."[49] After pointing out that Thorndike's two-year Latin and non-Latin groups (which scored 5.2 and 5.8, respectively) scored lower than the 6.9 achieved by their experimental group—and after noting that their own control group scored 2.2 as against 6.9 for their experimental group—Symonds and Penney concluded that the "time spent in English class on vocabulary is of much greater aid than time spent in the Latin class"[50] and that "a direct attack on vocabulary in the English class may be conducive to better results than with derivative study in either English or Latin classes."[51]

Apparently the conditions under which Symonds and Penney were obliged to work imposed certain limitations. Had it been possible, it would have been better to avoid the complication of having to determine the effectiveness of English instruction with students who were simultaneously studying Latin. Of course, the study involved too few students to be conclusive. But Symonds and Penney have put their fingers upon the basic, practical problems confronting teachers and students alike: namely, if the object is to teach the English language (spelling or other aspects), is the job best done by direct instruction in the English class? Or is it true that Latin study consciously directed toward English improvement gives students an advantage which no amount of direct instruction can overcome?

6. LATIN AND IMPROVEMENT IN ENGLISH SPELLING

Among the studies reviewed in the preceding section, the one by Douglass and Kittleson and the one by Otterman deal in part with the influence of the study of Latin upon the ability to spell English words. The following investigations may also be mentioned, some only briefly.

[46]*Loc. cit.*

[47]*Ibid.,* p. 98.

[48]E. L. Thorndike, "The Gains Made in Ability in English by Pupils Who Study Latin and by Pupils Who Do Not," *School and Society,* 18 (December 8, 1923), 690.

[49]Symonds and Penney, "The Increasing of English Vocabulary," *Journal of Educational Research,* p. 98.

[50]*Loc. cit.*

[51]*Ibid.,* p.99.

R. R. Rusk[52] and L. H. Allen,[53] who both analyzed English spelling, found that some errors could have been avoided by applying a knowledge of the spelling of the Latin words from which the English words were derived. In assessing the significance of these investigations, it should be remembered that the transfer of a knowledge of Latin to English spelling is not automatic and that it can take place to a significant degree only if Latin is taught so as to make the student conscious of the relationship between Latin and English spelling. Also, neither study is helpful on the crucial question of whether students with the ability to master Latin spelling and to apply that knowledge to English might do equally well or better—at a considerable saving in time—if taught English spelling directly and intensively.

Starting with the assumption that Latin is a highly practical language because "nothing is more 'practical' than our speech," Lynn Harold Harris set up an experiment "intended to establish. . .the connection between a knowledge of Latin and proficiency in the ordinary mechanics of English composition."[54] If one is looking for silver linings, all one can say is that it is refreshing to discover someone who is so frank about what he wants his study to prove.

To 324 freshmen at the University of Illinois, Harris gave a 50-word spelling test and a 10-word definition test. The words were of Latin origin, and many were "catch-words" having similar sounds or doubled consonants. By this device, Harris expected to show that Latin is a more advantageous method of improving spelling than are the "memory-methods of the spelling book."[55] All the test words were selected arbitrarily, but Harris indicated that in his opinion they were all words which one might properly expect a high school graduate to know. After comparing the number of correctly spelled words with the number of years of Latin study (0 to 4), Harris found that one-year Latin students had a slight advantage over non-Latin students, two-year and three-year Latin students scored slightly below non-Latin students, and four-year Latin students scored well above all others.

Harris concluded that "no amount of devotion to a spelling book can produce the same results as four years of Latin in the spelling of Latin-derived words. . . ."[56] This conclusion seems to rest upon a one-sided selection of evidence drawn from the total findings. How about those non-Latin students who scored better than those two-year and three-year Latin students? Another serious weakness is that Harris failed to provide for differences in mental ability among the several groups whose spelling scores he compared.

[52]R. R. Rusk, "Analysis of Spelling Errors of Adults," *Journal of Experimental Education*, 2 (June 1913), 119–122.
[53]L. H. Allen, *Some Errors in Spelling Made in Leaving Certificate Examination of 1917* (Sydney: New South Wales Teachers College, 1919), pp. 1–19.
[54]Lynn Harold Harris, "A Study in the Relation of Latin to English Composition," *School and Society*, 2 (August 14, 1915), 251.
[55]*Loc. cit.*
[56]*Ibid.*, p. 252.

An investigation by Warren W. Coxe undertook to answer these questions: Does Latin study increase students' ability to spell English words of Latin and non-Latin derivation? If so, what teaching methods and materials are most effective? Coxe also undertook to "determine whether spelling can be taught better in Latin classes than in English classes. . . ."[57] Coxe organized 5 groups consisting of several classes each. Group I studied beginning Latin without relating Latin to English spelling. Group II studied beginning Latin, but teachers were instructed to indicate spelling similarities between certain listed English words and their Latin ancestors. Group III studied beginning Latin, but teachers were instructed both to show Latin-English spelling similarities and to develop spelling rules. Group IV studied ninth grade English (no Latin) but received no special work in spelling. Group V studied ninth grade English (no Latin) but received special work in spelling which required no knowledge of Latin and which accorded with the "best current practice in the teaching of spelling."[58]

Coxe concluded that "Latin automatically improves the spelling of Latin derivatives" by a ratio of 3 to 2 over students not taking Latin; that "merely pointing out similarities in spelling between a Latin word and derivatives, produces considerable gain, but not as much as when rules or principles are used"; that Latin classes which used spelling rules or principles produced the best results of all, better even than the results produced in English classes using the "best current practice in the teaching of spelling"; and that Latin as presently taught "does not improve the spelling of non-Latin words."[59]

One wonders whether the value of rule formation has not been somewhat overstressed by Coxe. As another researcher, Lillian B. Lawler, pointed out in commenting upon Coxe's study, several of the rules have numerous exceptions which might make rules less valuable in a normal linguistic situation.[60]

The purpose of Lawler's investigation was to identify those spelling errors actually made by high school students which "are potentially remediable by the study of high school Latin."[61] Lawler pointed out logically that her sort of study should precede "attempts to correlate English spelling and Latin, in order that we may know, before we start to correlate, whether the correlation would be worth while."[62] "The words used. . .were the 1,459 of classical Latin origin in the first 2,977" of William N. Andersen's list[63] which is "a scientifically compiled list obtained from a study of the correspondence of adults of various callings. . . . "For each of these words 200 actual spellings from each of the three

[57]Warren W. Coxe, "The Influence of Latin on the Spelling of English Words," (Ph.D. dissertation, Ohio State University, 1923), p.10.
[58]*Ibid.*, pp. 26, 37–38.
[59]*Ibid.*, pp. 107–110.
[60]Lillian B. Lawler, "The Potential Remediability of Errors in English Spelling through the Study of High School Latin," *Classical Journal,* 21 (November 1925), 135.
[61]*Ibid.*, p.35.
[62]*Loc. cit.*
[63]William N. Andersen, "Determination of a Spelling Vocabulary Based upon Written Correspondence," *University of Iowa Studies in Education,* 2, 1 (1917).

grades of junior high school . . . were examined." Approximately a million spellings were examined in all. Only spellings by junior high school pupils who had never studied Latin were used in order to "preclude the possibility that work in Latin might have already influenced spelling ability."[64] Only misspellings occurring two or more times were included.

The main conclusion which Lawler reached was that correlating Latin with English spelling "would seem to be worth trying, since about two-thirds of the errors made by seventh-, eighth-, and ninth-grade pupils . . . in spelling . . . are potentially remediable by Latin."[65] Some limitations of this study, which Lawler carefully reviewed, are, first, that it is based on only one spelling list and, second, that errors potentially remediable by Latin may not turn out to be remediable by Latin because psychological and physical factors causing poor English spelling may also prevent learning Latin spelling or may hamper transfer of Latin spelling to English.

It should be recognized that Lawler's study was not designed to deal with the problem of what to do about the English student whose spelling is poor. Should he study Latin in a Latin class or Latin derivations in an English class? Clearly, the study was intended for the Latin teacher who wishes to improve students' English spelling. Such a teacher should be stimulated to greater efforts by Lawler's evidence that about two thirds of Latin-derived words that are actually misspelled by students are potentially remediable through Latin study.

Without implying a criticism of Lawler for not doing what she did not intend to do, it may be observed that it would be interesting if someone would investigate whether, say, two thirds of all misspelled words—not just Latinate words—are potentially remediable through Latin study. Also, it would be valuable to know how many of the most frequently misspelled words, regardless of derivation, are potentially remediable through Latin study. A large finding of potential remediability from such studies as these might encourage English and Latin teachers to begin to consider approaching spelling, at least in part, through Latin. But a final decision should await evidence that potential remediability can be converted into actual remediability. In sum, because Lawler dealt with only the potential remediability of Latinate words through Latin study and because potential remediability is not actual remediability, it would be both premature and a misapplication to cite Lawler as grounds for believing that there is a Latin highway to improved English spelling.

By means of general school averages obtained from school records and by administering a silent reading test, M. Theresa Dallam paired two groups of 17 students each. These groups, she believed, were approximately equal in mental ability. One group had 4 years of Latin, the other "little or no Latin." All students were high school seniors. Dallam gave tests in spelling, reproduction, dictation, Latin derivation, definition, composition, and English grammar in order to

[64] Lawler, "The Potential Remediability," *Classical Journal*, p. 136.
[65] *Ibid.*, p. 147.

discover whether Latin is "advantageous to the study of English."[66] Her conclusion with respect to spelling is that there is no significant statistical difference between the scores of the Latin and non-Latin groups.

However, Dallam did find a significant advantage for the Latin group in derivation and grammar. Regarding derivation, it should be noted that—although her report is obscure on the point—Dallam apparently tested for information which was more likely to have been included in Latin courses than in English courses taken by non-Latin students. Thus, the study with respect to derivation may have been slanted, however unconsciously, in favor of the Latin group. Regarding the finding that the strongest correlation existed between Latin study and proficiency in English grammar, it should be remembered that, at the time of this investigation, grammar in the high schools and, indeed, colleges meant prescriptive grammar modeled after Latin and in accord with principles enunciated in the eighteenth century. Some correlation between Latin study and Latinate English grammar should, therefore, be expected; but contemporary linguistic researches would maintain that the correlation lacks genuine significance because it is a correlation with a grammar that is not adequate to the job of portraying the workings of English.

Overlooking the grammar portion of Dallam's study, which is badly out of date, it is still not possible to give the study more than tentative status because the number of students involved was quite small and because the pairing technique was crude.

The object of Frederick M. Foster's study was to "discover whether the study of Latin during the high-school course had been of any value for inculcating ability to spell Latin derivatives."[67] He gave a 50-word spelling test to 503 university freshmen, 238 girls and 265 boys. Test words were chosen from Lodge's list[68] and represented, in Foster's opinion, the 4 years of Latin study. For girls, the big spelling improvement came in the fourth year, a drop in errors from 24 to 17. For boys, the big improvement came in the second year, a drop in errors from 37 to 29. Since girls consistently spelled Latin derivatives more accurately, it is curious that their big improvement came two years later and was slightly smaller. Foster did not interpret this finding. Nor did he say anything about girls with no Latin scoring better than all but the girls who had taken 4 years of Latin.[69] However, after correlating general mental ability with

---

[66]M. Theresa Dallam, "Is the Study of Latin Advantageous to the Study of English?" *Educational Review,* 54 (December 1917), 500–501.

[67]Frederick M. Foster, "The Results of a Recent Spelling Test at the University of Iowa," *School and Society,* 5 (April 28, 1917), 507.

[68]Gonzalez Lodge, *The Vocabulary of High School Latin* (New York: Bureau of Publications, Teachers College, Columbia University, 1907).

[69]Foster's silence about the non-Latin girls may mean only that—unknown to him—the table on p. 507 contains an arithmetical error or a misprint or both. The number of spelling errors for girls who did not study Latin seems to be either 23 or 28, the print being unclear. Neither figure enables one to calculate exactly the average error that Foster later reports, although 23 makes possible a figure closer to Foster's.

spelling ability, Foster concluded that the relationship between mental ability and spelling was "quite remarkable" and that the correlation between Latin study and the spelling of Latin derivatives was "not sharp enough to warrant the conclusion that the study of Latin has been of material aid for the correct spelling of Latin derivatives."[70]

Even if Foster's conclusions are correct, his means of arriving at them do not inspire wholehearted confidence. It would have been prudent of him, for example, to have sampled students' spelling performance before and after taking Latin because this procedure, if corrected for "normal improvement" during the elapsed time, would then serve as a check whether Latin or some other factor was influencing spelling ability. Also, if the test Foster gave was, as he believed, representative of the 4-year Latin vocabulary, it would still not be representative of the commonly used vocabulary of people not studying Latin; thus, the test probably discriminated against the non-Latin or little-Latin students.

7. LATIN AND MASTERY OF ENGLISH GRAMMAR

Surprisingly few studies deal exclusively or in part with the idea that the study of Latin greatly increases one's mastery of English grammar. The Classical Investigation of 1921-24,[71] which deals in part with the influence of Latin study upon English mastery, is especially weak in its discussion of the value of Latin in helping students master English grammar. Its conclusion that Latin does help is based on one unpublished study, one study which was never completed, and upon a few others which erred in using Latin-derived grammatical rules for correctness in testing the power of Latin to improve students' English grammar.[72]

To the foregoing may be added the studies by Dallam, Rivlin, and Douglass and Kittleson—all discussed elsewhere in this chapter. It may be recalled that the part of Dallam's study dealing with grammar was regarded as out of date, that Rivlin found that half the grammatical items considered essential by foreign language teachers (including Latin teachers) were considered unessential by English teachers, and that Douglass and Kittleson found that Latin students had a slight but insignificant advantage over non-Latin students in grammar.

There are no studies available at this writing which test the power of Latin to increase students' mastery of a descriptive, linguistically oriented, English grammar. Though prophecy is a dangerous business, it seems safe to predict in this instance that such a study would show Latin to be of little or no help in mastering an English grammar of that sort.

To date, the best evidence of the relationship between Latin and English

[70] Foster, "The Results of a Recent Spelling Test," *School and Society,* p. 508.
[71] American Classical League, *The Classical Investigation, Part I, General Report* (Abridged ed.; New York: New York University, 1924). This investigation is discussed in more detail in section 8 of this chapter.
[72] *Ibid.,* pp. 49-51.

grammar is historical, which tempts one to say that teachers of English might conceivably avoid some gross instructional blunders if they really understood the growth and structure of the English language.

It is perhaps worth mentioning here a prevading weakness which happens to be especially obvious in the grammar, vocabulary, and spelling studies. One study after another set up Latin and non-Latin groups and tried to render variables, such as intelligence, constant. All this is proper, but one inequity seems somehow to remain. The Latin students study Latin, which is usually an elective course, and also study English, which is a required course. The English students with whom the Latin students are compared have only their work in English to benefit them. There is thus a built-in extra-time advantage for the Latin students. It is not enough to reply that English is the same for all (a constant) and that the studies are valid because they test the difference Latin makes. After all, instruction under Latin (or other) auspices in grammar, vocabulary, or spelling may make a difference merely because of the extra time and attention given it; any increased mastery in English among Latin students, therefore, may be unrelated to the fact that Latin supplied the context of the instruction. It would seem advisable that future studies should build in a statistical correction or allow a longer instructional period to the English students.

8. RELATED STUDIES

The investigations included here are tangentially related to the problem of whether the study of Latin helps students to master English. The first is the single, organized, large-scale attack upon the question of whether Latin has a place in the curriculum. The second study points to the probable effect of the first. The third seeks to test the oft-made assertion that Latin students are superior to other students.

One of the most ambitious undertakings in the history of American education is the Classical Investigation which sought by experimental means to assess the status of Latin instruction, discover means of improving instruction, and test the validity of the aims of Latin instruction. The Classical Investigation had its origin in May 1920 in an offer by the General Education Board to finance a comprehensive study of the classics in American secondary schools. In February 1921 the Board accepted the American Classical League's plans for an investigation. The *General Report,* which summarized the results, appeared in 1924. Many of the most prominent figures in education at the time were involved directly or in an advisory capacity. The precise role that each played was not made explicitly clear in the *General Report,* but even a partial list of the names is impressive: W. L. Carr of Oberlin College; Thomas H. Briggs, E. L. Thorndike, and William C. Bagley of Teachers College, Columbia University; S. A. Leonard, M. V. O'Shea, and V. A. C. Henmon of the University of Wisconsin; Leo J. Brueckner of the University of Minnesota; W. W. Charters of the University of Pittsburgh; Ernest Horn of the State University of Iowa; and Charles H. Judd of the University of Chicago.

It would be interesting to know what role specialists in the teaching of English played in the formulation of studies dealing with comparisons between students of English and students of Latin. Specifically, what was the function and what was the influence of such a scholar as Sterling Andrus Leonard, who was listed as a principal collaborator and who later wrote two important studies relating to the teaching of the English language?[73] Leonard's fine command of the historical and philosophical ramifications of the problem contrasts with the neglect of these matters in the *General Report.*

The studies on which the *General Report* was based vary greatly. Some were conducted by candidates for the master's and doctor's degree and not by the established scholars themselves. For the most part, the studies, though part of a comprehensive plan, were each limited in scope and within the capacity of a single investigator with restricted research assistance. As a result, no single study of the sort that cooperative, research-team effort makes possible was undertaken. A further weakness is that the *Report* tended to accept the results of its commissioned studies uncritically; the presentation of L. V. Walker's and R. I. Haskell's studies illustrate this tendency. Last of all, it is disconcerting to discover that one study cited in the *Report* (and, incidentally, also in the 1950 edition of the *Encyclopedia of Educational Research*) was not completed, is nowhere obtainable, and, thus, cannot be said to exist.

Among other things, the *Report* concluded that the evidence goes "far to show that, aside from its direct and cultural values, Latin does something for those who study it which gives them in other fields of mental effort a margin of advantage that may fairly be called substantial."[74] Perhaps this positive conclusion springs from the evidence, but there is still a question about the significance of the evidence.

. . . . .

What did the mighty labors of the Classical Investigation bring forth? Certainly those involved hoped to improve and encourage Latin study. An indication of the influence of their efforts may be found in a 1958 dissertation by Joan Marie Madsen, who studied the status of Latin in the public schools of Illinois.

Madsen found that 57.45 percent of the high schools in Illinois in 1956-1957 offered Latin and that these schools enrolled 80.57 percent of the total high school population in the state. However, only 8.22 percent of the students were actually taking Latin courses. (The Classical Investigation of 1921-1924 claimed that 30 percent of all high school students were enrolled in Latin

---

[73] *The Doctrine of Correctness in English Usage, 1700-1800.* University of Wisconsin Studies in Language and Literature, No. 25 (Madison, Wis.: University of Wisconsin, 1929); *Current English Usage.* English Monograph Series, No. 1 (Chicago: National Council of Teachers of English, 1932).

[74] American Classical League, *The Classical Investigation,* p. 243.

classes.) Also, 68.11 percent of the schools offering Latin offered only two years of study, and 26.77 percent offered work in Latin beyond two years.[75]

According to Madsen, 68.78 percent of the teachers relied heavily upon the translation method of instruction, 53.59 percent relied heavily upon the translation-grammar method, and 42.61 percent relied heavily upon the grammar-translation method. Madsen concluded that Latin teaching "appeared to remain static in its stress upon translation and grammar rather than upon the reading method and socio-cultural objectives vigorously proposed by learned opinion since the Classical Investigation of 1921–24."[76]

. . . . .

"Conjecture and surmise," observed Edith I. Newcomb, "have long been rife as to the superiority of the Latin pupils . . . ."[77] In an attempt to settle the question, Newcomb obtained test results from more than 100 schools in 35 states. The tests were given in September to students just beginning Latin study and to those not taking Latin. The tests were given at the start of the semester in order to prevent class instruction from influencing the results.

Newcomb found that the range of performance in reading was great but that, as a group, the Latin students did slightly better. With respect to word knowledge (vocabulary), Newcomb found a greater superiority for the Latin students and, again, a wide range of scores for both Latins and non-Latins with the former scoring higher. On the test for grammatical knowledge, the Latins surpassed the non-Latins. Again the range was great. This time there was an increase in low scores for both groups with the non-Latins supplying more low scores. Finally, the scores achieved on the several tests for general intelligence showed that the Latin group was superior to the extent that 65 percent of the Latin group reached or exceeded the median of the non-Latin group. To Newcomb, this 65 percent overlap did not indicate very great superiority and would be approximately the same degree of superiority that women display over men in ability to detect different tastes or that girls display over boys in ability to mark the letter A. Once again, ranges were wide for both groups and varied greatly from school to school; in one school, students' mental ages ranged from eleven years to seventeen and one half years, whereas in another they ranged from nine and one half to a point above the scale of measurement.

Newcomb drew the following conclusions: On the whole, Latin pupils are more able than non-Latin pupils; the superiority of the Latin pupils is not as great as it had been thought to be; the Latin group—like the non-Latin group—

[75] Joan Marie Madsen, "A Study of Current Practices in the Teaching of Latin in the Public High Schools of the State of Illinois, 1956–57" (Ph.D. dissertation, University of Illinois, 1958); in *Dissertation Abstracts,* 19, 10 (April 1959), 2550.

[76] *Loc. cit.*

[77] Edith I. Newcomb, "A Comparison of the Latin and Non-Latin Groups in High School," *Teachers College Record,* 23 (November 1922), 413.

includes students of vastly different abilities; and, last of all, group character-istics vary markedly from school to school.[78] Unless evidence comes to light that Latin and non-Latin groups have altered their composition since Newcomb's investigation, it would appear that Newcomb has settled the question. Inciden-tally, Newcomb's finding that group characteristics vary markedly from school to school explains why Otis, in the study referred to earlier, had such trouble matching the intelligence scores of pupils in his Latin and non-Latin groups.

9. SUMMARY AND CONCLUSION

Is there a *Via Latina* to English mastery? The claim that the study of Latin will help students master English continues to be made, and in order to assess its merits, it is necessary to examine both historical and experimental evidence.

a) A review of the development of the English language shows that English grammar of the familiar textbook sort was greatly influenced by Latin but that the structure of the English language itself grew to be quite different from the structure of Latin. However, Latin contributed heavily to English vocabulary. Whether this contribution is an enrichment, a handicap, or a not unmixed bless-ing, it is nevertheless correct to say that the significance of the Latin contribution to the English vocabulary is limited by the fact that the most commonly used words are of Anglo-Saxon stock and that changes in form and meaning of words over the years have often obscured their Latin origin. Consequently, the history of the language does not encourage one to suppose that Latin study will provide a ready avenue to the mastery of the structure or vocabulary of the English lan-guage.

b) Among the experimental studies, one group deals with the number of pure Latin words (i.e., not English words derived from Latin) and the number of classical references in newspapers, magazines, and literature. Although the studies identified thousands of Latin items, they were concerned with quantity expressed in so-many-thousands of Latin items and not in terms of the propor-tion of Latin items in the total body of writings, and further, they failed to con-sider the significance of their findings in terms of cultural value or plain com-munication. At this point, therefore, it would be premature to conclude that Latin should be studied in the Latin class or as part of the English course because English contains many Latin words and references. Whether, how, and to what degree Latin words and classical references should be studied are questions which at this time can be answered only in terms of a personal estimate of their cultural and communicative significance.

c) Does translating Latin improve students' ability to write English? Studies dealing with this question are agreed that "translation English" is likely to be poor English and that students' translations are likely to be inferior to the same students' English compositions.

d) Another group of studies investigated the benefit supposed to exist in studying one language as preparation for the study of another. One study found

[78]*Ibid.*, p. 422.

French and Spanish more efficacious than Latin and German and found, also, that English usage benefited from foreign language study whereas vocabulary and spelling did not. Another study found that Latin definitely aided the study of French and Spanish, but another found that Latin was only slightly related to probable success in French. In addition, a study of the opinions of the English and foreign language teachers showed that the English teachers considered unimportant half the grammatical items considered important by their foreign language colleagues. The conclusion is that Latin is not known to have special powers to confer upon the student of some other foreign language or upon the student of English. Among related languages, the study of one is likely to be of some help in the study of another. But no language has yet been identified experimentally to be of such great help that it should be studied because it paves the way to the mastery of another.

e) By far the most attention of the researchers was given to the problem of Latin study as a means of improving the English vocabulary. Almost all the studies showed some vocabulary gain for the Latin students. Although some of the studies on both sides of the issue were criticized, the studies which seemed more competent showed that the Latin students in comparison with the non-Latin students made either no special gains or made very slight gains. The conclusion here is that Latin is either suspect as an improver of vocabulary or of slight value and that intelligence seems to be a more important factor in predicting students' vocabulary achievement.

f) The investigations dealing with the value of the study of Latin to improve English spelling established that perhaps as many as two thirds of English spelling errors in Latin-derived words are potentially remediable through the study of Latin. Potentially remediable, however, means only that some Latin words resemble their English descendents so closely that a knowledge of the Latin word will enable one to spell or deduce the spelling of the English word. If spelling help from Latin is potentially possible two thirds of the time and if the total vocabulary is about 60 percent Latinate, then only two thirds of 60 percent, or 40 percent, of the words in the total vocabulary are potentially remediable through Latin study. Since this estimate of potential remediability is not an estimate of actual remediability and since actual remediability will be influenced by the number of exceptions to each spelling rule governing the application of Latin spelling to English and since remediability through Latin assumes an ability to spell Latin, it is apparent that even a generous allowance of 40 percent potential remediability promises only a much diminished practical aid in any attempt to improve English spelling.

Other studies dealing with Latin and spelling produced mixed results. One study found no significant difference between the spelling scores of Latin and non-Latin students. One group found an insignificant advantage in favor of the Latin students. Another group concluded that Latin study did help students to master English spelling. The final estimate, after allowing for the limitations in the studies on both sides, is that the study of Latin affords students a slight advantage in mastering English spelling but that this advantage is too slight and achieved by too circuitous a path to constitute either a substantial justification for the study of Latin or a practical adjunct to the study of English.

g) Undoubtedly, Latin is a substantial help in aiding students to master and (with less certainty) to apply the Latin-derived rules of English grammar that are familiar to past and present readers of secondary school textbooks. However, to define English grammar in terms of rules of Latin origin is to stack the deck in favor of a particular experimental outcome. Because the grammatical picture is quite different when considered from a descriptive, linguistically oriented viewpoint, it seems probable that Latin study would be of little help to the student seeking to understand the linguistic picture of English.

There are no experimental investigations testing whether Latin study can increase one's grasp of a non-Latinate English grammar. The best evidence, at present, on the relationship between Latin and English grammar is historical, and what it reveals most importantly is a basic structural dissimilarity between the two languages.

h) Among the studies presented as tangentially related to the problem of Latin as a route to English mastery, the first, really a series of studies sponsored by the Classical League, sought primarily to improve Latin teaching. In those aspects dealing with the relationship between Latin and English, the Classical Investigation seemed lacking in a number of respects. Another study, which dealt with the status of Latin in Illinois in 1956–1957, demonstrated that Latin instruction had been static since the date of the Classical Investigation and that Latin teachers still retained such primary educational objectives as to increase English vocabulary and to increase understanding of English grammar. Finally, a study designed to test the assumption that Latin students are superior to other students found that the Latin students are, taken as a group, superior but are far less superior than had been thought. It would seem that the more able students are attracted to Latin but that in both Latin and non-Latin groups there is a very wide range of abilities and that the quality of the students in both groups varies widely from school to school.

. . . . .

There is no *Via Latina* to English mastery, but, then, neither is there a royal road to geometry, as Euclid is reported to have said to Ptolemy I. The way to master English is the same as the way to master Latin—attend to it diligently and, if possible, with the help of a good teacher. Any benefit transferable from the study of one to the study of the other is likely to be a meager and insufficient reward for one's efforts. Until the widespread notion that Latin is the handmaiden of English is dispelled, both Latin and English instruction will suffer, and Latin will neither function in the schools nor be regarded at large as a body of knowledge with intrinsic merit.

Chapter **II**

Eggys, Egges, Eyren:
The Problem of Spelling

There are those who share Napoleon's view that a man occupied with important business cannot, need not, concern himself with spelling. Similarly, there are those who agree with Whitman that niceties in spelling lead to impotence in literature. There is a band of undetermined size whose contempt is for the fellow who knows only one way to spell a word. Perhaps—this is a guess—the largest group is essentially ambivalent. But all, no doubt, would lament with William Caxton the creation of the problem: "Loo! what sholde a man in thyse dayes now wryte, egges or eyren? certaynly it is harde to playse every man by cause of dyversite and chaunge of langage."

The irony is that Caxton, the first English printer, helped to aggravate the very situation he found so distressing. By introducing printing, he strengthened the tendency toward standardization of word form without, at the same time, slowing or directing changes in pronunciation. The result is an orthography that is less consistent between sound and graphic symbol than would otherwise be the case. Beyond any question, the difficulty of modern English spelling and conflicting contemporary attitudes regarding the importance of spelling have together greatly complicated the task of teaching spelling.

Research in spelling has followed many paths. Some studies are frankly practical. Should the teacher point out hard spots in words? Should words be taught by rule? Is test-study or study-test the better method? Other studies seek clues to the basic processes by which spelling is learned. There is no shortage of studies; the problem, as usual, is to find food value before one succumbs to verbal engorgement.

1. WHAT IS A MISSPELLING?

The first problem, of course, is to decide what words to teach. Two studies carry a clear warning about what *not* to teach. It is obviously foolish to waste valuable class time on words which are not spelling problems. But when is a word misspelled? Donald W. Emery's study says that there are many "fairly common words" which may be spelled in two or more ways, according to respectable dictionaries, and that even the dictionaries do not always agree on the number and spelling of the variant forms of a word. Emery reports that at

29

times it was "difficult to decide which form a dictionary considers the more common spelling and which the variant."[1]

What Emery did was to document what any observing user of dictionaries must have noticed, namely, that dictionaries, even good dictionaries, do not always agree on spelling. Emery compared entries in the *American College Dictionary* (1957), *Webster's New Collegiate Dictionary* (1956), *Webster's New World Dictionary* (1957), *Thorndike-Barnhart Comprehensive Desk Dictionary* (1957), and *Funk & Wagnalls New College Standard Dictionary* (1956). The resulting list is most interesting, but it is unclear what Emery meant by "fairly common words." Some words, like *socks* and *swat,* seem much more "fairly common" than others, like *umiak* and *pavan.* The main point, at any rate, is sound enough; the teacher should not be too quick to assume a misspelling; the student may know ways to spell that are unfamiliar to the teacher.

There is no present information about how much of the so-called spelling problem is owing to people's, especially teachers', unfamiliarity with variant spellings or hostility to variant spellings. One piece of evidence does, however, support the contention that people's rigid attitudes toward spelling have made the problem seem at least a little worse than it really is. In 1950, Thomas Clark Pollock set out to find what spelling errors college students actually make. He asked 599 college teachers in 52 colleges and universities in 27 states to send him the "next fifty words" their students misspelled in their compositions. The results of this study will be discussed in another connection later, but for now it is enough to report Pollock's statement that "a number of college teachers. . . assumed that a student misspells when he writes *judgement. . .or fulfill. . . .*"[2] Tactfully, Pollock refused to reveal the exact number, but clearly he thought it significant. Pollock's experience strengthens the suspicion that some part of the hubbub over poor spelling comes from those who either know or like only one spelling for a word. More important, however, is the fact that spelling instruction, if it is to be more than the perpetuation of teachers' spelling prejudices, must be grounded in the facts of the language as reported in major dictionaries compiled in accordance with modern lexicographical principles.[3]

2. DO WE SPELL AS WELL AS WE USED TO?

A legion of commentators, both in and out of the professional journals, maintain that students are poor spellers. After granting that people are hard to please and that any misspelling is likely to provoke some criticism, the hard

---

[1] Donald W. Emery, *Variant Spellings in Modern American Dictionaries* (Champaign, Ill.: National Council of Teachers of English, 1958), pp. 14, 15.

[2] Thomas Clark Pollock, "Spelling Report," *College English,* 16 (November 1954), 102-103.

[3] For a brief statement of the modern lexicographer's job, see Clarence L. Barnhart, "General Introduction," *American College Dictionary* (New York: Harper & Brothers, 1951), pp. xix-xx; for a history of dictionaries, see Mitford M. Mathews, *A Survey of English Dictionaries* (London: Oxford University Press, 1933); for the controversy over what a dictionary should be and do (generated by the publication of *Webster's Third New International Dictionary*), see James Sledd and Wilma R. Ebbitt, *Dictionaries and THAT Dictionary* (Glenview, Ill.: Scott, Foresman and Company, 1962).

question remains: How does the spelling skill of present-day students compare with the spelling skill of students a generation or more ago?

Fred C. Ayer compared the median scores of ninth grade students on the same words contained in standardized tests given in 1915, 1925, and 1950. The results, according to Ayer, "indicate a deplorable falling-off in current high-school spelling ability."[4] He found, for example, that *trouble* was correctly spelled 100 percent of the time in 1915, 95 percent of the time in 1925, and 91 percent of the time in 1950; for *stomach,* the results for the 3 years were 94 percent, 82 percent, and 78 percent.

Andrew M. Doyle sought to discover how present-day students compare with students of yesteryear. His method is ingenious.

> If properly determined, the norms of a standardized test reflect the achievement of the entire population from which the standardizing sample is drawn. Two populations can, then, be compared as to achievement if we have two tests—one standardized on each population. The two tests can be administered to any group of pupils all of whom take both tests. If the average score on one test is higher than the average score on the other, it can be concluded that the groups upon which the tests were standardized were not equal in achievement, for the tests are not of equal difficulty. If one of the tests represented the achievement of the pupils of today and the other that of pupils of thirty years ago, then the difference in the difficulty of the tests would reflect a difference in the achievement of the two groups.[5]

Doyle administered one contemporary spelling test (part of the Stanford Achievement Test, Form D) and one dated 1918 (the Buckingham Extension of the Ayres Spelling Scale). Both tests were given to 1,415 students, grades two to eight, in 6 schools in 5 states. Doyle's tabulation shows that at each grade level the students performed less successfully on the Buckingham test, indicating that the Buckingham test was harder for them and that, consequently, the Buckingham test was standardized for a group in 1918 that spelled more ably than do contemporary students. After ruling out the possibility that the results were influenced by students' lack of familiarity with the words in the Buckingham test, Doyle concluded that the "earlier group emerges. . .superior" in spelling.[6]

Neither Ayer nor Doyle attempted to explain the decline in spelling proficiency. All reasons that have been advanced, such as the existence of a more select student body years ago or the declining respect for spelling skill among students today, are essentially speculative. The fact remains. Spelling shares the fate of the Old Grey Mare.

3. THE PRESENT STATE OF AFFAIRS

After allowing the possibility that our predecessors might be able to outspell

---

[4] Fred C. Ayer, "An Evaluation of High-School Spelling," *School Review,* 59 (April 1951), 236.
[5] Andrew M. Doyle, "A Study of Spelling Achievement," *Catholic Educational Review,* 48 (1950), 171.
[6] *Ibid.,* p. 174.

us, it is still worth asking how well, or poorly, our students are doing and how well, or poorly, we are teaching. The evidence is not encouraging.

Doris Hagman and H. R. Laslett characterized the performance of 204 students whom they tested as "not very commendable."[7] Hagman and Laslett gave a series of 16 tests consisting of 20 words each to students in required freshman, sophomore, junior, and senior classes in a high school. The tested words were "widely used in everyday speech and writing" and were "relatively simple."[8] The investigators then counted spelling mistakes and noted any relationships between students' performance and their intelligence. They found that students with lower IQ's made the greater number of mistakes; that girls spelled better than did the boys; that spelling ability improved steadily from grade to grade; and, finally, that the general level of spelling ability for the entire 4-year group was uncommendable—the students having misspelled a mean of 80 words out of 320.

The authors' claim that the students were representative of high school students in general is based only on the fact that the students were in a required course. Maybe they were a representative group, but the reason for believing it is insufficient. Did the school draw its students from a cross-section of the American population or largely from a particular socioeconomic group? On this question the study is silent. Other studies have found a wide range of spelling ability from school to school. In any case, Hagman and Laslett, in their study dealing with students in one school, found a level of spelling performance which they regarded as unsatisfactory.

It would be possible to dismiss the situation Hagman and Laslett found as merely an isolated case were it not for the fact that other researchers have concluded much as they did. Oliver E. Harris, for example, investigated the average spelling achievement and range of achievement of students in grades eight through twelve. He constructed 8 tests of 20 or 25 words each, taking his words from *The Stanford Speller* (Laidlaw Brothers, 1937) and from the *Teachers Manual for Directed Spelling Activities and Guide to Spelling Progress,* by Emmett A. Betts and Mabel Louise Arey (American Book Company, 1941). After satisfying himself as to the validity, reliability, and discrimination of the grade-level tests, he administered them in the order of increasing difficulty to 1,235 students in grades eight through twelve with the help of 35 teachers. Test scores were checked by Harris and an assistant. Harris then computed and recorded the percentage of words spelled correctly on each test and on the total of 8 tests. In order to determine the level of achievement for each student in a given grade, Harris defined level of achievement as "the highest level for which he scores ninety percent or higher, provided he has failed to make ninety percent on no more than two consecutive tests at lower levels."[9] The range of

[7]Doris Hagman and H. R. Laslett, "The Spelling Ability of High-School Pupils," *School and Society,* 73 (June 2, 1951), 348.

[8]*Ibid.,* pp. 347, 348.

[9]Oliver E. Harris, "An Investigation of Spelling Achievement of Secondary-School Pupils," *Educational Administration and Supervision,* 34 (1948), 213.

achievement was identified, first, by recording the highest and lowest scores for students in each grade and, second, by recording the highest and lowest assigned grade level for each student in each grade.

Harris' estimate of the students' achievement was low. "The average achievement of Grade VII pupils was approximately high third or fourth grade level; of Grade VIII, fourth or fifth; Grade IX, fifth or sixth; Grade X, sixth or seventh; and Grades XI and XII, seventh grade level." The picture in terms of ranges offers little encouragement. "With the exception of Grade XII pupils, whose lowest achievement level was second grade, the achievement levels ranged from below second grade to a substantial high school level."[10]

Harris' study dealt with students in grades seven through twelve in one school district. Another study by William H. Fox and Merrill T. Eaton dealt with 3,547 classes and 82,833 pupils in grades two through eight in urban public and parochial schools in Indiana. The Fox-Eaton study was designed to reveal whether students were on, above, or below the norms for their grade as defined in a standardized test. The study also sought to uncover relationships between spelling performance and such variables as length of school year, size of school, length of spelling period, time of day when spelling is taught, use of progress charts, and use of pretests. But the findings dealing with how well students performed in comparison with the norms for the grade were the most startling and among the most clear cut. Fox and Eaton found, first, that "At no grade level did the average pupil deviation for all students equal or exceed the norm. . ." and, second, that "On the average, the. . .pupils were .6 grade below the norm in tested spelling achievement."[11]

Another study to add to this discomfiting catalog is by Henry Lester Smith and the same Merrill T. Eaton who coauthored the research summarized in the passage immediately preceding. Smith and Eaton examined the English usage, vocabulary, and spelling of an unselected group of 251 first-year graduate students in education at Indiana University. The average scholarship of the group was 91.64. Approximately 70 percent were men, and approximately 70 percent of the group were between twenty and thirty-four years old. Most were preparing to teach high school subjects.[12]

Smith and Eaton gave the Cooperative English Test, Provisional Form OM, to the 251 students and compared the results with the publisher's norms Type III which were based on 14,000 students in 35 colleges who most closely resembled the students in the Smith-Eaton group. "Since norms in Type III are not provided for graduate students, the norms used in this study were those found for seniors. The seniors. . .were tested at the end of the senior year so that

[10]*Ibid.*, p. 216.
[11]William H. Fox and Merrill T. Eaton, "Analysis of the Spelling Proficiency of 82,833 Pupils in Grades 2 to 8 in 3,547 Teaching Units in the City Schools of Indiana," *Bulletin of the School of Education of Indiana University,* 22 (1946), 43.
[12]Henry Lester Smith and Merrill T. Eaton, "A Study of the English Usage, Spelling, and Vocabulary of 251 Graduate Students at Indiana University," *Bulletin of the School of Education of Indiana University*, 16 (1940), 22.

they do not differ greatly from beginning graduate students so far as semesters of schooling are concerned."[13]

What Smith and Eaton found, among other things, was that the graduate students, as a group, "were much less efficient in English usage and spelling than were the seniors."[14] "Perhaps the most significant aspect of this phase of the study was the poor aptitude by all. . .groups in usage and spelling, as even the English group did not reach the senior standard norm. . . ."[15]

It is possible to temporize a little in interpreting studies such as the last two which compare students' spelling performance to norms established for a standardized test. What is being compared, really, is the performance of the group studied with the performance of the group used to establish the norms. If, as in the Fox-Eaton and Smith-Eaton studies, the experimental groups performed less ably than did the norms groups, all that has been shown is that one group did better than another. One could even argue that the norms show that people can spell fairly well or, at least, can spell better than can the subjects in the experiments and that this is grounds for encouragement. However, the fact remains that Fox-Eaton's thousands of Indiana school children did not measure up and neither did Smith-Eaton's graduate students. This fact alone should effectively forestall rejoicing in the streets and should add to the suspicion that spelling instruction could be much improved.

In an attempt to get to the heart of the problem, Dwight L. Arnold, in 1941, tried to find out whether teaching spelling helps students to spell. His study was designed to test the conclusions of two earlier studies; one had found that spelling ability developed at about the same rate whether or not the word had been taught, and the other had found that more spelling is learned before and after instruction than during the time of instruction.

Arnold gave spelling tests to 2,250 students in grades three through six in 10 elementary schools. Arnold calculated the percentage of pupils each semester who spelled a given word correctly. Then he constructed a graph for each word showing percentages of students at each semester who could spell the word correctly and showing the semester during which the word was taught. He also prepared graphs for words that were not taught but which, of course, had been tested.

After examining the graphic record, Arnold concluded that "teaching a particular set of words in a particular semester. . .does not make a distinct and continuing contribution to the growth of ability. . .to spell. . . ."[16] In support of this conclusion he showed that for most words teaching merely disturbed, but did not seriously change, the general growth curve and that—for at least 15 of

[13]*Ibid.*, p. 23.
[14]*Ibid.*, p. 65.
[15]*Ibid.*, p. 64.
[16]Dwight L. Arnold, "Spelling Lessons and Ability to Spell," *Elementary School Journal*, 42 (September 1941), 40.

19 words—teaching "seems to have had no permanent beneficial effect on the curve of mastery."[17] The finding that the graphs of untaught words were "not distinctly unlike"[18] the graphs of taught words provides additional evidence in support of Arnold's contention that instruction was ineffective. The fact that the schools in the study used the much recommended test-study method would suggest either that the method is overrated or, at least, insufficient to overcome the handicap imposed by the absence of cumulative lists or periodic reviews.

The significance of Arnold's study is limited in that his conclusions can apply only to one kind of teaching—a list method in which a word is taught, however thoroughly, only once. There is no information about how prevalent this method is, although Arnold, at the time he wrote, thought the method quite common. In any case, the thousands of children in the school system Arnold studied were apparently not getting much benefit from the 15 minutes of each day devoted to spelling instruction. Until that thing called "articulation" ceases to be an educational problem and until the efforts of all teachers at all grade levels coordinate their efforts smoothly, it seems a fair assumption that there will be places aplenty which could profitably take Arnold's study to heart.

A study by E. R. Sifert is worth mentioning in spite of its 1926 date and its flaws. Sifert gave 78 students in grade eight a 200-word test of words they had studied and a 200-word test of words they had not studied. Both tests were of equal difficulty as determined by the Iowa Spelling Scale (1918). Sifert found that his students spelled "studied words better than unstudied words by a mean difference of only 1.8%."[19]

The study suffers because few students were involved and, primarily, because no effort was made to control the kind of instruction students received during and before the experiment. There is the possibility, in spite of Arnold's findings, that had instruction been better the results might have been different. But even after disregarding problems of method, there is the problem of the interpretation of the results. In spite of the small gain on the test of studied words, did students really profit from instruction so that they were able to learn unstudied words in an incidental way? Sifert suggested this possibility.[20] But it seems unlikely because students with such expertise at incidental learning would surely have achieved higher scores on each of the two tests, regardless of their showing in a comparison of test results. What we have here, in any case, is a thin strand of evidence that instruction of the kind in use at the time of the experiment did not pay off very well.

Worth mentioning, last of all, is Robert S. Thompson's study which undertook an assessment of the effectiveness of spelling instruction. Writing in 1930

---

[17]*Ibid.*, p. 39.
[18]*Ibid.*, p. 40.
[19]E. R. Sifert, "A Comparative Study of the Abilities of 8th Grade Children to Spell Studied and Unstudied Words" (Master's thesis, State University of Iowa, 1926), p. 27.
[20]*Ibid.*, p. 28.

("the good old days"?), Thompson concluded that the "state of affairs can hardly be regarded as satisfactory even by the most confirmed optimist."[21] An interesting feature of the study is that it scrutinized "children with relatively permanent habits of correct spelling" in a school "reaching or exceeding" nationwide norms and using methods held to be in conformity with the "best scientific knowledge."[22] The disappointment evident in Thompson's just cited conclusion must be owing in large measure to his having deliberately stacked the cards in favor of a far more happy result.

The experiment was conducted under regular school conditions, and the teachers, who were accustomed to a data-collecting principal, were not informed that anything special was going on. Teachers used their customary method of teaching spelling, the test-study method. The words for the week were pretested on Monday. The words were pronounced, used in a sentence, and defined if necessary. Students spelled the word and, after the test was corrected, added their misspellings to their "demon" lists. Words missed were studied on Tuesday. A second test was given on Wednesday, and missed words were studied on Thursday. After a third test on Friday, each student recorded his mistakes for further study the following week. Reviews were held every fourth week. Students were urged to study spelling by pronouncing a word, visualizing the syllabicated word with eyes closed, recalling the word, looking at the word, writing the word, comparing the word, writing it again, comparing it again, and writing it a third and last time.

Each week, except for review weeks, the teachers in grades two to eight reported the number of mistakes in the 20-word spelling assignment. The number of errors on the Monday prestudy test was recorded along with the percentage of correct spellings for each word and the number of pupils who spelled each word. Teachers also kept records on the spelling performance of each ability group in the school. To obtain information about retention, the teachers gave 50-word tests every 4 weeks using the words taught in the previous semester.

Thompson did not say what, precisely, in his findings led him to conclude that spelling instruction is "hardly...satisfactory," but he did say that he thought schools should strive for "95 to 100 percent mastery"[23] of words specifically taught and that he found specific teaching to be "only about 50 percent efficient in all grades except the upper grades, where the efficiency is only a little more than one-third."[24] In short, Thompson, who studied what he regarded as a superior teaching situation, was dissatisfied with the results that were being obtained and was doubtful of the effectiveness of the methods being employed.

The several studies mentioned here have sought in various ways to discover

[21] Robert S. Thompson, *The Effectiveness of Modern Spelling Instruction* (New York: Bureau of Publications, Teachers College, Columbia University, 1930), p. 73.

[22] *Ibid.*, p. 22.

[23] *Ibid.*, p. 73.

[24] *Ibid.*, p. 71.

how well we are teaching and how well our students are learning. All the writers agree that the results are beneath what they regard as their legitimate expectations. Maybe these expectations are unrealistic when applied to mass education, but it would be premature to reach such a conclusion before all imaginable means of improvement have been tried and found wanting and before future researches into the psychology of spelling have proved to be a light that failed.

4. THE SPELLING CURRICULUM

Imagine a spelling teacher staring at the imposing bulk of *Webster's Third New International Dictionary* and praying softly, "Which words, O Lord, which words?" It is easy to sympathize, and the problem is real—real enough to have stimulated some mighty efforts to discover which words deserve inclusion in a spelling curriculum. Some investigators have sought to identify difficult words, "demons" or frequently misspelled words; others have investigated the frequency with which words occur in student writing, adult writing, and publications; others have tried to find means for deciding at which grade a word should be taught.

Typically during the nineteenth century and to a lesser extent even today, spelling lists consisted of words which were thought to be appropriate to adult writing and speech. Noah Webster's *Elementary Spelling Book,* the so-called Blue-backed Speller, is the best example of a book written in this tradition, and it was easily the most influential. In 1850 it sold more than a million copies, or approximately one copy for every 23 people in the nation. Whole generations of pioneer children memorized such words as *vellum, foppish, temporal.* Spelling bees (also called spelldowns because it was the custom for a contestant to be seated as a sign of defeat when the word he missed was correctly spelled by another contestant) were considered social and recreational as well as educational activities. Spelling bees are still with us. Although they seem to have lost their local social and recreational character, they are still contests in spelling hard words. Although spelling bees and spelling lists were supposed to give students spelling skills necessary in adult life, it now seems abundantly clear that the words learned were uncommon even in adult use. If spelling instruction in the public schools is supposed to be practical and useful, then a calculation of the time wasted in learning to spell rarely occurring words must be astronomically large.

The twentieth century has seen the production of many lists intended to identify frequently occurring words. The first, published in 1910 by W. E. Chancellor, listed the 1,000 spelling words which the author considered most important. But Chancellor recorded no frequencies for the words he listed, and the study is of no scientific value, whatever its historical value may be.[25] Another early study by L. P. Ayres is worth mentioning only because it stirred great interest in research in the frequency of occurrence of words and in

[25]W. E. Chancellor, "Spelling: 1,000 Words," *Journal of Education* (Boston), 71 (May 5, 12, 19, June 2, 1910), 488–489, 517, 522, 545–546, 573, 578, 607–608.

establishing an objective spelling word list.[26] The results of the Ayres and the
Chancellor studies and of several other early studies[27] were compiled by Ernest
Horn and were included in his further investigation, *A Basic Writing Vocabulary*.[28] Horn's work is widely regarded as influential and is deserving of additional comment.

Horn started with a compilation of about 864,334 running words obtained
from previous investigations. He then supplemented this body of information by
conducting additional investigations into the vocabulary of business correspondence; personal correspondence; well-known writers' letters printed in magazines
and newspapers; letters of application and recommendation; excuses written by
parents to teachers; minutes, resolutions, committee reports; and letters of a single
individual. In all, 5,136,816 running words were involved in the study, including
the original 864,334. Horn's frequency count of the millions of running words
enabled him to identify the 10,000 most frequently occurring words. Estimates
were made of the frequencies of 372 words which had first been omitted from
the study but were later included.

Horn's count is probably not representative of the adult vocabulary. In commenting elsewhere about his study, Horn acknowledged the probability that "a
disproportionate amount of material was sampled from the writings of persons
at higher educational levels."[29] The study itself reports that approximately
44 percent of the running words "were from business and professional
letters."[30]

The first claim that Horn made for his list was that it "affords a scientific
basis for selecting the words to be taught."[31] Granting the appeal to science and
allowing for the distortion in favor of a more educated vocabulary, the question
remains as to how valuable the list is for school use. It would seem that the
lower the grade, the less useful the list because, after all, it is a list of words in
the adult, not the child, vocabulary. Again, granting an overlap of children's and

[26]L. P. Ayres, *The Spelling Vocabularies of Personal and Business Letters* (New York:
Russell Sage Foundation, 1913).
[27]Anne Nicholson, *A Speller for the Use of the Teachers of California* (Sacramento:
California State Printing Office, 1914); W. A. Cook and M. V. O'Shea, *The Child and His
Spelling* (Indianapolis: Bobbs-Merrill Company, 1914); W. N. Andersen, "Determination of
a Spelling Vocabulary Based upon Written Correspondence," *University of Iowa Studies in
Education*, 2,1 (1921), 1-66; J. D. Hauser, "An Investigation of the Writing Vocabularies of
Representatives of an Economic Class," *Elementary School Journal*, 17 (1916-1917),
708-718; W. F. Clarke, "Writing Vocabularies," *Elementary School Journal*, 21 (January
1921), 349-351; Ernest Horn, "The Vocabulary of Bankers' Letters," *English Journal*, 12
(June 1923), 383–397; Ernest Horn, "The Vocabulary of Highly Personal Letters," 1922
(unpublished). For a discussion of each of these studies, see Ernest Horn's *A Basic Writing
Vocabulary*, pp. 8ff. Horn also lists (pp. 45–46) eight early studies dealing with children's
in-school writing vocabulary.
[28]Ernest Horn, *A Basic Writing Vocabulary*. University of Iowa Monograph in
Education (Iowa City: University of Iowa, 1926).
[29]Ernest Horn, "Spelling," *Encyclopedia of Educational Research* (New York: The
Macmillan Company, 1960), p. 1339.
[30]Horn, *A Basic Writing Vocabulary*, p. 185.
[31]*Ibid.*, p. 193.

adults' vocabularies, it seems clear that Horn's list should be used cautiously and should not be the sole determiner of the spelling curriculum. As Horn pointed out, studies of the adult vocabulary tell us about the demands that later life will make upon the spelling skills of today's children, and studies of the child's vocabulary tell us about either the present status of the child's vocabulary or about the child's present spelling needs. Studies of the child's vocabulary are not proper measures of the adult's vocabulary any more than studies of the adult's vocabulary are proper measures of the child's vocabulary. Both types of studies are needed. [32]

The Teacher's Word Book, surely the best-known word list, was compiled in 1921 by Edward L. Thorndike. Originally a list of the 10,000 most frequently occurring words, it was expanded in 1931 to include the 20,000 most frequently occurring words, and in its last revision was expanded (with the assistance of Irving Lorge) to include the 30,000 most frequently occurring words. Unlike Horn's list, this list is not exclusively concerned with adult's vocabulary—nor, for that matter, with children's vocabulary. It is, instead, a list which, according to Thorndike, "tells. . .how common the word is in standard English reading matter."[33] The trick, of course, was to establish "standard English reading matter." Thorndike examined a great variety of printed material. Samplings were taken from such categories as textbooks, popular magazines, newspapers, mail order catalogs, postal regulations, juvenile books, the Bible, and literature assigned in school. Lacking criteria, it is impossible to say whether this conglomeration is really what it is supposed to be. Assuming that it does indeed represent standard English reading matter, it is more important to observe that Thorndike, in his 1921 edition, warned against using his list as a spelling list because derived forms of a word were not recorded and because derived forms are often more difficult to spell than the base form. That this important (and neglected) warning was not repeated in subsequent editions is regrettable. Of course, the *Word Book* does supply spelling information about those word forms it does list.

Probably both the Thorndike and Horn lists tell us most about the spelling vocabulary that the student should have at his command when he is grown and no longer a student. Important as this is, it is only a part of what teachers and curriculum makers need to know. To supplement the information it is necessary to turn to studies of words that children write.

The chief study of children's vocabulary was published by Henry D. Rinsland in 1945. Rinsland examined 6,012,359 running words and found 25,632 different words of which 14,571 occurred 3 or more times. Rinsland obtained samples of writing from children in grades one through eight. Of 1,500 schools invited to participate—schools in all kinds of geographic and socioeconomic areas—708 or 47.2 percent responded. Rinsland considered this a statisti-

---

[32] Ernest Horn, "Spelling," *Encyclopedia of Educational Research,* p. 1339.
[33] Edward L. Thorndike and Irving Lorge, *The Teacher's Word Book of 30,000 Words* (New York: Bureau of Publications, Teachers College, Columbia University, 1944), p. x.

cally satisfactory response which also represented adequately the types of schools in his original selection of 1,500.[34] Unlike Thorndike and like Horn, Rinsland counted derived forms, contractions, and abbreviations as separate words.

Within its area, the Rinsland study is easily the most extensive and most thorough. Yet it is not without problems. For example, Rinsland found that children in first grade used 5,099 different written words, but Madeline Horn found that kindergarten children used more than 7,000 *spoken* words.[35] But at least part of the inconsistency between Madeline Horn's and Rinsland's lists may be explained by differences in what each chose to accept as a different word. However, Rinsland did acknowledge the possibility of a problem with respect to his data for first graders.[36] Also, Ernest Horn has pointed out that there are "inconsistencies" in the frequencies reported for individual words at different grade levels which are hard to explain and are "contrary to the evidence from other counts of children's writing."[37] Nevertheless, the Rinsland study is valuable and the most useful instrument of its kind that we possess.

Different from the three studies previously mentioned is James A. Fitzgerald's *A Basic Life Spelling Vocabulary*. This work is entirely based upon other lists, yet it makes a genuinely original contribution. It is, all in one, a summary of research, an interpretive discourse of "procedures for selecting and grading words for a spelling curriculum," and a basic vocabulary list for both children and adults.[38] The 2,650 words listed by Fitzgerald were "selected from a much larger tentative list which had been compiled by a careful study of child and adult writing vocabularies."[39] This tentative list was unpublished and had been compiled with the assistance of Paul McKee. Judging from the comparisons Fitzgerald made between his list of 2,650 words and other lists, it appears that Fitzgerald derived his list principally from Horn's *A Basic Writing Vocabulary* and Rinsland's *A Basic Vocabulary of Elementary School Children* and from several other less extensive but informative studies.[40] One could wish that Fitzgerald had been more explicit about the sources of his list. According to Fitzgerald, these words and their repetitions comprise 93.54 percent of the run-

[34] Henry D. Rinsland, *A Basic Vocabulary of Elementary School Children* (New York: The Macmillan Company, 1945), pp. 6, 10, 20.

[35] Madeline Horn, *A Study of the Vocabulary of Children Before Entering the First Grade* (Washington, D.C.: International Kindergarten Union, 1928).

[36] Rinsland, *A Basic Vocabulary*, p. 8.

[37] Ernest Horn, "Spelling," *Encyclopedia of Educational Research*, p. 1340.

[38] James A. Fitzgerald, *A Basic Life Spelling Vocabulary* (Milwaukee, Wis.: Bruce Publishing Company, 1951), p. 3.

[39] *Ibid.*, p. 50.

[40] Frederick S. Breed, *How to Teach Spelling* (Dansville, N. Y.: F. A. Owen Publishing Company, 1930); Frances Brittain and James A. Fitzgerald, "The Vocabulary and Spelling Errors of Second-Grade Children's Themes," *Elementary English Review*, 19 (February 1942), 43-50; Edward William Dolch, *Better Spelling* (Champaign, Ill.: Garrard Press, 1942); James A. Fitzgerald, "The Vocabulary and Spelling Errors of Third-Grade Children's Life-Letters," *Elementary School Journal*, 38 (March 1938), 518-527.

ning words from which the Rinsland list was derived and approximately 95 percent of the running words in the unpublished McKee-Fitzgerald list.[41] All of the 2,650 words are in McKee-Fitzgerald's list and in Rinsland's list, all but 16 are in Horn's list, 2,151 are in Breed's list of 3,481 words, 1,611 are in Dolch's list of 2,000 most common spelling words, 669 are in Fitzgerald's list of 692 spelling errors of third graders, and 750 are in Brittain's list of 810 words misspelled in the themes of second graders.[42] "These 2,650 words," Fitzgerald asserted, "are a basic vocabulary for child and adult writing."[43]

The last of the "big lists" to be mentioned is B. R. Buckingham and E. W. Dolch's *A Combined Word List* (1936). It is a "combined" list in that it brings together the findings of Horn and Thorndike and several other vocabulary researchers. Preceding Rinsland's and Fitzgerald's lists, it is of interest here primarily because of its introduction of the free association technique for identifying words that children know. Twenty-one thousand six hundred ninety-five children in grades two to eight from New York City and "various towns in New England" supplied 2,714,857 words. These words were obtained by "having the children write any words which came to their minds" in a 15-minute period.[44] The list was not intended as a spelling list, but it does tell something about what words are important enough to children for them to think of them of their own accord. The list should be useful to writers of children's literature as well as to spelling teachers. In using the free association technique, Buckingham and Dolch sought to avoid the limitations imposed upon other studies which relied upon children's oral or written language. "As soon as a subject is selected by a child, it restricts his association to a narrow field." Free association, according to Buckingham and Dolch, permits the child's mind to wander far and wide "in accordance with certain general principles."[45]

It would be reassuring to have more than Buckingham's and Dolch's say-so that familiar school surroundings will not long limit the child's train of associations. It would seem that Buckingham and Dolch actually succeeded in trading one set of limitations for another. In place of the limitations imposed by assigned topics they have instead the limitations imposed by lack of imagination, by puzzlement at a suddenly unstructured situation, and the like. Nevertheless, the free association technique cannot be cavalierly dismissed. The faultless method for plumbing the depths of the mind is yet to be devised, and, until it is devised, any method that will reveal a portion of what we seek to know should be prized. It is regrettable that there have been no attempts by spelling and vocabulary investigators to refine the Buckingham-Dolch technique and carry the research further.

[41]Fitzgerald, *A Basic Life Spelling Vocabulary*, p. 53.
[42]*Ibid.*, pp. 50-51.
[43]*Ibid.*, p. 53.
[44]B. R. Buckingham and E. W. Dolch, *A Combined Word List* (Boston: Ginn and Company, 1936), pp. 3-5.
[45]*Ibid.*, p. 4.

One clear answer that research has provided is that children's and adults' vocabularies overlap. Bennie Joe Davis studied Horn's and Rinsland's lists and found evidence of considerable overlap. Of 2,999 words of highest frequency in Rinsland's list, 2,392 also appear in Horn's and Fitzgerald's lists.[46] Fitzgerald summarized the earlier evidence on overlapping and concluded that there is "important overlapping in child and adult writing vocabularies."[47] The interpretation of this finding is that spelling instruction should concern itself neither exclusively with spelling preparation for adulthood nor with spelling instruction for immediate needs but, rather, with teaching words every step of the way which reflect the present spelling needs of children as well as their preparation for the demands of the future. This can be done by teaching the words of highest frequency of occurrence in the children's vocabulary as well as the words of highest frequency which both children and adults use. This instructional view has been vigorously presented by Gertrude Hildreth[48] and also by Fitzgerald.[49] That, in general, words studied should be of high frequency is clear from the evidence reviewed by Fitzgerald.[50] The point is that relatively few words make up the bulk of written discourse; as the spelling list lengthens, the less need the student will have to use the additional words.

Frequently occurring words which are also troublesome words are called spelling demons. A genuine list of demons will provide a good start for the construction of a spelling curriculum. Fitzgerald has pointed out that his list of 222 demons accounted for 55 percent of the spelling errors he recorded. A composite list of 100 demons prepared by Fitzgerald from several previous lists accounted for about 39 percent of the errors in 682,082 running words of writing.[51] "It is obvious that, if persistent demons. . .could be taught. . .and mastered, a considerable percent of misspellings would disappear from the writing of children and adults."[52]

To the studies just mentioned, which review and build upon previous spelling demon lists, may be added Thomas Clark Pollock's study of the mistakes in spelling made by college students. Pollock's study, previously referred to, contains some preliminary findings about misspellings in seventh, eighth, and twelfth grade. The findings for the college years consist of 5 lists of words misspelled 100 times or more, 50 to 99 times, 40 to 49 times, 30 to 39 times, and 20 to 29 times. These lists were based on reports by 599 college teachers in

[46] Bennie Joe Davis, "A Study of the Vocabulary Overlap between Words Written by Children and Words Written by Adults" (Master's thesis, University of Texas, 1954), pp. 32, 132.

[47] Fitzgerald, *A Basic Life Spelling Vocabulary*, pp. 31ff.

[48] Gertrude Hildreth, "An Evaluation of Spelling Word Lists and Vocabulary Studies," *Elementary School Journal*, 51 (January 1951), 262-265.

[49] Fitzgerald, *A Basic Life Spelling Vocabulary*, p. 34.

[50] *Ibid.*, pp. 44-47.

[51] James A. Fitzgerald, "Spelling Words Difficult for Children in Grades II-VI," *Elementary School Journal*, 53 (December 1952), 223, 225.

[52] *Ibid.*, p. 227. See also Fitzgerald, *A Basic Life Spelling Vocabulary*, pp. 21, 141-152, for a detailed presentation of research on spelling demons.

52 institutions in 27 states. Each teacher reported "the next fifty words he found misspelled. . .in the compositions of his students."[53] Although Pollock did not actually say so, it seems probable, judging from the reference to compositions, that most or all of his data came from freshman writing. If this is true, then his study is really a study of mistakes made by first-year college students and is not a study which properly may be said to reflect the spelling condition of students throughout the four college years. A further limitation springs from the fact that college assignments were the source of the data. The topics on which the students were obliged to write must have influenced the vocabulary employed and, in turn, influenced the vocabulary of misspellings. However, this limitation is less than serious because, as the lists show, students used commonly occurring words as well as a more specialized and less frequently occurring vocabulary. Pollock found that only 9 percent of the words account for more than half the spelling errors and that 70 percent of the words were involved in only 18 percent of the spelling errors—and these words (the 70 percent) were misspelled fewer than 5 times each.[54] This confirms the findings of others that a limited number of spelling demons accounts for the largest number of errors.

Like Pollock, Edna L. Furness and Gertrude A. Boyd concluded that a "relatively small number of words. . .cause a great deal of the trouble."[55] In order to identify the most troublesome of troublesome words at the college level, Furness and Boyd compared 6 spelling lists, one of which was the Pollock list. Important information about the compilation of some of these lists is not available, but at least the Pollock list and the list by Kenneth B. M. Crooks (in "Reading and Science Instruction," *The American Biology Teacher,* 19 [May 1957], 134-143) are defensible. Furness and Boyd's collation identified 335 words which surely qualify as dreadful demons.

The grading of words has long been a touchy problem. Emmett A. Betts, in 1949, compared the grade placement of words in 8 spelling textbooks and found that among 8,652 words only 65 were graded in the same way by the 8 authors and that most of the agreement existed in the lower rather than the higher grades.[56] Of the 8,652 words in 8 textbooks, only 483 words were common to all 8 books.[57] In 1934, Carl T. Wise reported his examination of 20 spellers which claimed to be based on scientific investigations. Wise found 208,771 words including repetitions, 13,641 being different words. Of the 13,641, 30.72 percent appeared in only one book, 50.29 percent appeared in no more than 3 books, 73.39 percent appeared in no more than 10 books, and 26.61 percent appeared in 11 or more books. Only 6.48 percent of the words (or 884 words) appeared in all 20 books. This situation Wise described as an

---

[53] Pollock, "Spelling Report," *College English,* p. 102.

[54] *Ibid.,* pp. 103-104.

[55] Edna L. Furness and Gertrude A. Boyd, "335 Real Spelling Demons for College Students," *College English,* 20 (March 1959), 292.

[56] Emmett A. Betts, *Second Spelling Vocabulary Study* (New York: American Book Company, 1949), p. iv.

[57] *Ibid.,* p. v.

"extraordinary lack of agreement among authorities concerning the particular words that should form the basic spelling vocabulary. . . ."[58]   But, according to Wise, the situation with respect to grade placement is worse. "The initial grade placement of words shows far greater variability than does the selection of words for the spelling vocabulary. Only 54 words common to 5 or more spellers are placed in the same initial grade."[59]

There are some sensible, general principles to guide the would-be grader of spelling words, but very little has been done to supply prepared lists of graded words. Unfortunately, graded lists in spelling textbooks are not dependable, as Wise has shown.[60] As for the general principles to guide curriculum construction and word grading, one may readily find these summarized in the 1960 edition of the *Encyclopedia of Educational Research* (p. 1344). Additional help, in the form of studies by George Spache and Harry A. Greene, is welcome but hardly decisive.

Spache, in 1939, computed the average grade placement for selected words to be taught in the elementary school. Spache was primarily concerned with the reading-spelling vocabulary for remedial work, but the principal limitation of his study is that he relied upon three previous studies which assigned grade levels by averaging the grades assigned in spelling textbooks and "primers." To determine grade level by this scheme is to beg the question. If textbooks and primers had been properly graded to begin with, there would be no need for Spache's investigation. To take an average of doubtful guesses by textbook authors is even less inspiring of confidence than to make one's own guesses.[61]

Somewhat more useful is Greene's study which, among other things, was designed to give teachers "reliable information on the average or typical difficulty" of words in each elementary grade.[62] The sources of Greene's spelling list are Horn's, Rinsland's, Fitzgerald's, and Thorndike-Lorge's lists, and other less comprehensive lists. The resulting list of 5,507 words was sent to 230,327 students in 8,793 classrooms in 645 school systems in communities across the country with populations ranging in size from under 2,500 to a half million or more. The 5,507 words were divided into 111 tests of 50 words each. (Greene did not explain the arithmetical discrepancy.) Each 50-word test contained words of approximately the same range of frequency. Cooperating teachers received two different, randomly selected tests with directions for administering

---

[58]Carl T. Wise, "Selection and Gradation of Words in Spelling," *Elementary School Journal*, 34 (June 1934), 759.

[59]*Ibid.*, p. 765.

[60]Confirming evidence may be found in Douglas F. Dickerson, "Misleadings vs. Actualities in Spelling," *American School Board Journal*, 120 (February 1950), 33-34. Apparently the situation has changed little since 1950, judging from Horn's article in the 1960 edition of the *Encyclopedia of Educational Research*, p. 1344.

[61]George Spache, "A Minimum Reading-Spelling Vocabulary for Remedial Work," *Journal of Educational Research*, 33 (November 1939), 161-174.

[62]Harry A. Greene, *The New Iowa Spelling Scale* (Iowa City: State University of Iowa, 1954), p. 1.

and scoring the tests. The tests were the standard dictation type in which a word is pronounced, used in a sentence, and pronounced again before being written by the student. According to Greene, the scores "represent the spelling of all pupils in all classes sampled on a nation-wide basis."[63] Greene disclaimed any attempt to provide grade-by-grade lists of spelling words, but he did say that his study does "make available a highly useful source of words of established social importance and difficulty suitable for testing purposes at specific grades."[64] Obviously, if the Greene list provides preinstruction test words at a given grade, it may well provide the means for deciding what words will be taught at a given grade. It is no long step between a list recording the percent of student error at each grade and a list which tells at any teacher-selected point which words still need to be taught at a given grade. The big remaining question is how much recorded error should the teacher allow before deciding that a word should be included in her diagnostic test. This is the bread that each would-be word grader must eat alone.

Before leaving the subject of the spelling curriculum there is one largely unresolved problem that should be mentioned, namely, the problem imposed by the introduction of new words and the falling into disuse (or lesser use) of other words. There are no major studies specifically designed to identify what, if any, words have lost their importance in the spelling curriculum. Fred E. Bryan, who studied the size of children's vocabularies, has pointed out that there is a danger in relying exclusively on lists compiled even 15 years ago.[65] Words like *radioactive* and *jet-propelled* may now have an unsuspected frequency and may also be spelling problems. However, the danger may not (yet) be great. Paul M. Hollingsworth compared 1,245 different words culled from newspapers with Horn's list and found only 153 words which did not appear in any form in Horn's list. Of these 153, only 16 appeared two or more times in the newspapers. [66]

Letitia Moerke McCann, in 1955, investigated new words in the vocabulary. She assembled the results of 8 previous counts of words used in letters to the editors of 4 newspapers and 4 magazines, and she compared this composite list with the Horn and Rinsland lists to discover, first, the overlap between adults' and children's writing vocabularies and, second, the "incidence of words new to the English language in either form or meaning. . . ."[67] The finding of relevance here is that approximately 1.7 percent of the 22,485 different words in McCann's compilation (or 390 words) were new in form or meaning as indicated

[63]*Ibid.*, p. 11.

[64]*Loc. cit.*

[65]Fred E. Bryan, "How Large Are Children's Vocabularies?" *Elementary School Journal*, 54 (December 1953), 214.

[66]Paul M. Hollingsworth, "Spelling Lists—Outdated?" *Elementary English*, 42 (January 1965), 152.

[67]Letitia Moerke McCann, "Writing Vocabularies: A Comparison of the Nature, Extent, and Mobility of Child and Adult Writing Needs" (Master's thesis, University of Texas, 1955), pp. 8-10.

by their not having been recorded in the 1950 edition of *Webster's New International Dictionary.* [68]

It might seem that McCann did not find a large enough group of new words to justify concerning ourselves about them. But it should be remembered that she gave no information about their frequencies and that they *may* be more important in terms of frequency of occurrence than their gross number would indicate. Furthermore, it should be borne in mind, in interpreting McCann's finding, that new words tend to have a timeliness and a social importance that frequency counts may or may not reflect. The child today who cannot spell *rocket* surely obtains a censure even from his coevals which the child who cannot spell *receive* does not suffer.

Like McCann, Julia M. Browning investigated words added to the writing vocabulary. She also analyzed the same group of letters. Out of 22,485 running words written by adults in letters to editors of magazines and newspapers, Browning found only 216 new words (.96 percent). She concluded that the writing vocabulary is "not changing to any great extent."[69] The same considerations mentioned in connection with the interpretation of McCann's study apply equally here, and, in addition, it should be noted that 22,485 running words are far too few for a study of this kind and that using only letters to the editor imposes a further handicap. The large question of the place of new words in the spelling curriculum is yet to be carefully and thoroughly explored. Until it is explored, it would be sensible for teachers to make small, cautious additions to the spelling vocabulary of those new words which appear to be important in the lives of their students.

The research reported in this discussion of the spelling curriculum points to frequency of use and frequency of error as the pivotal considerations in determining which words to teach. The assumption is that spelling is largely "chaotic" and that individual words or small groups of words are best taught as individual spelling problems. There are, however, those who contend that English orthography is not so chaotic as it appears to be and that rules derived carefully and inductively according to linguistic principles will provide an accurate guide to the workings of English spelling. This view is encouraged by the work of Paul R. Hanna, who sought defensible orthographic generalizations (rules) but did not seek to test whether rules would improve students' ability to spell (see section 14, below).

5. THE ROLE OF RULES

Not only have different writers disagreed over the utility of spelling rules but individual writers have changed their minds over a period of time. The controversy on the experimental level began with J. M. Rice,[70] in 1897, whose

[68]*Ibid.,* pp. 40, 56.
[69]Julia M. Browning, "Writing Vocabularies: A Study of Significant New Words in the United States Since 1926" (Master's thesis, University of Texas, 1957), p. 57.
[70]J. M. Rice, "The Futility of the Spelling Grind," *Forum,* 23 (April and June 1897), 163-172, 409-419.

study was later seriously questioned by W. F. Tidyman.[71] Rice is mentioned because his recommendation that no more than 15 minutes a day be spent on spelling seems to have stood the test of time and because he stimulated experimental research. Rice believed, among other things, that rules make it possible to teach spelling efficiently. Oliver P. Cornman's study, undertaken in reaction to Rice's, found that dropping the spelling period entirely and teaching spelling in an incidental way did not affect spelling performance.[72] Although today Cornman's study seems methodologically imperfect, his study during the years immediately following its appearance was cited as grounds for believing that formal instruction utilizing spelling rules or other methods was inefficient in comparison with incidental instruction.

In 1911, nine years after Cornman's study appeared, J. E. W. Wallin[73] claimed to have exceeded Cornman's results by using a drill method to teach 10 words a week to about a thousand school children in Cleveland. The experiment, like Cornman's, lasted 3 years. After every eighth week, Wallin held spelling contests using the 80 words studied during the preceding 8 weeks. At the start, the children's average spelling achievement was 75 percent; 3 years later their average achievement was 94 percent. Although Wallin thought he had refuted both Rice, who advocated rules, and Cornman, who advocated incidental teaching, he was probably self-deceived into believing that his results could be compared with theirs. For one thing, it is impossible to determine whether Wallin and Cornman gave tests of equal difficulty. For another, Wallin's students had prior experience with test words and Cornman's did not. Also, Wallin's experiment introduced frequent, highly competitive contests which represent an influence that the other studies did not allow for and which may possibly have been a crucial factor in determining Wallin's results. Even if contests rather than drill account for the spelling improvement among Wallin's students, it is still a question whether such an instructional method is desirable. Many of the principals and teachers who worked with Wallin expressed concern about the time consumed by contests, the consequent neglect of other subjects, and (most important) the emotional strain engendered among students by the contests.

Briefly, then, this was the situation in the early 1900's. There were, however, other less noticed studies of varying quality, and more studies were to appear later on. In 1917, Myron J. Wilcox compared the effectiveness of the *ie-ei* rule with the effectiveness of drill. The experiment involved 2,695 students in grades six, seven, and eight in two Nebraska school systems. Students in each grade were placed by random selection in either a "check" (that is, control) group which received no instruction in the *ie-ei* words, or in a rule group which developed the rule inductively, or in a drill group. The experiment included a

[71] W. F. Tidyman, "A Critical Study of Rice's Investigation of Spelling Efficiency," *Pedagogical Seminary,* 22 (September 1915), 391-400.

[72] Oliver P. Cornman, *Spelling in the Elementary School* (Boston: Ginn and Company, 1902), pp. 1-98.

[73] J. E. W. Wallin, *Spelling Efficiency in Relation to Age, Grade, and Sex and the Question of Transfer* (Baltimore: Warwick and York, 1911).

preliminary test, an instructional period of four 10-minute lessons, a final test given on the day following the last lesson, and a readministration of the final test given 11 months later.[74] After comparing all the scores of all the groups, Wilcox concluded that (1) in spelling words that are exceptions to the rule, the "use of the rule acts as a confusing element to a much greater extent than the drill"; (2) in securing long-term improvement, instruction by rule is less effective than instruction by drill; and (3) the rule approach proved superior only when students were called upon to spell untaught words governed by the rule.

The study is unclear as to what, if any, provision was made to teach exceptions to the *ie-ei* rule to the rule group. If none was made, it is hardly surprising that the rule group should have been confused by exceptions. The second and third conclusions point in opposite directions. It is an important finding that instruction by rule imparts a less enduring mastery than instruction by drill; on the other hand, since most of the words involved conform to the *ie-ei* rule, it is an important finding that knowledge of the rule helps students to spell untaught words. In view of all this, it would seem that Wilcox's overall conclusion, namely, that teaching by rule is generally less effective than teaching by drill, should be interpreted to mean something more tentative.

What is more, as Wilcox himself acknowledged, the conclusions apply only to the experimental conditions described in the study. The *ie-ei* rule might have been shown to be a most efficient means of instruction if the rule group had "reviewed and applied the rule frequently."[75] It is probably true that the study created experimental conditions that handicapped the rule group. Although the rule was taught inductively, it probably cannot be best taught in one, intensive, 4-day campaign without review or reenforcement. In short, the experimental conditions do not seem fair, and the results, which are contradictory, are neither win nor lose, but draw.

Whereas Wilcox studied the effectiveness of one rule, the *ie-ei* rule, and compared it with the effectiveness of drill, Robert L. Tone, in 1924, sought to compare the effectiveness of 4 rules with the effectiveness of direct instruction. The studies differ, also, in that Tone's 4 rules dealt with the spelling of derivatives and Wilcox's single rule did not. Tone clearly sought to eliminate Wilcox's major flaw, that is, his failure to provide "reviews designed to habituate the use of the rules."[76]

The 4 rules Tone dealt with concerned (1) adding *s* or *es* to singular nouns to form plurals, (2) changing *y* to *i* and adding *es* to form plurals of nouns ending in *y*, (3) doubling the final consonant before adding a suffix beginning with a vowel in words of only one syllable, and (4) doubling the final consonant before adding a suffix beginning with a vowel in polysyllabic words accented on

[74]Myron J. Wilcox, "The Use of a Rule in Teaching Spelling" (Master's thesis, State University of Iowa, 1917), pp. 6, 7, 16.
[75]*Ibid.*, pp. 83-84.
[76]Robert L. Tone, "The Value of Rules for Teaching Derived Forms in Spelling" (Master's thesis, State University of Iowa, 1924), p. 5.

the last syllable and ending in a single consonant preceded by a single vowel. The problems Tone set for himself were to discover (1) whether teaching rules for inflection and derivation would result in more rapid and permanent improvement or (2) whether the same time devoted to direct study would result in the same improvement. He also sought to discover whether learning the rules would help students spell words they had not studied.[77]

The experiment involved 4 schools; in two schools the spelling of derivatives was taught by using rules, and in two the spelling of derivatives was taught by the direct (nonrule) method. Tone was able to pair 25 students in the rule group with 25 in the nonrule on the basis of initial spelling ability. Tone's findings, thus, were derived from the performance of 50 students. Both groups spent 15 weeks on derivatives, but the rule group spent a week at a time on each of the 4 rules; no rule was reviewed fewer than 3 times or studied for fewer than 3 weeks.

Both groups were tested 5 times. Both took a preliminary test, a final test upon completion of the fifteenth week of instruction, a posttest which was administered two months after the completion of instruction, and a test on unstudied words governed by the rules, which was administered on the day following the posttest. Last of all, students in the rule group were tested for their recall of the rules.

Tone reported that he could find no significant difference between the rule and the nonrule groups in rate of improvement or permanence of learning. He was able to report that the rule group fared slightly better than the direct study group fared in mastering words that had not been studied. But Tone conceded that the small advantage of the rule group could have been the result of "other influences" (which he did not specify).[78]

Tone also reported that two rules appear to have "a slight value as a supplement to direct study."[79] These are the rule about changing *y* to *i* and the rule about polysyllabic words doubling the final consonant. Because the rule about polysyllabic words is the most complex and the one which might be expected to fare most poorly, this finding is particularly puzzling. No doubt the basic defect in the study is that too much is wrung from too few students.

An interesting study by Ernest Horn throws light upon a problem related to the use of rules in teaching spelling. Horn asked 195 first and second graders to spell *circus, tease,* and *miscellaneous.* Horn found that not only were the words typically misspelled but that the variety of misspellings was very great. *Circus,* for example, was written 148 ways, and only 6 children spelled it correctly.[80] Horn's analysis of the misspellings shows a probable influence of phonics and a probable attempt by children to spell in ways indicated by their past experience

[77]*Ibid.,* p. 6.
[78]*Ibid.,* p. 53.
[79]*Ibid.,* p. 60.
[80]Ernest Horn, "The Influence of Past Experience upon Spelling," *Journal of Educational Research,* 19 (April 1929), 284.

with spelling. What Horn has demonstrated is that the generalizations children make which are based on their previous experience do transfer—but transfer in ways that are likely to produce an unhappy spelling result. Of course, Horn's findings are not evidence against the deliberate application of children's tendency to spell in terms of their past experience, nor are they evidence that rules which aim at clarifying past experience are useless. The point is that the application of generalizations derived from past experience will probably produce a disadvantageous result and that caution, therefore, in the use of rules should be exercised. Certainly the successful teacher of spelling (or of anything else) is one who helps students apply what they have observed or been led to observe in a way which will achieve the desired result—in this case, the proper spelling. Horn did not say it outright, but his article obviously suggests that negative transfer will take place unless the teacher carefully guides the process by which students bring their past experience to bear upon a present spelling problem.

The negative transfer that Horn noted, in the article just mentioned, was confirmed in two studies published two years later, in 1930, by Clifford P. Archer[81] and James E. Mendenhall.[82] The fact of negative transfer is by now so well established that it is unnecessary to dwell upon these studies. More important is Archer's observation that "different methods of teaching" rules might yield better results.[83] Archer investigated this hypothesis in another study in which he suggested that experiments comparing the performance of a rule group with the performance of a nonrule (control) group were inadequate because the experiments gave "little attention. . .to the best method of teaching the rule."[84] Archer set up an experiment in which 76 children in two classes served as a control group and 78 children in two classes served as an experimental group. All classes were taught by the same teacher, and both groups were closely matched for intelligence and spelling ability. The difference between this experiment and others is that the rule group was taught by a largely inductive, step-by-step, test-study process. Archer found that after one week of instruction the experimental or rule group made a statistically significant gain over the control group in the spelling of 20 words of which 13 conformed to a rule about doubling the final consonant and 7 were exceptions to the rule. Archer concluded, first, that teaching the rule for doubling the final consonant is helpful and, second, that the rule must be taught "in a psychological manner," that is, inductively.[85] The significance of the Archer experiment is limited by the brevity of the experimental period and by the absence of any provision for measuring delayed recall.

[81]Clifford P. Archer, "Transfer of Training in Spelling," *University of Iowa Studies in Education,* 5, 5 (1930), 1-63.
[82]James E. Mendenhall, *An Analysis of Spelling Errors* (New York: Bureau of Publications, Teachers College, Columbia University, 1930).
[83]Archer, "Transfer of Training in Spelling," *Iowa Studies in Education.*
[84]Clifford P. Archer, "Shall We Teach Spelling by Rule?" *Elementary English Review,* 7 (March 1930), 61.
[85]*Ibid.,* p. 63.

However, the immediate results after a brief instructional period are clearly in favor of the rule method.

To teach or not to teach spelling by rule is basically a question of whether it is efficient and effective to discover amid the great variety of English words certain patterns to which the words conform in their spelling and to abstract or generalize from these observations a number of rules which can then be applied to spelling problems. The whole matter is referred to in the literature as the problem of "generalization." As Horn and Archer have shown in the studies just previously mentioned, children do generalize, either negatively or positively. However, the issue remains as to whether some students, say the bright students, generalize more and more successfully than do other students. Herbert A. Carroll's dissertation sought to answer this question. He compared 100 fourth and fifth graders with average mean IQ's of 92 to 100 fourth and fifth graders with average mean IQ's of 124.9. An analysis of the spelling errors of the two groups showed that the bright children possess a "marked superiority. . .in. . . generalization ability."[86] Although Carroll did not make the point explicitly, his evidence implies that bright children can profit more from rule-oriented instruction than can less able children.

Even if bright children are born generalizers, it does not follow that the rules will be worth teaching. Ina Craig Sartorius, therefore, set herself the task of discovering what rules were being taught and the "frequency and consistency with which. . .rules can be applied to. . .spelling. . . .[87] Sartorius examined the rules in 20 spellers published since 1920 and found 27 rules that appeared in 5 or more spellers. Applying the 27 rules to a list of 4,065 common spelling words, Sartorius found that some rules applied to many words and had few exceptions and that others had a far narrower application and many more exceptions. Using the data supplied by Sartorius, Leonard B. Wheat was able to identify 4 rules which offer theoretical possibilities of wide application.[88] As Wheat pointed out, the actual teachability of these 4 rules can be shown only by controlled experiment in the classroom.

The studies previously mentioned by Mendenhall, Carroll, and Sartorius were all dissertations conducted under the sponsorship of Professor Arthur I. Gates of Teachers College, Columbia University. They were part of a brave and worthy effort, as Gates later expressed it, to contribute "something toward straightening out the tangle. . . ."[89] As has been shown, neither Mendenhall, Carroll, nor Sartorius attacked the central issue of whether teaching spelling by

[86] Herbert A. Carroll, *Generalization of Bright and Dull Children* (New York: Bureau of Publications, Teachers College, Columbia University, 1930), p. 54.

[87] Ina Craig Sartorius, *Generalization in Spelling* (New York: Bureau of Publications, Teachers College, Columbia University, 1931), p. 55.

[88] Leonard B. Wheat, "Four Spelling Rules," *Elementary School Journal,* 32 (May 1932), 697-706.

[89] Arthur I. Gates, *Generalization and Transfer in Spelling* (New York: Bureau of Publications, Teachers College, Columbia University, 1935), p. 13.

rule really functions to advantage in the classroom. Nor did Alice F. Watson, another of Gates's students, attack the central problem, although her study is, nevertheless, a valuable critical review of spelling research.[90] Among the Gates-sponsored studies, the one that comes closest to attacking the central issue is by Luella M. King, who sought to determine how well, comparatively, Sartorius' theoretically most promising rules could be learned and used by elementary school children.[91]

King's study tells us, for example, at what grade a rule can be satisfactorily restated by pupils, what the predominant errors in restatement are at different grade levels, and what the likelihood is of correct application of a rule at each grade level. Although the record of successes and failures that King's students made in trying to apply the rules suggests that the rules did not seem to be functioning efficiently, it must be admitted that King's study was not designed to test whether rules or some other instructional procedures function more effectively.

It remained, finally, for Gates himself to undertake an inquiry which, hopefully, would reveal whether instruction employing rules is better than instruction not employing rules. In Gates's words, "The purpose. . .was to determine the value of a program which employed a variety of generalization devices with one which made no effort to encourage or guide rationalization or transfer."[92] And again, "The study was designed merely to show whether a rather simple, easily organized and easily taught program in generalization would show to advantage in comparison with a 'specific learning,' or 'non-generalization,' program in the use of which the teachers were experienced. The experiment was conducted with the understanding of all concerned that if the generalization program used seemed promising, better ones could be developed and hence superior results obtained."[93]

Gates's experiment was conducted in a Brooklyn, New York, public school and involved 3,808 students. The first part of the experiment was conducted during the fall semester, 1929-1930. The second part was conducted during the fall semester, 1930-1931, and was "a repetition and continuation of the first."[94] Gates had earlier compiled a list of 4,065 words of frequent occurrence in spelling textbooks and children's usage. This is the list that Sartorius and others working under Gates had used. From this list Gates allocated from 12 to 20 different words to be taught each week in each grade, two through eight. Students at each grade level were placed in a generalization group (rule group) or in a nongeneralization group (specific learning group) which served as a control.

[90] Alice F. Watson, *Experimental Studies in the Psychology and Pedagogy of Spelling* (New York: Bureau of Publications, Teachers College, Columbia University, 1935).
[91] Luella M. King, *Learning and Applying Spelling Rules in Grades 3 to 8* (New York: Bureau of Publications, Teachers College, Columbia University, 1931).
[92] Gates, *Generalization and Transfer in Spelling*, p. 16.
[93] *Ibid.*, pp. 16–17.
[94] *Ibid.*, p. 35.

Students from both groups were ability-paired semester-by-semester on the basis of an initial word test of 100 items selected at equal intervals from the list of words to be taught. Gates considered the groups "substantially equal in initial spelling ability."[95]

To the students in the first part of the experiment, Gates gave a final test consisting of the same words used in the initial test. His purpose here was to detect any gain in ability to spell words that had been the subject of instruction. Gates also gave a final generalization test which was intended to detect any improvement in students' ability (1) to apply rules to unstudied words, (2) to verbalize the rules or principles the students had used in determining spellings, and (3) to spell by analogy with similar words. The last test taken by students in the first part of the experiment was a test of range and power in spelling which contained 76 words selected from the original, basal list of 4,065 words. These 76 words ranged from the easiest to the hardest in the basal list. In sum, the words in the test were chosen so as to sample "the major types of spelling difficulties" and to provide "opportunity to apply the main types of spelling rules and conventions found in a basal elementary school vocabulary."[96]

To the students in the second part of the experiment, Gates gave the initial test, the final test of 100 words, a test on studied words governed by the rules, a test on new words governed by rules, and a test of ability to state rules. The tests in the second part of the experiment were essentially a refinement of the tests used in the first part. The tests in both the first and second parts of the experiment sought to reveal pretty much the same information, but the later tests focused more sharply on the problem of whether a knowledge of spelling rules assists the student to spell both studied words and new words.

Both the experimental and control groups were taught by the test-study method, except that the study-test method was used in grades two and three and in the slowest sections. Detailed instructions were given to all teachers, including step-by-step lesson plans.

Having compared experimentally the generalization (or rule) method with the nongeneralization (or specific learning) method, Gates reached the following conclusion:

> . . .a broad and varied program of generalization, while it does not increase ability to spell the words studied during the term more than the Specific Learning Method, does tend to increase to some extent the power to spell new words and especially to handle the specific derivatives and other elements to which the generalization program was especially directed.[97]

Gates's study provides the best evidence to date to support the case of those who would teach spelling by rule, but Gates's study gives no blanket approval, and it supports spelling by rule only within certain limits and under certain

---

[95]*Ibid.*, p. 31.
[96]*Ibid.*, p. 30.
[97]*Ibid.*, p. 78.

conditions. Advocates of the rule approach should note where Gates's claims are strongest (as in the latter portion of the passage just quoted) and should remember that his teaching procedure was inductive and largely test-study. Furthermore, the rules which Gates examined were among those few found by Sartorius to be theoretically teachable. Even if the Gates study should be unreservedly accepted, it can justify only a circumscribed role for rules in any spelling program that seriously pretends to incorporate the findings of research.

That Gates, in 1935, did not have the last word is made clear by Alton S. Rogness, in 1953. This study tested what appears to be the improbable hypothesis that there is value in grouping words in a spelling list according to rule even though no mention is made of the rule. Rogness worked for 4 weeks with 8 teachers and 160 fifth graders in 7 public elementary schools in Rochester, Minnesota. His purpose, as he expressed it, was to discover "if words in a list. . .were grouped according to the rule to which they apply, the pupils may inductively arrive at some generalization, without having the teacher make any mention of the rule; and. . .they would use that generalization, not only in learning how to spell those words, but also in spelling other words to which the rule applies."[98]

Rogness set up a control group, which studied 100 words listed at random, and an experimental group, which studied the same words grouped, however, according to the spelling rule which governed them. Students in the two groups were matched on the basis of the scores they made on a pretest. Students took weekly tests, a final test, and an "applications test" which was used "to determine if the experimental group. . .had any advantage over the control group in spelling new words to which the rule applied, and which they had not previously studied."[99]

The 100 spelling words were those recommended for fifth graders by Ernest Horn and Ernest J. Ashbaugh in *Spelling We Use* (1946). The rule illustrated in Rogness' arrangement of words in the experimental group's list was the rule about dropping final *e* before a suffix beginning with a vowel and retaining *e* before a suffix beginning with a consonant.

The teacher variable was controlled as much as possible by assigning the same teacher to a control and to an experimental group. Teachers received written directions for handling materials and written versions of everything they were to say to the students.

The experiment conformed to usually recommended teaching practices in the following respects: (1) the procedure was fundamentally inductive rather than deductive; students began with the words rather than with rules or statements about the words; (2) the grouped words illustrated only one rule rather than a plurality of rules; (3) reviews were regularly conducted; and (4) the spell-

---

[98] Alton S. Rogness, "Grouping Spelling Words According to the Rule" (Ed.D. dissertation, Colorado State College of Education, 1953), p. 2.

[99] *Ibid.*, pp. 9–10.

ing of the word was emphasized rather than the memorizing of a verbal statement of the rule.

The experiment deviated from usually recommended teaching practices in the following respects: (1) no mention was ever made of the rule; this deviation, of course, was essential to the experiment; (2) no opportunity was provided for students to examine or pronounce words prior to being tested; the justification here is that Rogness was seeking to forestall the teachers' giving some clue to the rule prior to the test; and (3) the usually recommended 15-minute study period was reduced to 10 minutes in the hopes of reducing the possibility that students in the experimental group would learn each word independently. "It was hoped that the restricted time would increase the possibility that each pupil in the experimental group, while correcting his paper and studying from the list of words grouped according to the rule, would rely more upon the order in which the words were grouped than upon any method previously used in studying each word independently."[100]

Rogness found that the scores of the control group were slightly better than the scores of the experimental group but that the superiority was not statistically significant. He concluded that the experiment did "not support the thesis that there may be some value for pupils studying spelling to have their words grouped according to a spelling rule, without any mention being made of that rule."[101]

There is just a chance that Rogness might have gotten somewhat more positive results if his subjects had been older—junior or senior high school students rather than fifth graders. There is a bare possibility that more mature—one is tempted to say more sophisticated—students might be able to do what Rogness' fifth graders were apparently unable to do. In any case, Rogness' study, as it stands, suggests that the inductive procedure alone will not show to advantage. It may be that to function to advantage rules must be brought to the level of conscious understanding (not necessarily memorized) and discovered and clarified as part of a deliberate program of instruction, but Rogness' study did not explore this matter.

Sister Evangelist Marie, unlike Rogness, attempted to test the worth of rules when they are taught at the level of conscious understanding. The study compared an Inductive (rule) Method and a Deductive (rule) Method with a Thought (no rule) Method. The precise nature of the Thought Method is unclear; it involved explaining and discussing the meanings of spelling words and asking pupils to " 'figure out' what the letters should be." The subjects of the experiment were 3,230 third, fourth, and fifth graders. The 3 instructional groups into which the 3,230 children were divided were "comparable" in socioeconomic background, size, and intelligence, but how this comparability was established was not explained. After 8 weeks of instruction, it was found that the Thought

[100]*Ibid.*, p. 29.
[101]*Ibid.*, p. 58.

Method had a clear advantage. Because the report of the study omits some important details, it is impossible to estimate its worth. It is no more than another indefinite indication that the rule method has failed to justify the faith that many teachers have placed in it.[102]

6. HARD SPOTS

There is a seductive idea that attention to the "hard spots" in words will forestall errors by anticipating them. Although the idea seems simple and sensible enough at first, it gets more complicated and improbable the more one looks into it. It will be remembered that Horn[103] documented the great variety of children's misspellings; also Mendenhall revealed both the great variety of children's misspellings as well as the ratio between the number of forms of misspelling in a given word and its total number of errors. (*E.g., trouble* is misspelled 15 different ways and 29 different times; 15 divided by 29 is 52 percent, which is Mendenhall's ratio; a high ratio signifies that students misspelled in many different ways, and low ratio signifies that students misspelled in few different ways.) To Mendenhall it appeared that the "mean per cents. . .are high, ranging from 54 to 79 (median of means, 63 per cent)."[104] Obviously, if students display as great a degree of creativity in the way they spell as Mendenhall and others have shown, then it will become an impossible job for teachers to anticipate their errors and eliminate them through instruction. In other words, it appears that many children found too many hard spots in too many words to make this instructional technique practical.

The Horn and Mendenhall studies concern the spelling of elementary school children. But what of older children? Harry V. Masters gave a spelling test to 200 eighth graders, 200 twelfth graders, and 200 college seniors. Test words were those which appeared in the first 5,000 in Horn's *A Basic Writing Vocabulary* and which were misspelled by 40 percent or more of eighth grade pupils as determined by Ernest Ashbaugh's Iowa Spelling Scales (1922). Masters found a significant continuation of error through the college years. *Accommodate*, for example, was misspelled 134 times by eighth graders, 95 times by twelfth graders, and 118 times by college seniors. There were 16 different forms of *accommodate* used by eighth graders, 14 used by twelfth graders, and 10 used by college seniors. College seniors fared better with some other words, such as *dropped* which they misspelled 11 times in 3 different ways as against twelfth graders who misspelled it 20 times in 7 different ways and eighth graders who misspelled it 41 times in 8

[102]Sister Evangelist Marie, "A Study of Teaching Rules in Spelling," *Elementary English,* 40 (October 1963), 602-604, 647; a "thought approach showed to advantage in Frogner's study on the teaching of grammar (see Chapter III, section 2). However, see also Hanna's study (mentioned in section 14, below), which provides evidence that spelling is not so "chaotic" as has been thought and that, therefore, linguistically defensible spelling rules might, theoretically, be more helpful to writers than previous rules have been.

[103]Horn, "The Influence of Past Experience on Spelling," *Journal of Educational Research.*

[104]Mendenhall, *An Analysis of Spelling Errors,* p. 19.

different ways.[105] It would seem that the situation in the elementary school so clearly described by Horn and Mendenhall may be found to a disquieting degree on the college level as well.

In an attempt to overcome the objections apparent in the findings of the previously mentioned studies, Arthur I. Gates, in 1937, published a study with the following descriptive title: *A List of Spelling Difficulties in 3876 Common Words, Showing the "Hard Spots," Common Misspellings, Average Spelling Grade-Placement, and Comprehension-Rating of Each Word.* Gates's purpose, basically, was to identify the hard spots in commonly taught words so as to help "the teacher or a pupil to realize in advance what difficulties to guard against."[106]

The list was composed of the most commonly occurring words in state and large-city lists and in 25 popular spelling textbooks. Gates made no claim for his list beyond saying that it presented words which textbook writers and curriculum makers thought were important. Although the list was arbitrarily limited to 3,876 words, Gates pointed out that this number was "close" to the average number of words in the texts and lists he examined.[107]

In order to discover the characteristics of students' misspellings, Gates gave spelling tests composed of unstudied words to an unspecified number of students in "various" public schools in New York City. The familiar dictation method of testing was used in which a word is pronounced, used in a sentence, pronounced again, and finally written by the student.

One of Gates's findings is identical with the findings of other investigators, namely, that the variety of misspellings is great. As he expressed it, "it is much easier to define the part of a word in which the error occurs than to give the specific total misspellings."[108] But what did Gates contribute, after so much labor, to the case in favor of teaching hard spots? For one thing, he demonstrated that 95.9 percent of misspellings have either one or two hard spots. For another, he demonstrated that when a word is misspelled, the error will appear in a hard spot 78.2 percent of the time. Again, he demonstrated that 66.4 percent of the words had one common misspelling and 88.8 percent had up to two common misspellings. All of this would be tremendously convincing except for one thing. Most of the time, fewer than half the students made any one error. For example, *recipe* was misspelled 100 percent, that is, by everyone who attempted it, but the most common misspelling, *resipe,* appeared only 14 percent of the time. One trouble with teaching hard spots, as illustrated dramatically but not unfairly by *resipe,* is that the teacher may be slighting a majority of those students who misspell a word while he goes about eliminating the

---

[105]Harry V. Masters, "A Study of Spelling Errors," *University of Iowa Studies in Education,* 4, 4 (1927), 19.

[106]Arthur I. Gates, *A List of Spelling Difficulties in 3876 Common Words* (New York: Bureau of Publications, Teachers College, Columbia University, 1937), p. 5.

[107]*Ibid.,* p. 1.

[108]*Ibid.,* p. 7.

greatest single problem with the word. Such a time-wasting procedure could be avoided simply by giving a pretest or diagnostic test and directing the attention of all students who made mistakes to the specific nature of their mistakes.

If the evidence with its interpretation presented thus far bodes ill for advocates of the teaching of hard spots, it must be admitted in their favor that the evidence shows only what the probable difficulties are. The key question is still: How do things work out experimentally?

The major experimental effort to "settle" the issue was made by L. S. Tireman. He rejected the procedural plan which calls for equating two groups on the basis of intelligence and giving words marked for hard spots to an experimental group and unmarked words to a control group. This method, he said, "presupposes that the effects of marking versus non-marking would be reflected in the comparative number of errors made after equal periods of study." The trouble, he added, is that the "correlation between spelling ability and intelligence. . .is not sufficiently high to insure that two classes equated on the basis of intelligence quotients would be equal in spelling ability."[109] Instead, Tireman equated two sets of marked and unmarked words for each group of fourth, fifth, and eighth grade students. There were 58 fourth grade classes, 68 sixth grade classes, and 45 eighth grade classes involved in the study. Tireman worked out a careful rotation plan so that classes would receive different lists during the first and second weeks of the experiment and different combinations of marked and unmarked lists. In this way, Tireman sought to nullify any slight differences that might exist among his lists. Incidentally, a hard spot in a word is said to be marked if it is indicated by some attention–getting device such as underlining, capitalizing, or italicizing.

Since Gates's study locating hard spots had not yet appeared, Tireman located the hard spots in his lists by "taking each correct letter in turn and going through the list of misspelled forms to determine the presence or absence of the correct letter. . . ."[110] He determined the percent of error by dividing the total number of errors in each letter by the total number of misspelled words. Tireman defined a hard spot arbitrarily as "any part of, or place in, the word which is misspelled by 40 percent or more of those who misspell the word.[111] Approximately a half million spellings were returned by 4,182 students.

Teachers participating in the experiment received detailed, written instructions. Teachers were told exactly what to do with their classes and were told word-for-word what to say to their classes. These procedures were first refined with the help of a class in the Experimental School of the University of Iowa and then sent to a "friendly superintendent for trial."

The method of instruction was the one recommended in *Lippincott's New*

[109]L. S. Tireman, "Value of Marking Hard Spots in Spelling," *University of Iowa Studies in Education,* 5, 4 (May 15, 1930), 8.
[110]*Ibid.,* p. 11.
[111]*Ibid.,* p. 13.

Horn-Ashbaugh Speller (1926), a test-study method. All tests were given by the familiar dictation method. Each student took a preliminary test which was used to check the validity of the equated spelling lists. This test was followed by tests on Wednesday and Friday of the first and second weeks of instruction. After a lapse of 5 weeks, each teacher gave a recall test.

The findings at each grade level were remarkably consistent. For fourth graders, Tireman found marking hard spots to be "valueless." For sixth graders, Tireman found that the practice "may be of value for immediate recall but for permanent results it has no value." For eighth graders, Tireman found that marking hard spots was "not. . .warranted."[112] Tireman's conclusion is unequivocal. "The essential fact in spelling is to write all the letters and have them in the right order. Anything that diverts the pupils from this does harm. The fact stands out that the pupils who studied words with the hard spots marked made poorer scores than those who studied lists with words unmarked. In other words, the people who advocate marking the hard spots are not only suggesting a useless device but possibly a harmful one."[113]

In spite of Tireman's hopes, his study failed to settle the issue. Gates's study of the hard spots in 3,876 words appeared 7 years after Tireman's, and there have been a few small investigations since. The reason the issue survives, if one may hazard a guess, is that advocates of the hard spots approach apparently distinguish between *marking* hard spots (by underlining, using color, using different type faces) and teaching students to avoid the pitfalls in words by nonmarking means. The distinction seems to be farfetched. Even if a teacher could find a practical way of directing students' attention to hard spots without physically marking the word, he would still probably be altering the students' visual image of the word, which is exactly what physical marking does.

There are some experimental studies, of course, which urge the hard spots approach. Unfortunately, they have serious methodological flaws or do not show what they have been said to show. W. S. Guiler (like Tireman, writing in 1930) tested a program to improve the spelling of a fifth grade class. One of several features of the program was the marking of hard spots, and one of his conclusions was that marking hard spots is worthwhile.[114] The trouble with the study is that it failed to isolate the several instructional innovations contained in the spelling program examined. Perhaps the attention given to motivation accounted for the improvement in the children's spelling performance from the fourth grade level to the sixth grade level. Another difficulty is that the experiment involved only 21 students. On the other hand, an interesting feature of the study is that it identified the parts or spots of words that were difficult for each child in the class, which suggests that if teaching hard spots has a value, it is realized

---

[112]*Ibid.,* pp. 30, 39, 47.

[113]*Ibid.,* p. 47.

[114]Walter Scribner Guiler, "Improving Ability in Spelling," *Elementary School Journal,* 30 (April 1930), 597, 603.

when instruction is highly individualized. There are no studies which inquire into this particular point. Anyone who attempts such a study will have to distinguish the influence of individualization from the influence of attending to hard spots.

Twelve years later, in 1942, W. S. Guiler and Gilbert A. Lease conducted an experiment to see if a "systematic program. . .based on individual diagnosis of spelling difficulties"[115] would improve spelling ability. As in the Guiler study just mentioned, the authors individualized instruction and also used the technique of underlining hard spots. One hundred ten matched pairs of students participated, one member of each pair being assigned to a control group and the other to an experimental group. Students in the control group were not asked to observe the spots in the words that were difficult for them, nor did the students or the teachers keep any record of "specific pupil weaknesses."[116] Guiler and Lease found that both experimental and control groups made gains but that the gains of the experimental group were far greater. The Guiler-Lease study is methodologically more impressive than Guiler's earlier study, but, again, it was not set up to isolate the separate factors that led to the result they reported. Neither the Guiler study nor the Guiler-Lease study can properly be said to tell us anything reliable about the effects of marking hard spots.

7. INDIVIDUALIZING INSTRUCTION

The "old hand" who has sat in countless department and faculty meetings knows that there is a strong preference among teachers for small classes. Although, paradoxically, the range of what is defined as small is great, there is no mistaking teachers' preference for a class size which they consider small. Class size is a problem that has come into public prominence less because of its genuine educational importance than because of its burgeoning economic dimensions. The usual argument advanced by the schoolmen is that small classes make it possible to individualize instruction and that individualized instruction is better instruction. Considering the impact that a decision in this matter would have upon the number of teaching positions, upon the general economic status of the profession, and upon the size of school budgets, it is surprising that there has not been a flood of studies from all who are concerned with the outcome. The following should give some indication of how much and how little we know about the worth of individualized spelling instruction.

In 1923, B. J. Rohan, a principal, published an account of an experiment conducted by a sixth grade teacher under (apparently) Rohan's supervision. The class was divided into small groups on the basis of grade level ability in spelling as determined by the Ayres Spelling Tests and class standing. It developed that the group of children in the class had spelling abilities ranging from the fourth grade to the eighth grade level. The groups that were below the sixth grade level were taught the spelling words for the grade level at which they qualified. Rohan

[115]W. S. Guiler and Gilbert A. Lease, "An Experimental Study of Methods of Instruction in Spelling," *Elementary School Journal,* 43 (December 1942), 234.

[116]*Ibid.,* p. 235.

did not report what was taught to the groups that tested above grade level, but presumably they consolidated their hold on the sixth grade words and went as far beyond as possible. Instruction was by the test-study method, and students were required to keep a notebook record of all words misspelled. Students were motivated in different ways, primarily by being able to graduate from a lower grade level group into a higher group as their achievement warranted it. According to Rohan, all below grade students had reached the sixth grade level by the end of the year. All 30 students in the class took the same final examination. Half scored 100 percent, 13 scored between 90 and 99, one scored 89, and one scored 84. Rohan drew no conclusions, but the tone of the article, especially in the final paragraphs, leaves no doubt that he considered the experiment a good demonstration of the value of individualizing spelling instruction.[117] That the experiment, as reported, is far short of proof must have been as clear in 1923 as it is now. Rohan did not attempt to explain the crucial final examination, nor did he explain the activities of the above grade level spellers, nor did he isolate the effects of motivation. Had the examination been too easy, the same dramatic results could have been obtained. The study, in fact, has a delightful, unsophisticated air in comparison with others which may be no better but which bristle with statistics, pilot studies, and controls. In its defense it may be said that there is a chance that it demonstrated what it intended to demonstrate, but so much is obscure and so few safeguards were employed that the most one can do is wait for confirming evidence.

Another study by E. E. Keener, published in 1926, compared group instruction with individualized instruction. Four hundred eighty-eight pairs of students, matched on the basis of initial spelling scores, were divided into groups. One member of each pair was placed in a class in which spelling was taught by a group method, and the other was placed in a class in which spelling was taught by an individual method. Except in a few instances, the same teacher taught one individual method class and one group method class. The same 100 words were taught to each pair of classes. Because classes from grades two through eight participated in the experiment, it was necessary to have different lists of 100 words that could appropriately be taught at the different grade levels. Students worked 15 minutes a day and were responsible for 20 words a week for 5 weeks.

Keener calculated that the individual method achieved a 3.5 percent better result at a 12 percent saving of time.[118] However, this finding must be considered in connection with certain methodological complications. The individual instruction classes used the test-study method, and the group instruction classes used the study-test method. Although both kinds of classes were encouraged to syllabicate words, only the group instruction classes were asked to note hard spots.

[117]Ben J. Rohan, "An Experiment in Spelling," *Journal of Educational Method, 2* (June 1923), 414.
[118]E. E. Keener, "Comparison of the Group and Individual Methods of Teaching Spelling," *Journal of Educational Method,* 6 (September 1926), 34.

In other words, it is possible that more than just the difference between group and individual instruction affected the results.

The Guiler-Lease study referred to in Section 6, above, was designed to compare group instruction with a program "based on individual diagnosis."[119] It may be recalled that 110 pairs of seventh and eighth graders were involved. The control group used a spelling book which made no provision for diagnostic self-testing, and there was no record kept by teachers or students of specific difficulties that individual students encountered. The experimental group used a book which enabled each student to identify beforehand the words that he did not know. All students in the experimental group were taught words with which the majority had trouble, but when smaller numbers of students had trouble with a word or words, the teacher gave individual instruction to the children concerned. The experiment lasted for one school year. Before the conclusion of the experiment, the investigators gave a final test which they regarded as "equivalent. . .in content and difficulty" to the initial test. This enabled them to compute student achievement. Guiler and Lease found that the improvement of the experimental pupils was "consistently and significantly greater than that made by the control pupils. Interpreted in terms of the test norms the mean growth in spelling ability amounted to 1.8 grade levels for the experimental pupils and 1.1 grade levels for the control pupils."[120]

As was pointed out in section 6, the Guiler-Lease study is inadequate as a gauge of the worth of marking hard spots, which was one of the instructional devices employed by the experimental group. However, the rest of the study stands up better. Since the attention given to hard spots by the experimental group may not have been an advantage, it is possible to attribute the superior performance of the experimental group to the other factor in the situation, namely, the individualization of instruction. Nevertheless, the findings of the Guiler-Lease study are hardly conclusive, if only because the report is not sufficiently specific about the precise way instruction was conducted from day to day and because the information about the key initial and final tests is sketchy.

Last in this enumeration is Edward Eisman's study which appeared in 1963. There were 17 fifth graders and 13 sixth graders in Eisman's Individualized Program and 17 fifth graders and 15 sixth graders in his Group Program. Data for third graders, based on an earlier study, were included. In mean IQ and mean MA (mental age) the groups were "either identical or very similar."[121] Students in both groups were average or above average in ability.

Students in the Group Program followed the California-approved method which consisted of class study of weekly lists "with a substitute list for slow learners."[122] Students in the Individualized Program worked with the same

[119]Guiler and Lease, "An Experimental Study," *Elementary School Journal,* p. 234.
[120]*Ibid.,* p. 238.
[121]Edward Eisman, "Individualized Spelling: Second Report," *Elementary English,* 40 (May 1963), 530.
[122]*Ibid.,* p. 539.

words that their colleagues in the Group Program were studying, but the words were alphabetized and rated 1 (easiest) through 10 (most difficult). Each student in the Individualized Program selected the number of words he felt he could master and compiled his own weekly list on his self-determined level of difficulty. Words missed on the weekly test were added to the list for the following week. When a student showed he could spell the words on the level of difficulty at which he was working, he was permitted to attempt the words on the next higher level.

The study lasted for 3 years. Different teachers participated at different times in order to protect the results from being influenced by the interests, abilities, or instructional philosophies of any one group of teachers. Eisman found, after 3 years, that students in the Individualized Program were "on the average .8 to 1.5 grades higher in spelling than children in the Group Program."[123] However, the degree of superiority of sixth graders in the Individualized Group declined sharply, suggesting that individualization tends to lose its advantage as the age and grade level of the students increase.

The obvious limitations of this study, which Eisman acknowledged, are the small number of students involved and the failure to control "pupil motivation and other variables."[124] There is a further complication implicit in Eisman's brief reference to a substitute spelling list for slow learners which was part of the Group Program. This sounds like the introduction of a degree of individualization into the Group Program. How serious a flaw this is, or whether it is a flaw at all, cannot be determined because Eisman did not explain the details of the Group Program. All that can be said, finally, is that the Eisman study, like those previously discussed, finds evidence in favor of individualization of instruction but is too insecure in method to support any confident generalization about the merits of individualization in spelling instruction.

8. SYLLABICATION

The term *syllabication* refers to the practice of indicating by any of several means the portions or segments into which words are customarily divided. These segments or syllables are assumed to correspond to patterns of sound. However, researchers using sensitive decibel meters have shown that English syllables tend to merge, become less distinctly separate, as tempo increases. What is more, the pattern of stresses within a word is affected by the rhythm of the sentence in which the word occurs.[125] Indeed, the conventional syllabic transcription of some words would appear to be unrelated to their sound (e.g., *anx·ious*). The implication of all of this is that the common sense view that syllabication should help in teaching spelling is not, after all, a simple matter. Nobody has yet published an investigation of whether spelling is better taught by way of some

123*Ibid.*, p. 530.
124*Loc. cit.*
125Simeon Potter, *Modern Linguistics* (New York: W. W. Norton and Company, 1964), pp. 69, 73-74.

linguistically accurate system of syllabication or by the traditional system. But there are some studies which purport to tell whether spelling is better taught by the familiar method or by omitting syllabication entirely from spelling instruction.

The first study, published in 1909 by Edwina E. Abbott, succeeded in demonstrating the need for a better study. Abbott's word lists were presented with diacritical marks and in syllabicated form, thereby making it impossible to identify whether one or the other was responsible for the results.[126]

In 1918, J. D. Heilman published a study intended to discover "whether the syllabicated or unsyllabicated form of a word was more favorable to the task of learning how to spell."[127] Seventy-three children in fourth, fifth, and seventh grades were the subjects. They were divided at each grade level into two groups equated for size, spelling ability, and sex. One hundred misspellings garnered from students' writing comprised the material of the study. One class at each grade level studied the words in syllabicated form, and the other studied the words in unsyllabicated form. Ten words a day were taught, and each word was reviewed 3 times. Including the time required for testing, the experiment occupied 35 school days.

The words were presented on cards held up to view. The experimenter pronounced the word twice. For the syllabication group he pronounced the word once with clearly defined pauses between syllables and once as a unit. For the nonsyllabication group he pronounced the word both times as a unit. After a few seconds, the card was turned down and the children wrote the word. Following the writing of the tenth word, the children's papers were collected, and a test of the words was dictated. A final test was also given. Heilman concluded that "in general, the syllabized form of the word promotes the learning process in spelling."[128]

Two "limitations" of Heilman's study have been noted by Harry A. Greene. First, Heilman used doubtful methods for equating the two groups whose performance he was comparing. Second, Heilman did not, apparently, control the pronunciation of the words dictated to both groups. Greene considered it "fair to conclude that the differences which appear in this experiment are due partly to variation in pronunciation, and partly to the inequality of the two groups of children."[129] Heilman himself has listed other methodological problems.[130] In sum, the study probably has too many flaws to be considered seriously as a guide to teaching.

[126]Edwina E. Abbott, "On the Analysis of the Memory Consciousness in Orthography," *Psychological Monographs,* 11 (November 1909), 127-158.
[127]J. D. Heilman, "A Study in Spelling," *Colorado State Teachers College Bulletin,* Research Bulletin No. 2, 18 (October 1918), 3.
[128]*Ibid.,* p. 209.
[129]Harry A. Greene, "Syllabication as a Factor in Learning to Spell," *Journal of Educational Research,* 8 (October 1923), 210.
[130]Heilman, "A Study in Spelling," *Colorado State Teachers College Bulletin,* p. 3.

H. Alena Wolfe and F. S. Breed[131] reported a study in 1922 which sought to improve on the study by Abbott, mentioned previously. Briefly, what Wolfe and Breed did was to divide 52 students into two equivalent groups and teach each the same way, except that one group was presented with syllabicated words and the other was not. Wolfe and Breed found syllabication to be slightly more effective. However, the study fails to convince because of the small number of students participating, the possibility that the control and experimental groups were not really equated, and the possibility that the differences noted were not statistically significant.

In addition to commenting upon some earlier syllabication studies, Greene also reported a study of his own. His experiment, Greene explained, "involved too few cases to be used as a basis for any but tentative conclusions," but he believed that the method of the experiment might be "sufficiently significant to warrant presentation."[132]

Fourth, fifth, and sixth grade teachers in the University of Iowa Elementary School conducted the experiment under Greene's direction. The experiment was designed to use the plan of individual instruction already in use in the school in which "each child worked only on the words he missed in a preliminary test on the words assigned." Difficult words were chosen in order to "magnify the differences between the two methods" being compared. A novel feature is that syllabic and nonsyllabic presentation were compared "as to the way they operate on the *same* children when learning words of equal spelling difficulty."[133] Greene felt that it was easier to equate spelling lists than to equate groups of children. Also, he specifically avoided the use of diacritical marks. The pronunciation of the words was the same for both methods of presentation. In this way Greene was able to rule out aspects of method which he thought might distort his results.

Using data gathered for the Ashbaugh-Iowa Spelling Scale, Greene selected 50 words at each grade level. Greene then divided each group of 50 words into two 25-word lists (Lists A and B) which he equated for difficulty by means of a preliminary test. Each of the two 25-word lists at each grade level was then prepared in a syllabicated and nonsyllabicated form.

Each class at each grade level was divided into two groups of equal size. During the first week of the experiment, Group I in each class studied List A in unsyllabicated form, and Group II studied the same List A but in syllabicated form. During the second week of the experiment, Groups I and II in each class at each grade level studied List B, but this time the groups received the kind of list, syllabicated or unsyllabicated, which they had not received at first. Greene's day-by-day outlines of instructions to his teachers reveal that students had

[131] H. Alena Wolfe and F. S. Breed, "An Experimental Study of Syllabication in Spelling," *School and Society,* 15 (June 3, 1922), 616-622.
[132] Greene, "Syllabication as a Factor in Learning to Spell," *Journal of Educational Research,* p. 211.
[133] *Ibid.,* pp. 211–212.

4 opportunities to study the same words, not counting test experiences during which learning might take place.

Two weeks following the completion of instruction of List A, Greene's teachers dictated the 25 words on the list to test delayed recall. The same procedure was followed two weeks after the completion of instruction of List B.

Greene's experiment was constructed with care and ingenuity. Its only apparent defect is the one Greene himself noted, namely, the small number of students involved. What did Greene find? Although the scores Greene obtained show a slight superiority for the syllabicated form of presentation, the difference was not statistically significant. He, therefore, was unable to urge the superiority of either method of word presentation.[134]

Undoubtedly the best study to date on the subject is Thomas D. Horn's dissertation which was completed in 1947. The purpose of the study was to discover the "effect of...syllabic presentation...upon learning to spell" and to identify which "type of words, if any, benefit from...syllabic presentation."[135] Horn's study is alone in its recognition of the key role of the words selected for study. He identified 18 classes of words, each representing a different problem in syllabication which might conceivably affect the learning of the word. Among these are the following:

> Words in which syllables are commonly omitted in mispronunciation (mod·er·ate, priv·i·lege)
>
> Words in which syllables, rightly pronounced, may lead to misspellings (fur·nace)
>
> Compound words with which syllabication may lead to misspelling as two words (some·thing, base·ball)[136]

In Part I of his study, Horn dealt with the "general effect of a syllabified presentation" of words contained in a regular sixth grade spelling text. In Part II, he dealt with the effect of a syllabified presentation upon classes of words such as those just illustrated.

Part I involved 768 sixth grade students and lasted for 4 weeks. The 25 words studied each week came from Ernest Horn and Ernest Ashbaugh's *Progress in Spelling* (Lippincott, 1946), which happened to be in use in the cooperating school system. Whole classes rather than individual students were used as the sampling unit. A random procedure determined which students in each class would be taught by one method or the other.

Each week students received a booklet containing directions, words for the week, and space for tests on Monday, Wednesday, and Friday. Half of every class received booklets with words in syllabicated form, and half received book-

---

[134]*Ibid.*, pp. 218-219.
[135]Thomas D. Horn, "The Effect of Syllabic Presentation of Words upon Learning to Spell" (Ph.D. dissertation, State University of Iowa, 1947), p. 9; reported also in "Learning to Spell as Affected by Syllabic Presentation of Words," *Elementary School Journal,* 49 (January 1949), 263-272.
[136]*Ibid.*, pp. 10-12.

lets with the words in unsegmented form. Instructional conditions for both groups in a class were identical, except that one group used the booklet with the syllabicated list.

Each student took a preliminary test covering all 100 of the words to be studied during the 4-week experimental period. Thirteen days after the conclusion of the experimental period, the students took a recall test, and 19 days later, students took another recall test.

Part II of the study, which investigated types of syllabication problems, lasted 5 weeks and involved 1,000 fifth grade students in 3 school systems. Each week students studied one of the following 5 classes of words:

Words in which there is no obvious connection between syllabication and learning to spell, e.g., *remind, travel*

Words which have been found to provide difficulty in pronunciation, e.g., *business, strictly*

Words which have been found to contain suffix-prefix difficulties, e.g., *inspection, collection*

Words which have been found to contain double consonant difficulties, e.g., *already, thankful*

Words which, if syllabified, may cause spelling errors, e.g., *awhile, whatever*[137]

On Monday of each week the students took a 25-word test which they corrected themselves; then the students were tested again on the same words. As in Part I, prepared booklets were used, and half of each class received the syllabicated list and half the unsyllabicated list. In other respects the experimental conditions for Parts I and II were the same, except that in Part I the experimental procedure was substituted for the regular spelling activity, and in Part II the experimental procedure was administered in addition to the regular activity.

Horn concluded that the data on recall, delayed recall, and word groups reveal no advantage to presenting words in syllabicated form. For one group of words—those like *therefore* and *awhile* which may cause errors in spelling if they are syllabicated—there is evidence in the study to suggest that "syllabic presentation of such words may have a negative effect on learning to spell."[138] Horn recommended, finally, that the unsyllabicated presentation be retained because "there is no advantage in presenting words in syllabified form."[139]

Thomas Horn's experiment did not examine the effect of pronunciation upon syllabic presentation. Worth J. Osburn, in 1954, reported that careful pronunciation of syllables increases the effectiveness of instruction. Unfortunately, Osburn was not explicit about his groupings and about the number of students participating. What is more, his pronunciations appear to have been over precise;

[137]*Ibid.*, pp. 26-27.
[138]*Ibid.*, p. 78; Marana O. Humphrey was unable to confirm Horn's finding of a negative effect of syllabication; see her "The Effect of a Syllabic Pronunciation of Words upon Learning to Spell" (Master's thesis, University of Texas, 1954).
[139]*Ibid.*, p. 79.

thus they must have given some spelling clues that would not be afforded by a pronunciation conforming to common usage.[140]

In 1956, the same Thomas D. Horn wrote an article about syllabication which contained an oddly contradictory conclusion. In the first sentence he urged "continuing attention to syllabic elements" because good spellers seem to have a " 'feel' for syllables." In the second sentence he recommended that the "regular *method*" should use the undivided presentation of words. Finally, he said that for the sake of variety and enrichment only, words can be presented "orally or visually and. . .by syllables."[141] It would appear that in 1956 Horn was having trouble accepting the full implications of his study of 1947. The only portion of the 1956 statement that is substantiated by research—his own research—is the second sentence. That is where the matter should rest until better experimental evidence comes along.

By way of concluding the discussion of syllabication, it is worth noting that the syllabic division of words currently in use was established by eighteenth century English printers who did not, unfortunately, identify unerringly the sound segments of the language. The common definition of the syllable as a single voice impulse is at best an oversimplification. The value of syllabication to spelling instruction cannot at last be known until the syllable itself has been fully explored and until the findings of such studies have been used in carefully constructed educational experiments. Meanwhile, studies of conventional syllabication do not encourage faith in its value to spelling instruction; and if it turns out that linguistic researches finally establish an accurate system of syllabication revealing syllabication to be a variable and relative thing dependent upon other factors, such as tempo, then it may be that syllabication will be shown to have even less value to spelling instruction than the conventional system appears to have.

9. WORD GROUPING

No single study or group of studies has ever explored fully and systematically the value of grouping spelling words. There are, of course, many different bases for grouping. For example, words may be grouped because they are homonyms (*write, right*), because they differ in only one letter and sound (*hit, pit*), or because they contain some identical sound which is spelled differently *(cherry, bury)*. Obviously, there is no disadvantage to grouping words like *red, bed, led.* Even if these words can be learned equally efficiently if ungrouped, it is still true that the grouping does no harm and wastes no time provided that all the words in the group need to be learned and are appropriate to the grade level at which they are being taught. A more difficult issue, however, appears in connection with homonyms in which typically there are only slight spelling clues and in

140Worth J. Osburn, "Teaching Spelling by Teaching Syllables and Root Words," *Elementary School Journal,* 55 (September 1954), 32-41.

141Thomas D. Horn, "How Syllables Can Help in Spelling," *Education,* 76 (1956), 294-295.

which possibilities for spelling errors may be introduced. Homonyms provide the most difficult test of the merit of word grouping. All that homonyms have in common is sound. The spellings are different and, in some cases, widely different from the usual way or ways of representing the same sound.

Two studies need not detain us long. The first, by H. C. Pearson, in 1911, found an instructional advantage for the "together" method of teaching homonyms.[142] The second, by E. O. Finkenbinder in 1923, found an instructional advantage for the "separate" method of teaching homonyms.[143] Arthur I. Gates has criticized the Pearson study briefly,[144] and Keith C. Harder has listed at greater length the weaknesses in the Pearson and the Finkenbinder studies.[145]

Another study sometimes cited in discussions of the merits of grouping spelling words is C. A. Wagner's, which appeared in 1912. Wagner taught 200 words containing similar structural and phonic characteristics to two fairly well-matched sixth grade classes. For one class the words were grouped according to common difficulty and structural and phonic similarity. For the other class the words were presented in chance order. The class that studied the grouped words for 10 lessons made a 29 percent gain in spelling accuracy, whereas the class that studied the ungrouped words made only a 20 percent gain in spelling accuracy. These results may be attributed in part to the design of the study which did not isolate different kinds of word groupings; consequently, words of nearly similar spelling and identical sound—which are most profitably grouped—served to improve the score of the experimental class. Had the experimental comparison been between ungrouped words and homonyms, the scores achieved by the two classes might have been different. At this point, any doubts about the method of the study can only be strengthened by recalling that the number of students involved was small and that a rating by the principal was the only means of insuring that the teachers of the experimental and control groups were of equal ability.[146]

Twelve years later, in 1924, W. F. Tidyman and Edith Johnson published a study in which they stated their intention "to test the value of grouping words" and "to substantiate if possible" Wagner's experiment.[147] Twenty-three fifth graders were taught 80 words appropriate to the grade and "representing typical spelling difficulties."[148] On the basis of a test previously given, the 80 words

[142]Henry C. Pearson, "The Scientific Study of the Teaching of Spelling," *Journal of Educational Psychology*, 2 (May 1911), 241-252.

[143]E. O. Finkenbinder, "The Spelling of Homonyms: An Experimental Investigation of Teaching Them," *Pedagogical Seminary*, 30 (September 1923), 241-251.

[144]Gates, *Generalization and Transfer in Spelling*, p. 5.

[145]Keith C. Harder, "The Relative Efficiency of the 'Separate' and 'Together' Methods of Teaching Homonyms," *Journal of Experimental Education*, 6 (September 1937), 7-8.

[146]C. A. Wagner, "Experimental Study of Grouping by Similarity as a Factor in the Teaching of Spelling" (Ph.D. dissertation, University of Pennsylvania, 1912).

[147]W. F. Tidyman and Edith Johnson, "Value of Grouping Words According to Similar Difficulties in Spelling," *Journal of Educational Research*, 10 (November 1924), 208.
[148]*Loc. cit.*

were divided into two lists of equal difficulty. One was a Nongrouping (chance order) List and the other a Grouping List. A test was given to determine the initial ability of the students to spell the words on both lists. The same students were taught the words in the Nongrouping List and then taught the words on the Grouping List. Ten words were taught in each 20-minute daily lesson. Conditions were identical—same teacher, same students, same methods of teaching—except that for 4 days the words were presented in chance order and for 4 days the words were grouped "according to similar difficulties" and according to "like peculiarities of form."[149] Students took a final test at the end of the week in which the words were studied. A delayed recall test was given 11 weeks after the conclusion of the experiment. After compiling the results, Tidyman and Johnson found that the grouping method was 13 percent more effective than the nongrouping method, as measured by the final test, and 10 percent more effective than the nongrouping method, as measured by the delayed recall test.

The Tidyman-Johnson study satisfied its authors' desire to confirm Wagner's study, but we would be wise not to attach great significance to the findings. One reason is that only 23 students were involved. Another is that the Grouping List contained words like *sought* and *ought,* and *least* and *feast* which are the sort most likely to be grouped to advantage. The list contained no homonyms, such as *wait* and *weight,* which offer, at least, the possibility of confusion by virtue of the very fact that they are grouped. The objection, then, is that in setting up this study the researchers stacked the deck in favor of a positive finding by including only those words with the greatest transfer possibilities. The more similar the words being tested, the less important the findings. After all, it is no shattering revelation that *screw* and *drew* reinforce each other. The study tells us nothing about the more controversial problem of grouping homonyms, like *blue* and *blew.* Although this cannot be said to be a fault in the study, it is a sharp limitation of the significance of the study.

Additional sources of information about grouping are the studies dealing with what is known in the literature as transfer of training and generalization. Both transfer and generalization studies have, in the past, found it suitable to use word groupings as a means of determining experimentally whether and what students transfer and generalize. Both the transfer and generalization studies are different ways for formulating the same problem. Transfer studies formulate it in terms of applying, or transferring, insights obtained from experience in one situation to another situation; and generalization studies formulate it in terms of perceiving guiding principles in one situation which, presumably, can be applied, transferred, to another situation. The previously mentioned studies by Mendenhall and Carroll demonstrated that students' attempts to spell are influenced by their prior spelling experience, that is, that students generalize from their past spelling experience and apply or transfer their learnings to new spelling problems. The resulting spelling may be correct, or it may be incorrect owing to

[149]*Ibid.,* p. 299.

the vagaries of English orthography. But transfer and generalization, as these studies have shown, clearly influence what the student finally writes down. Misspellings, thus, are not likely to be original, spontaneously generated creations; rather they are misapplied earlier learnings.

Archer's study, "Transfer of Training in Spelling," also mentioned previously, pointed out the hazards in teaching which would stress transferring learnings from one spelling situation to another. "If a child studies forms like *preferred*, he is likely to double the *l* in *counseled*, and the *t* in *benefited*."[150] Archer's study did not deny that some benefits from transfer may occur if words are grouped or if other teaching devices encouraging transfer are used. But his experiment did not examine the efficacy of teaching devices; instead it emphasized the perils implicit in any attempt, through groupings or by other means, to teach spelling by relying heavily upon transfer-encouraging techniques.[151]

Gates's *Generalization and Transfer in Spelling*, discussed earlier in connection with spelling rules, presented groups of words to one set of students. The words were grouped according to common visual or phonetic elements (for example: *in, eep, able, ly, tion*), according to the way the words add *s, es,* or *d,* and according to other common features. Another set of students studied words listed according to difficulty or frequency and not according to any characteristic of their form or spelling. Gates found that a generalization program in which word grouping was a part did enable students "to some extent" to increase their "power to spell new words and especially to handle specific derivatives"[152] that had been the subject of study. However, in his final evaluation of his own and others' work, Gates said, "it must be admitted that the general value of groupings and other devices to foster generalization in the spelling course is not clearly proved."[153] Now, after a reinspection of the literature and after more than 3 decades have elapsed since Gates wrote these words, one can do no more than add an affirmation.

If Gates's not exactly sanguine appraisal of the worth of groupings in general is fair and accurate, what can be said of grouping homonyms, a practice which offers even fewer theoretical possibilities of being worthwhile? According to Archer, negative transfer (spelling mistakes resulting from transfer) increases as words become more dissimilar and reaches "its maximum when. . .the words have many similar sounds but different spelling."[154] Probably the best study of the value of grouping homonyms was published by Harder in 1937. "The purpose of this investigation," he said, "is to determine whether the 'separate' or 'together' method of presenting homonyms in lessons would result in greater

---

[150] Archer, "Transfer of Training in Spelling," *Iowa Studies in Education*, p. 58.
[151] *Ibid.*, pp. 57–60.
[152] *Ibid.*, p. 78.
[153] Gates, *Generalization and Transfer in Spelling*, p. 13.
[154] Archer, "Transfer of Training in Spelling," *Iowa Studies in Education*, p. 59.

spelling accuracy."[155] His experiment was conducted in 7 school systems in Iowa and Nebraska, involving 30 third grade and 24 sixth grade classes enrolling about 1,150 students. All classes followed the same weekly routine:

Monday—test of words to be studied for the week

Tuesday—study of words missed on the Monday test

Wednesday—second test of the words for the week; review test of words taught one month previously

Thursday—study of words missed on the Wednesday test

Friday—test of all words tested the previous Wednesday

Harder selected 219 homonyms from several studies of spelling errors. Of these 219 words, Harder chose 60 for use in the third grade and 86 for use in the sixth grade, the selection having been made on the basis of difficulty, grade placement, and frequency of usage. The list of third grade words and the list of sixth grade words were each divided into two lists of equal difficulty. Students in each grade studied one list by the "separate" method and one list by the "together" method. Students received the lists in the form of two booklets. One booklet received by the "separate" group contained homonyms arranged so that at least two weeks would intervene between the study of the homonyms in a cluster. The "together" group received a booklet arranged so that homonyms appeared in clusters or groups.

A pretest enabled Harder to equate the "separate" and "together" groups. Harder controlled the teacher variable by devising a rotation scheme which required each teacher to teach both lists at his grade level and to teach both "separate" and "together" groups. Each teacher received instructions stressing that in presenting words to the "separate" group he was not to call attention to words with the same sound and that in presenting words to the "together" group he was required to emphasize the presence of words with the same sound but with different spelling and meaning.

The experimental period lasted for 8 weeks. Upon its conclusion, Harder repeated the pretest, which served as an immediate recall test for those homonyms studied during the last 4 weeks and as a delayed recall test for those homonyms studied during the first 4 weeks.

The findings are as interesting as they are tricky. On the immediate recall test the sixth graders in the "together" group did significantly better (critical ratio 9.57) than did their colleagues in the "separate" group. Third graders in the "together" group also outperformed their classmates in the "separate" group, but the third graders' score fell just short of statistical significance (critical ratio 2.82). "These results indicate that for immediate recall the 'together' method is much better than the 'separate' method."[156] However, on the delayed recall test it was the "separate" group which showed to advantage, albeit less dramatically.

[155] Harder, "The Relative Efficiency of the 'Separate' and 'Together' Methods of Teaching Homonyms," *Journal of Experimental Education*, p. 8.

[156] *Ibid.*, p. 13.

"A consistent, but not statistically significant difference is found for the 'separate' method in the third grade (critical ratio .22) and in the sixth grade (critical ratio 2.32) on the delayed recall test."[157] Since Harder considered permanent recall "the final measure of spelling accuracy," he gave greater weight to the results of the delayed recall test. He concluded, "Considering the consistency of the findings on the delayed recall test, a reasonable interpretation is to favor the 'separate' method as giving slightly better results than the 'together' method."[158]

There is no doubt that Harder was correct in considering the learning that "sticks" to be more important educationally than the learning which, no matter how great, is merely immediate. There is no doubt, also, that the advocates of separatism will find small comfort in the statistical insignificance of the long-range superiority of the "separate" method. About the most that can confidently be said on Harder's evidence is that neither method proves to have a special advantage over the long haul. The probable justice of this interpretation is reenforced by Harder's acknowledgment in his last paragraph that "average differences. . .between the methods were small."[159] It is surprising that a study of homonyms, which would seem to be such a hard test of the efficacy of grouping, should produce so indecisive a result. But then, after the necessary allowances are made for methodological crudities, no one of the other studies produced a decisive result. To the teacher we can say again with Gates, ". . . the general value of grouping. . .is not clearly proved," and we can add the only advice that research might support, namely, "Group if you must, but remember it confers no special advantage and may even introduce errors unless the grouping illustrates consistently followed spelling patterns; do not group if you find it bothersome or time consuming; ordinarily your students will learn either way so that you will be unable to tell the difference without a micrometer."

Though Gates's position may serve as a good guide for the present, it may be of some value to speculate just a little (and very warily) about the future. Linguistic researches suggest that English words fall into 3 classes of sharply diminishing size: regular, semiregular, and irregular. That is, the actual sounds of the language (phonemes) are symbolized with unexpected consistency by the written shape-units (graphemes) of the language. In other words, spelling is not so irregular and capricious as many have supposed. At this writing, the proof of this contention is not available, but the results of a large-scale study approaching completion by Paul R. Hanna are expected to support the contention (USOE Cooperative Research Project, No. 1991). Without any prejudgment, it is enough to say that if phoneme-grapheme relationships are closer than has been supposed, then surely further experimental studies should be conducted to discover whether linguistic groupings do indeed enable spelling to be taught more effectively. (See section 14, below, for a report of the work of Hanna and others.)

[157]*Ibid.*, p. 15.
[158]*Loc. cit.*
[159]*Ibid.*, p. 22.

In the meantime, the clearest (if somewhat polemic) statement of the case for linguistic grouping is a pamphlet by Robert A. Hall, Jr., *Sound and Spelling in English* (Philadelphia: Chilton Company, 1961).

10. TEST-STUDY VS. STUDY-TEST

On this topic the experimental evidence accumulated over the years is fairly consistent. But because consistency is no guarantee of worth and because the consistent evidence has not always been interpreted consistently, it will repay us to look anew at the studies.

Test all words before teaching is the advice Ernest Horn gave in "Principles of Method in Teaching Spelling as Derived from Scientific Investigation" (*Eighteenth Yearbook,* National Society for the Study of Education, Part II, 1919). But the only evidence he cited was an unpublished study by himself and E. E. Ritter showing that children already know many words on the spelling list and that more than 75 percent of instructional time would be wasted if children were obliged to study every one of the listed words. Earlier, in 1913, W. H. Winch's study recommended the test-study method because it promised to save some time. Winch's study focused on audio-visual-kinesthetic methods of teaching spelling and should not, therefore, represent more than an insightful approach to the problem of whether test-study or study-test is the better method.[160]

In 1923, John H. Kingsley, a public school teacher in Albany, New York, reported his attempt to discover experimentally which of the two methods is superior. First, Kingsley convinced a sixth grade teacher who was discouraged with the results of the study-test method to try the test-study method. When at the end of one month the teacher was pleasantly surprised, it was possible for Kingsley to interest an eighth grade and a seventh grade teacher to try the test-study method. A year later, 3 grades in another school (which grades and how many teachers were not specified) joined the experiment. One fifth grade and one seventh grade class were taught by the study-test method in order to provide a basis for comparison. In order to provide a uniform measure of achievement, Kingsley gave the Ayres Measuring Scale for Ability in Spelling to each class each month. After all classes had participated for at least a year, Kingsley found that the test-study classes made better gains and had a higher average performance than the study-test classes were able to achieve.[161]

Regrettably, Kingsley did not say anything about the number and composition of his experimental and control groups and did not calculate the statistical significance of the differences he found. His terse comment that some classes "changed from the old plan to the new plan" is disconcerting.[162] Its procedural

[160]W. H. Winch, "Experimental Researches on Learning to Spell," *Journal of Educational Psychology,* 4 (November 1913), 524–537.
[161]John H. Kingsley, "The Test-study Method Versus the Study-test Method in Spelling," *Elementary School Journal,* 24 (October 1923), 129.
[162]*Loc. cit.*

flaws being what they are, it is unlikely that the study tells us anything reliable about the worth of the test-study and study-test methods.

Another study which also changed its procedures along the way was reported in 1924 by Hughes Mearns, a teacher in the Lincoln School of Teachers College, Columbia University. In some ways, what Mearns reported is less an experiment than an account of an on-going, self-critical program in spelling.

Having grown dissatisfied with their pupils' level of spelling achievement, the teachers at the Lincoln School undertook to review the professional literature to discover improved means of teaching spelling. After a review lasting 6 months, the teachers decided that spelling improvement would not result from "studying words in general, or rules, or mnemonic or other devices" but would be the result of "direct and persistent attack on the words that must eventually be learned."[163] They decided to use the Horn-Ashbaugh lists which contain the most frequently occurring 4,000 words out of 750,000 words appearing in correspondence.

Between March and May of 1921 the teachers worked out a test-study procedure for grades four to eight. "Each Monday the grade teacher tested the class on twenty words not previously seen, an inventory to discover the spelling problems of each pupil; these misspellings were the pupil's task for the week. The same list was tested on Wednesday and on Friday, the aim being to make sure the spellings were mastered, and to discover the new misspellings among words not completely learned. Four weeks later the list was given again to test retention. In an individual record sheet, containing a printed list of words, the pupil kept an account of his failures and of his progress in mastering them."[164]

Prior to the Monday inventory test, students read aloud from their printed word lists and pronounced each word. During the Monday test they heard the teacher pronounce each word, and they heard it pronounced and properly spelled by the teacher while they corrected their tests. Similarly, on Wednesday and Friday they heard the word pronounced twice and corrected spelling once. Also, each child was given printed instructions on how to spell a word. The instructions were adapted from Horn and Ashbaugh and stressed "repeated visualization. . ., repeated vocalization. . ., and repeated muscular control of the right form."[165] The results of the March to May preliminary experiment were uniformly encouraging to the teachers.

The teachers decided to make certain procedural changes for the year 1921-1922. Among these were the introduction of a second inventory test to be taken immediately after the first in order to increase the likelihood that students' spelling deficiencies would be revealed and, also, the introduction of a system to enable students to dictate to each other the words they missed on the previous test. For the third year, 1922-1923, the teachers dropped the second inventory,

[163] Hughes Mearns, "A Report on a Specific Spelling Situation," *Teachers College Record,* 26 (November 1924), 220.
[164] *Ibid.,* p. 121.
[165] *Loc. cit.*

which turned out to be a work of supererogation. Also, the teachers decided that it was unnecessary to have pupils dictate words to each other.

The results of the whole enterprise, as it turned out, did not apply to grades seven and eight because "the junior high school schedule did not permit the same daily attack on spelling."[166] Continuous records covering all 3 years were available for only 39 pupils—a fact which makes it exceedingly difficult to interpret differences in scores from year to year. There was, of course, no control group, since students' performance was compared to their own previous performance during the experiment or to their performance prior to the initiation of the test-study procedure. It is apparent that the students improved noticeably after the introduction of the experimental procedures. But the improvement did not seem to be affected by alterations in details of procedure.

Mearns did not report what spelling instruction was like prior to the experimental period. Perhaps spelling was neglected. Perhaps it was taught by the incidental method or by some other method which did not concentrate student attention upon spelling. Perhaps spelling was taught in so poor and boring a fashion that learning was actively discouraged. Therefore, it is impossible to say whether the improvement Mearns noted was the result of the merits of his test-study plan or the result of the deficiencies of the instructional program that preceded it.

This much can be safely said—the test-study procedure worked well during the experimental period for 39 students in the Lincoln School. Whether such a statement has practical importance for the education of the children in the public schools of the nation seems unlikely. Surely the students in the Lincoln School at the time of the Mearns experiment represented a minority whose ability and whose social, economic, and linguistic background were well above the national average. With such a group, it might have been enough for the teacher to frown a little, hand out a spelling list, admonish the students to learn the list on pain of incurring his or their parents' displeasure, and let it go at that.

The first large-scale comparison between the test-study and study-test methods was conducted by E. E. Keener and has been commented upon in section 7 in connection with individualizing spelling instruction. It may be recalled briefly that Keener found that the test-study method achieved a 3.5 percent better result at a 12 percent saving of time.[167]

The second large-scale attempt to assess the merits of the test-study and study-test plans was made by L. R. Kilzer during the academic year 1925-1926. Thirty high schools located in 8 states returned data on 777 students. Kilzer prepared two 25-word tests containing words of the same frequency and degree of difficulty. Half of the participating students were taught List A by the test-study method and, a few days later, List B by the study-test method. The other half were taught List B by the test-study method and, later, list A by the study-

[166]*Ibid.,* p. 228.
[167]Keener, "Comparison of the Group and Individual Methods of Teaching Spelling," *Journal of Educational Methods,* p. 34.

test method. Reversing the lists in this way served as a safeguard against any unknown inequality in the lists. All students took an immediate recall test following the completion of instruction by each method. All students took a delayed recall test 5 months after the conclusion of the experimental period.

Concerning immediate recall, Kilzer found that in one group of schools the chances are 226 to 1 that the test-study method is superior and that in the second group of schools the chances are 80 to 1 that the test-study method is superior. With respect to delayed recall, Kilzer found no significant difference between the two methods. He urged the adoption of the test-study method on the grounds of its superiority in immediate recall and its more economic use of time.[168]

A third study involving a substantial number of subjects was conducted by A. C. Senour in 1927. Senour obtained data from 694 pupils in 25 classes taught by 10 different teachers in the East Chicago, Indiana, school system. On Monday, before permitting students to study the words for the week, Senour's teachers gave an initial test. On Tuesday students studied the words they missed on the initial test. On Wednesday the teachers gave a second test. On Thursday students again studied the words they missed on both previous tests. On Friday the teachers gave a final test. The first recall test was given 4 weeks after the final test, and a second recall test was given 3 months later.

The assembled data show that students, although they failed to achieve perfect scores, improved to a "creditable and acceptable" extent. On the final test, the students improved 47 percent; on the first recall test, students improved 94 percent; and on the second recall test, students improved 92 percent.[169]

It should be observed that the study did not compare methods of instruction. What it did was seek to show that the test-study method gets results, aside from the question of how good or bad other methods may be. It is, therefore, not likely to convince those who are disposed to claim that other methods will do as well or better. Unfortunately, Senour did not construct his word lists so that they would be suitably difficult at the grade levels at which they were taught. What is more, the study was, apparently, loosely supervised—as indicated by the fact that data supplied by 8 of 18 teachers had to be ruled out of the study, and data supplied by 2 other teachers could be explained by Senour only by assuming that the teachers had not reported accurately what they had done.[170] Since no other study has reported recall results of the magnitude of Senour's, it would appear best for this and other reasons to value his findings at a much discounted rate.

In 1931, Arthur I. Gates published a study which he had conducted in a New York City public school for approximately 20 weeks beginning on Febru-

[168] L. R. Kilzer, "The Test-Study Method Versus the Study-Test Method in Teaching Spelling," *School Review,* 34 (September 1926), 523, 525.

[169] A. C. Senour, "An Investigation of the Effectiveness of the Test-Teach-Test Method of Instruction in Spelling," *Elementary School Journal,* 30 (May 1930), 703, 706.

[170] *Ibid.,* pp. 701, 706.

ary 1, 1928. For the first 10 weeks, half of the students in each class used the study-test method and half used the test-study method. For the second 10 weeks, the students in each class used the method they had not used at first. By this means Gates was able to control substantially the pupil variable, avoid elaborate pairing schemes, and isolate the differences that it appeared reasonable to attribute to the methods of teaching employed. In all, Gates obtained 3,236 completed scores from students in 49 classes in grades two through eight during both halves of the experimental period. The final test, given in the tenth week, contained an equal number of words from the 9 lists taught during the preceding 9 weeks; thus, the final test did double duty as a short-term delayed recall test.

Gates expressed the view that the test-study method has "fewer" and "less serious" faults. He expressed surprise that the test-study method did "not show to greater advantage" in his own study and in the studies of others.[171] Gates found that, although differences were small, the study-test method obtained better results in the second grade and in the first half of the third grade and that the test-study method obtained better results in the other grades through grade eight. Gates found that low ability students through grade four fared better when using the study-test method and fared equally well in grades five through eight regardless of which method they used. But brighter students learned more from the test-study method, except in second and fourth grade where neither method showed to advantage.

These findings did not conform to what Gates, on theoretical grounds, had been led to believe. He suggested that a possible explanation might be the inadequacy of pupils' methods of study and the failure of teachers to supervise pupils adequately during self-study periods. Beyond doubt, such deficiencies as Gates suspected could skew the findings to the disadvantage of the test-study method. Unlike its opposite, the test-study method depends to a far greater extent upon teachers' zealousness in supervising self-study sessions and upon teachers' ability to resist the temptation to use the time during self-study sessions to catch up on any uncompleted chores of their own. If improperly supervised students cannot, or will not, use the self-study time to advantage, then there is no hope for the test-study method, in spite of its theoretical possibilities. Fortunately, there is no reason to suspect a student plot against self-study nor anything inherently in opposition to self-study in the nature of students. The most likely hopothesis may very well be what Gates suggested, namely, that the test-study method, which relies heavily upon self-study, did not fare better because supervision by teachers was inadequate and the students did not work as they should have.

Gates's study leaves one with the impression that the test-study plan is still sound in theory and promising in practice and that—if properly taught and skillfully assessed—it will demonstrate its superiority. It is too bad that the Gates study did not create the proper experimental conditions to settle the matter.

[171] Arthur I. Gates, "An Experimental Comparison of the Study-Test and Test-Study Methods in Spelling," *Journal of Educational Psychology,* 22 (January 1931), 18.

The studies since 1937 have tended to favor the test-study plan. Two which find evidence instead for study-test are by Leslie W. Johnson and Dorothy M. Beatty. After one year of instruction in which the same students in 6 schools, grades three through eight, learned spelling by both methods, Johnson found that the study-test method was 35 times more effective than the test-study method. This finding is not surprising in view of the inadequacy of the test-study procedure employed in the experiment. Apparently all that Johnson did was to give a test on Monday and Friday, and apparently Johnson made no use of the corrected test. Apparently, also, the experiment was completely uncontrolled.[172] Beatty's study, though better constructed than Johnson's, failed to produce an unequivocal result.[173]

Among the post 1937 studies that see merit in the test-study plan, the first, by C. W. Dupree, found a statistically significant difference in favor of the test-study method, but the results might have been affected by the fact that Dupree promised exemption from further spelling study to students in the test-study group who achieved two consecutive perfect scores on the spelling test.[174]

In another experiment, Sister M. Gervase Blanchard taught spelling demons to 160 pairs of eighth graders. For 2½ months, one member of each pair used the test-study method and the other used the study-test method. The mean score on a recall test given at the end of the experimental period revealed that the test-study group made 3 times the improvement of the study-test group.[175]

Helen M. Shubik matched two groups of third graders for intelligence, spelling ability, and achievement and taught the same list of demons to both groups for 7 weeks. The mean score of the test-study group was 4.77 greater than the score for the study-test group, a statistically significant difference.[176]

Three masters theses by Gladys H. Hibler, Margaret A. Montgomery, and Bernice K. Ledbetter urge the superiority of the test-study method.[177] Since all

---

[172] Leslie W. Johnson, "Study-Test Method Is Superior in Teaching Spelling," *Nation's Schools*, July 1950, pp. 51–52.

[173] Dorothy Marie Beatty, "A Comparison of Two Methods of Teaching Spelling," (Ph.D. dissertation, State University of Iowa, 1955), in *Dissertation Abstracts*, 15, 11 (November 1955), 2110–2111.

[174] C. W. Dupree, "A Comparative Experimental Study of the Pupil-Self-Study Method and the Modern-Systematic Method of Teaching Spelling," *Journal of Experimental Education*, September 1937, pp. 1–6.

[175] Sister M. Gervase Blanchard, "An Experimental Comparison of the Test-Study and Study-Test Methods of Teaching Spelling in the Eighth Grade" (Master's thesis, Fordham University, 1944).

[176] Helen M. Shubik, "An Experimental Comparison of the Test-Study and Study-Test Methods of Teaching Spelling in the Third Grade" (Master's thesis, Fordham University, 1951).

[177] Gladys Hunt Hibler, "The Test-study Method versus the Study-test Method of Teaching Spelling in Grade Two: Study I" (Master's thesis, University of Texas, 1957); Margaret Ann Montgomery, "The Test-study Method versus the Study-test Method of Teaching Spelling in Grade Two: Study II" (Master's thesis, University of Texas, 1957); Bernice Katheryn Ledbetter, "The Test-study Method versus the Study-test Method of Teaching Spelling in Grade Two: Study III" (Master's thesis, University of Texas, 1959).

three studies were completed at the same university within 2½ years of each other, employ identical language at many places, and contain identical concluding chapters, it is assumed that they report the same experiment. For convenience, therefore, references will be made only to the last of these, the study by Ledbetter.

Four hundred ninety-eight students in second grade were randomly divided into an experimental (test-study) group and a control (study-test) group. Both groups worked with the same spelling list of 50 words drawn from a spelling textbook. Both groups took a pretest, a recall test given 13 days after the conclusion of the experimental period, and a delayed recall test 34 days after the conclusion of the experimental period. In order to reduce the teacher variable, each teacher taught both test-study and study-test groups.

The study is not without methodological handicaps, as Ledbetter and her colleagues recognized. The experimental period should have been longer. The delayed recall test might well have been delayed longer. The list of words tested was probably much too easy, thereby obscuring to some extent the effects of instruction. Last of all, the experimental procedures should have been more closely supervised.

In experiments of this kind, supervision seems to be a crucial problem. It may be recalled that Gates—no amateur—also had trouble with supervision. The experimenter must supervise his teachers to see that they, in turn, supervise their students during the critical phase of the experiment in which each member of the test-study group is supposed to be studying the words he missed. If supervision by the teachers is unreliable and the test-study method fares poorly, there is no way to tell whether the test-study method is at fault or whether it is merely that students were relaxing while their teacher's attention was elsewhere.

But in the Ledbetter experiment the test-study method showed a statistically significant advantage over the study-test method in spite of Ledbetter's doubts about supervision. Since deficiencies in supervision work to the disadvantage of the test-study method, it seems reasonable to suppose that the test-study method would have produced even better results than it did if the supervision by the teachers had been beyond question. It is ironic that the great virtue in the test-study method (its economical adaptation to students' individual needs) seems to be precisely why the method has not shown up better in experiments. Certainly any future experimenters should be at pains to insure the quality of supervision that cooperating teachers are supposed to give during students' self-study sessions.

Among the studies dealing with the value of the test-study method, the most recent and the most elaborate is by Hale C. Reid and A. N. Hieronymus. Working with second and third graders in 27 schools in the Cedar Rapids system, Reid and Hieronymus sought to discover the relative effectiveness of 5 methods of teaching spelling, namely, the (1) test–study–test method, (2) workbook method, (3) word perception method—with test, (4) word perception method—without test, and (5) proofreading and correction method. The first two of these methods involved simply the direct teaching of a basal word list. The second two involved direct teaching of the basal list and, in addition, the completion of exercises "intended to generalize spelling ability to other words."[178] The last method involved writing a student's theme on the chalkboard prior to working out corrections.

Novel features were the use of teacher rating scales and the assignment of teachers according to their preferences for a particular method. In this way the researchers hoped to minimize the teacher variable. Classes assigned to work with each of the 5 methods were of approximately equal ability, as determined by their average composite score on the Iowa Test of Basic Skills which had been administered in previous years. As a further check, intelligence scores and pre-experiment spelling scores were obtained after students had been assigned to classes. The intelligence and initial spelling ability scores provided a means for correcting statistically the gains which each experimental group made.

Reid and Hieronymus were unable to find a truly decisive superiority for any *one* method, but they did conclude that the test-study method and the word perception method—without test—appeared to have an advantage over all others. The workbook method and the proofreading-correction method, they found, provided the poorest results.

This experiment, which is methodologically impressive, serves at least to buttress the case for the test-study method. That it also supports the case for a dissimilar method (the word perception method—without test) should not be interpreted as a contradiction or a puzzle. After all, there is no reason to assume that learning can proceed effectively by only one means or by only one set of similar means. Many roads may lead to the Heavenly City, and the function of research is simply to discover which are the most direct and least rocky routes.

A study by Hugh Schoephoerster differs from those previously mentioned in that it starts by accepting the superiority of the test-study method and then undertakes to identify which form or version of the method should be preferred under given conditions. Schoephoerster's subjects were 155 fifth graders who were taught spelling by 3 test-study plans.

Plan I   Monday: exercises on pronunciation and meaning; initial corrected test
        Friday: mastery test

Plan II   Monday: same as Plan I
        Wednesday: corrected test
        Friday: same as Plan I

[178] Hale C. Reid and A. N. Hieronymus, *An Evaluation of Five Methods of Teaching Spelling in the Second and Third Grades,* United States Office of Education Cooperative Research Project No. 1869 (Washington, D. C.: USOE, 1963), p. 9.

Plan III   Monday: same as Plan I
            Wednesday: word study
            Friday: same as Plan I

The experimental period was 12 weeks long. All 155 students worked according to the Plan I method for 4 weeks and then spent 4 weeks under Plan II and, finally, 4 weeks under Plan III. By means of this arrangement Schoephoerster avoided having to match groups. The risk in this arrangement is that the results obtained during the last 4 weeks (Plan III) might be affected by the students' experiences during the previous 4 weeks (Plan II). The published report does not mention this possibility. There is, also, a possibility that a 4-week trial of each method may not adequately reveal its potentialities.

The spelling words used during each 4-week phase of the experiment were "equated for difficulty" with the help of the New Iowa Spelling Scales (1954). Six teachers participated in the study. A delayed recall test was administered 11 days following the conclusion of each of the three phases of the study.[179]

The students were divided into 3 spelling ability groups (above average, average, below average) on the basis of the initial corrected test—a rough grouping. Data were analyzed for each ability group. Schoephoerster concluded that (1) above average students fared equally well regardless of the method of instruction; according to Schoephoerster, above average students learned sufficiently rapidly and knew so many of the words prior to formal instruction that the best plan for them should be Plan I which would involve the smallest expenditure of time; (2) average students fared equally well under Plan II or Plan III; and (3) below average students fared best under Plan III.[180]

Schoephoerster's evidence suggests that the one plan which would serve the needs of the largest number of students (average and below average groups) is Plan III. His recommendation of Plan I for above average students (because it saves the time of those who know 97 percent of the words at the start) might better be a recommendation that the above average group be given a more challenging list. Were this done, then Plan III might serve all ability groups. This deduction, though following logically from the evidence, was not experimentally tested.

11. LIST METHOD VS. CONTEXT METHOD

The list method consists of teaching words from a printed (or some other) list and testing the words by dictating them. The context method typically involves presenting the words in some prose context, teaching the words in context, and testing the words by dictating the passage. There are, of course, variations. For example, "context" may mean anything from a phrase to a paragraph. What makes the context method interesting and controversial is its assumption that spelling learned from a list will transfer imperfectly when students use the

---

[179]Hugh Schoephoerster, "Research into Variations of the Test-Study Plan of Teaching Spelling," *Elementary English,* 39 (May 1962), 460–461.

[180]*Ibid.,* pp. 461-462.

word in a prose context and that spelling learned originally in a prose context will transfer more efficiently when students try to spell the word in a context of their own original composition.

On the face of it, the context theory seems appealing. Transferring the newly learned spelling of a word from context to context seems like less of a jolt than transferring it from list to context. But even when viewed from this theoretical vantage point, the advantage of the context method may be largely illusory because the student must learn the spelling within a context manufactured by the teacher or textbook writer, and, then, he must still transfer the spelling successfully to a context of his own composition before the method can truly be said to teach spelling. Looked at in this way, it is hard to say on theoretical grounds whether a spelling learned in a manufactured context or whether a spelling learned in a list will transfer more readily to an original composition.

It is extremely difficult to discover whether a method of teaching spelling has an effect upon the way a student spells in an original composition. Therefore, studies comparing the list and context methods employ conventional tests. To test the effectiveness of the list method, the studies simply require students to write down dictated words. To test the effectiveness of the context method, the studies simply require students to write down dictated passages containing the spelling words. Were one method or the other to give dramatically superior test results, it would at least be good circumstantial evidence for believing that the method is superior and would indeed improve spelling in a student's original writing.

Several studies published prior to 1920 found that students using the column method spell better than students using the context method. Somewhat more recent studies, to which attention is directed here, support these findings and serve adequately to represent the present state of knowledge on the list-context question.

W. E. Hawley and Jackson Gallup found that students "using the list method did better than those using the sentence method."[181] The subjects were 1,100 students in grades three through eight who were taught by 32 teachers in two Rochester, New York, elementary schools. The students in the schools were comparable in terms of language background, according to the researchers. Students at a given grade level in one school were taught by the list method, and students at the same grade level in the other school were taught by the context (in this case, sentence) method. It was arranged so that in each succeeding grade in a school the method should be the one not employed in the preceding grade. By means of this scheme, Hawley and Gallup sought to minimize the effects of any human variables in the experimental situation.

Hawley and Gallup devised a separate test for students at each grade to

---

[181] W. E. Hawley and Jackson Gallup, "The 'List' versus the 'Sentence' Method of Teaching Spelling," *Journal of Educational Research*, 5 (April 1922), 309.

determine their initial spelling ability. The experiment lasted for 30 lessons, that is for 6 school weeks. After the tenth and twentieth lesson, Hawley and Gallup gave a test covering the words taught during the preceding 10 lessons. After the thirtieth lesson, they gave a final test covering the work of the entire experimental period.

The initial test revealed that—prior to instruction—students made better scores on the list test than on the context test. The final test revealed that students typically made better scores on the list test than on the context test— regardless of the method they had used during instruction. Students who used the list method tested far better on a list test than on a context test containing the same words. Students who used the context method also tested better on a list test than on a context test containing the same words, although the advantage was smaller. Hawley and Gallup, unfortunately, did not calculate the significance of the scores they obtained.

It is noteworthy that fifth and sixth graders taught by the list method initially knew fewer words than did their fellow fifth and sixth graders who were taught by the context method. Yet these list-taught students achieved superior scores on the final test. In short, Hawley and Gallup's recommendation that teachers use the list method seems to be substantiated by the data they supplied.

A study by Paul McKee examined the "relative efficiency of the. . .column . . .and. . .context forms."[182] McKee conducted 3 separate experiments comparing the list or column method with presentation in phrases, sentences, and paragraphs. From the Horn-Ashbaugh speller, McKee selected 480 words—160 for each of his 3 experiments. Two hundred seventy-five students in seventh grade returned about 50,000 spelling papers.

Each of the 3 experiments lasted for 8 weeks, 24 lessons in all. Prior to the experimental period McKee gave a preliminary spelling test of 100 words from Ashbaugh's Iowa Spelling Scales (1922). By means of this test McKee divided his students into two groups of equal spelling ability. One group used the list method and the other the context method. Thus for 8 weeks one group studied words in lists while the other studied words in context-phrases; during the second 8 weeks, one group studied words in lists while the other studied words in context-sentences; during the third and last 8-week period one group studied words in lists while the other studied words in context-paragraphs.

Students studied 20 new words each week. Each lesson lasted 15 minutes. McKee provided an initial, midweek, and final test each week so that he would have a record of each student's improvement. Nine weeks following the conclusion of a week of study on 20 words, McKee gave a delayed recall test.

---

[182]Paul McKee, "Teaching Spelling by Column and Context Forms," *Journal of Educational Research,* 15 (April and May 1927), 246-255 and 339-348; a two-part report of McKee's "Teaching and Testing Spelling by Column and Context Forms" (Ph.D. dissertation, State University of Iowa, 1924).

According to McKee's delayed recall tests, students who used the list method spelled significantly better than did students who used either the phrase, sentence, or paragraph method. Also, McKee's immediate recall tests showed the list group to advantage over the groups which used the phrase or paragraph method, but the list group was only slightly superior to the sentence group. On the question of whether students using one method would more readily transfer newly learned spellings to a new context, McKee was unable to find any clear superiority for any one method.

The evidence so far presented is heavily in favor of the list or column method in comparison with the context method. But the evidence would be less persuasive if it could be shown that the context method is the better method for helping students to learn the meanings of their spelling words. In a study involving 383 fifth graders in 16 classes, H. W. Distad and Eva M. Davis sought to discover whether students learn word meanings tested in context form better than they learn meanings tested in column form.

Distad and Davis established 4 lists of words of equal difficulty in spelling and equal difficulty in meaning. The 16 classes were organized in 4 groups of 4 classes each, and each group began its study with a different list and studied all 4 lists in different order. Two lists were *tested* by the column dictation method and two by the sentence dictation method. All 4 lists were *taught* by the same method; specifically, the teacher wrote each word on the blackboard, pronounced each by syllables, had the students pronounce each, read a sentence to illustrate each word, and kept the word on view on the blackboard for one week. The delayed recall test consisted of repeating each test one month after it had originally been given.

The results of the Distad-Davis experiment revealed a significant advantage for the sentence dictation test over the column dictation test. The authors concluded that the sentence-dictation method of testing spelling is superior "in teaching the meaning of words."[183]

It may be that testing spelling by dictating the word and using it in a sentence is a useful device in that it clarifies at least one meaning that the word has. But there seems to be a tricky logical connection between Distad and Davis's procedure and the conclusion they reached. What they actually tested was how well students spell deliberately selected hard words when these are uniformly *taught* by using sentences to explain them and then are *tested* by sometimes using illustrative sentences and sometimes not using illustrative sentences. The experiment would, thus, seem to be examining whether illustrative sentences in tests lead to better spelling performance on tests. How, then, do the authors reach a conclusion that the sentence-dictation method is superior "in teaching the meaning of words"? The answer is that they selected words

[183] H. W. Distad and Eva M. Davis, "A Comparison of Column-Dictation and Sentence-Dictation Spelling with Respect to Acquisition of Meaning of Words," *Journal of Educational Research*, 20 (December 1929), 359.

above the fifth grade level of difficulty and then assumed that the meanings of these words would also be difficult. Perhaps their assumption is correct, since they included such words as *average, entitle, investment,* and *procured.* That these words were more often correctly spelled on the sentence-dictation test than on the column-dictation test did not necessarily mean that students knew the meanings of these words. The sentence-dictation test may simply have helped the students to recall the form (spelling) of the word they had previously studied in the same sentence context. Indeed, the students' superior record on the sentence-dictation tests may indicate no more than the possibility that a sentence-dictation test helps students to avoid mishearing a word by providing contextual clues which rule out the word he thought he heard.

There is no doubt that students' motivation is increased when the meanings of spelling words are made clear. No doubt, also, any resultant increase in students' vocabulary is educationally desirable. No doubt, again, providing clues to the meaning of spelling words by using the dictionary and by using the words in sentences during the instruction and during testing requires only an infinitesimal investment of time and effort and can do no harm. There is no conclusive proof that it does any good, but the possibility of good is present. One thing is certain. Dictated tests which include a sentence in which the use of a word is well illustrated will help to prevent the student from making mistakes which are not spelling mistakes but rather are errors resulting from something askew in oral-aural communication.

12. GAMES, FLASH CARDS, EYE MOVEMENTS, AND PROOFREADING

The four paths to improved spelling to be discussed here have all interested teachers at one time or another, and some continue to be popular. Very little, however, has been done to find out whether these paths actually lead to the posted destination.

Games. One thousand five hundred sixty-five students in 38 classes (grades two to eight) in a Brooklyn, New York, public school were the subjects of an experiment by Arthur I. Gates and Frederick B. Graham. Half the group served as a control and was taught by drill and by direct study using the test-study and study-test methods. The other half was taught by means of games and activities such as crossword puzzles, filling in letters to complete words, spelling matches, supplying words omitted in a sentence, writing words to identify objects, unscrambling letters to make words. Gates and Graham received usable data from 1,076 students.

Gates and Graham sought to keep their experimental and control groups at approximately the same average level of mental ability. To accomplish this they relied upon the ability groupings already in existence in the school. They also gave a test of initial spelling ability on the basis of which they paired students in the control group with students in the experimental group. There were two final tests, one designed to measure the influence of instruction on students' ability to spell studied words and the other designed to measure the influence of instruction upon students' ability to spell unstudied words (a general spelling ability test).

According to the two experimenters, the results were "obviously inconsistent."[184] But they thought that the experimental (game) group would have made a better showing if students in the lower grades had not had to deal with "instructions and activities which were a little too complex."[185] They pointed out that after an appropriate correction had been made, the experimental group fared at least as well as the control group and might even be said to have exceeded the achievement of the control group.[186]

Gates and Graham found, also, that the less able students profited least from participation in spelling games. The abler students profited most. This is an interesting outcome because games are frequently defended as a way of reaching the less able students. However, before accepting this finding and its practical corollary, it should be remembered that the less able students may have suffered because the games were conducted by means of written directions which (according to the participating teachers) the less able students had difficulty in following.[187]

Flash Cards. In the Gates-Graham study just mentioned, flash cards were included among the games and activities by which the experimental group learned to spell. In 1932, two years prior to the Gates-Graham study, L. C. Gilbert reported an investigation specifically designed to assess the value of flash cards in the teaching of spelling. Gilbert was unable to find anything in the educational literature "concerning experimental investigations of the relative worth of flash card methods of teaching spelling,"[188] and this writer has been unable to find anything on the subject since Gilbert's study appeared. Perhaps it is the only study ever to be devoted entirely to an evaluation of the flash card method.

The origin of Gilbert's study lay in the observation that eye movements of poor spellers are "characterized by many fixations, by long and irregular pauses, by frequent regressions, by narrow units of study, and by a general lack of systematic procedure."[189] He reasoned that if a "learner realizes. . .he has but a brief opportunity to see a word, it is legitimate to suppose that he will attempt to group as much as possible and thus his pauses will be shortened, the number of regressions and other fixations will be cut down, his study unit will be broadened, and a few related perceptions rather than a confusion of many minutiae will be given him."[190] Gilbert proposed, therefore, to see whether drill with words flashed rapidly within the view of a group of students would

[184] Arthur I. Gates and Frederick B. Graham, "The Value of Various Games and Activities in Teaching Spelling," *Journal of Educational Research,* 28 (September 1934), 3.

[185] *Ibid.,* p. 5.

[186] *Loc. cit.*

[187] *Ibid.,* p. 7.

[188] L. C. Gilbert, "Experimental Investigation of a Flash-card Method of Teaching Spelling," *Elementary School Journal,* 32 (January 1932), 338.

[189] *Ibid.,* p. 337.

[190] *Ibid.,* p. 338.

train the students in better perceptual skills and, consequently, improve their spelling and their ability to learn spelling.

The subjects of the experiment were 32 fifth graders who were of at least normal intelligence and who were free of any physical disability which might affect their ability to spell. The subjects were divided into 3 groups of approximately equal ability. This division was made on the basis of a test of 50 words previously studied during the semester, a test of 5 extremely difficult words which students studied individually before taking the test, and the record of the time each student required for study prior to taking the 5-word test.

Group I, the experimental group, was "drilled in the idea of learning quickly" and was shown words on cards for only a brief moment. Group II also used flash cards, but the students were permitted to view the words as long as they wished. Here the "flash" was removed from the flash card method. Group III, the control group, employed a study-test method previously used in the school. Spelling games and reviews were a part of the program for Group III. Students in Group III were permitted to study individual words for as long as they wished.

All students took a review test after the second, third, and fourth week of the experiment. After the fifth and last week, all students took a 50-word test of words they had previously studied, and all students also took an individually administered test on 5 difficult words which none could spell at the beginning of the experimental period.

In every respect the experimental group exceeded the performance of the other groups. At first, Gilbert prudently made no "final statement. . .with regard to the value of the flash card method of teaching spelling"[191] because his experiment involved only 32 students and lasted only 5 weeks. Inasmuch as his results were "definite" and positive, he did urge a large-scale investigation and did, finally, succumb in the last paragraph to the temptation to claim that the study "in itself demonstrates that teaching by flash cards with a limited length of exposure has definite value in cutting down perceptual time."[192]

There is no denying that the scores of Gilbert's experimental group are impressive. But it is also possible that his results are owing wholly or in part to the Hawthorne Effect. The Hawthorne Effect *"is a phenomenon characterized by an awareness on the part of the subjects of special treatment created by artificial experimental conditions. This awareness becomes confounded with the independent variables under study, with a subsequent facilitating effect on the dependent variable, thus leading to ambiguous results."*[193] In other words, Gilbert may have invalidated his study by telling his experimental group, "We are going to study in a new way." By so doing he created an artificial experi-

[191]*Ibid.,* p. 350.
[192]*Ibid.,* p. 351.
[193]Desmond L. Cook, "The Hawthorne Effect in Educational Research," *Phi Delta Kappan,* 44 (December 1962), 118.

mental situation which might be expected to affect the attitudes, motivation, and behavior of his subjects in an uncommon way. It is significant that Gilbert himself observed that the experimental group had the "keenest interest" in what was going on.[194] He thought that this interest was the result of his quickly paced flash card method of instruction, but it is at least as likely that any reasonable method which was not actively distressing to the students would have worked as well under the same experimental conditions.

Corinne B. Brown, in 1957, reported a study in which she used a tachistoscope to teach spelling. It flashes words or phrases at controlled speeds upon a viewer and thus resembles the older flash card method.

For 6 weeks Brown used a tachistoscope to teach 25 words a week to a class of 33 seventh graders. She recorded "a 43 percent increase in retention of each spelling lesson as tested weekly."[195] When Brown "abruptly discontinued" the use of the machine after 6 weeks, she found that her students made 27 percent more errors. When Brown resumed the use of the machine, but used it less often, she found that her students returned to their former high level of spelling achievement. Several months after the use of the tachistoscope had been entirely discontinued, Brown gave two 50-word tests containing words chosen at random from the period of tachistoscope instruction and from the more recent period of non-tachistoscope instruction. This resulted in the "startling discovery that 28 percent more of the words learned with the tachistoscope were spelled correctly than of those studied more recently without the tachistoscope."[196]

There is more enthusiasm than caution in Brown's conclusion that the "immediate effectiveness of the instrument is obvious, as is the permanence of the learning efficiency."[197] The study contains no mention of controls. When Brown speaks of a 43 percent increase in retention, it is unclear what groups or what performances are being compared. She fails to reveal her usual method of instruction. Dramatic results such as these can be obtained simply by teaching poorly during times when the tachistoscope is not plugged in. Finally, comments made in the immediately preceding discussion concerning the Hawthorne Effect also apply here.

It would seem that the case for teaching spelling by means of flash cards and tachistoscopes has neither been proved nor disproved. Stripped of novelty, it is hard to see how either method is potentially more suitable for mass instruction than any other common form of drill.

Eye Movements. The subject of eye movements, which has long interested those concerned with teaching reading and spelling, has been alluded to in connection with flash cards and tachistoscopes. It may not be amiss to mention

[194] Gilbert, "Experimental Investigation of a Flash-card Method of Teaching Spelling," *Elementary School Journal,* p. 342.

[195] Corinne B. Brown, "Teaching Spelling with a Tachistoscope," *English Journal,* 40 (February 1951), 104.

[196] *Ibid.*, p. 105.

[197] *Loc. cit.*

just briefly some studies dealing with eye movements before going on to discuss studies dealing with the relationship between eye movements and spelling.

Guy T. Buswell, in 1922, sought to discover whether there are stages of development in eye movements as the reader gains maturity. He found that the average number of fixations per line, the average duration of fixations, and the average number of regressive movements decreased as students moved from first grade through twelfth grade and college. The period of greatest development occurred during the first four grades. Also in 1922, Charles H. Judd and Guy T. Buswell published a study showing that various types of silent reading affect eye movements; that is, changes in difficulty or in the content of reading material and changes in the reader's purpose are reflected in changes in the pattern of eye movements. William C. Morse, in 1951, reported somewhat different results. He worked with students who were past the critical reading maturation point at the end of the fourth grade in order to eliminate any effects that might be attributable to reading maturity alone. To fifth and seventh graders he gave a passage two years below grade level, at grade level, and two years above grade level. The results show that both the fifth and seventh graders read in approximately the same way regardless of the difficulty of the material. Equally interesting is the finding that the range of students' individual variation in eye movements was very wide; differences from student to student are greater than differences introduced by moving from a passage at one level of difficulty to a passage at another level of difficulty. If Morse's study does indeed report the true nature of things, then one application to spelling instruction is that students might well profit from perceptual training because they tend to be improperly adaptive to different kinds of material and, as a group, range widely in their habits of eye movement. But a study of college freshmen by Frederick L. Westover, in 1946, did not show that training in eye movements is superior to other methods of improving reading; all three of the methods he studied produced about the same positive result. Furthermore, a study of third graders by Eloise B. Cason, in 1943, found that eye movement training is no more effective in the teaching of reading than is free reading in the library.[198]

Although studies dealing with eye movements and reading, such as those just mentioned, have implications for the teaching of spelling, there are a few other

[198] Guy Thomas Buswell, *Fundamental Reading Habits: A Study of Their Development.* Supplementary Educational Monographs, No. 21 (Chicago: University of Chicago Press, 1922); Charles Hubbard Judd and Guy Thomas Buswell, *Silent Reading: A Study of Various Types.* Supplementary Educational Monographs, No. 23 (Chicago: University of Chicago Press, 1922); William C. Morse, "A Comparison of the Eye-Movements of Average Fifth- and Seventh-Grade Pupils Reading Materials of Corresponding Difficulty," in *Studies in the Psychology of Reading* (Ann Arbor: University of Michigan Press, 1951); Frederick L. Westover, *Controlled Eye Movements versus Practice Exercises in Reading* (New York: Bureau of Publications, Teachers College, Columbia University, 1946); Eloise B. Cason, *Mechanical Methods for Increasing the Speed of Reading* (New York: Bureau of Publications, Teachers College, Columbia University, 1943). All the preceding have been summarized in detail in C. W. Hunnicutt and William J. Iverson, *Research in the Three R's* (New York: Harper and Brothers, 1958), pp. 19–38, 254–259.

eye movement studies which deal directly with spelling. First among these is a study by Ethel M. Abernethy based on 12 subjects—4 graduate students at the University of Chicago and 4 good spellers and 4 weak spellers in the sixth grade at the University of Chicago Elementary School. The sixth graders were tested on 10 common words all had misspelled on preliminary tests. The graduate students were tested on 10 unfamiliar botanical and chemical terms. All the subjects were photographed while studying their words. Then all were immediately given a spelling test. Although the study was methodologically less than pure, its results anticipate the results of other studies, particularly those by Gilbert, which also found significance in students' eye movements or value in training eye movements. Specifically, Abernethy found that those who spell best learn fastest and that good spellers have eye movements which indicate superior word attack patterns.[199]

Luther C. Gilbert compared good and poor spellers from third grade through twelfth grade. Sixty-seven people served as subjects, a rather small number considering the span of grades being covered. Each person was pretested on 5 words. Then he was photographed while he studied the same 5 words "in his usual manner." Then, immediately afterwards, he was tested again on the 5 words. Gilbert found that the good spellers had fewer fixations of shorter length, fewer regressions, and a shorter study time.[200] The significance of this finding is hard to assess. It would be illogical to conclude that since good spellers have good eye movements, learning good eye movements will make good spellers. This is as unreasonable as saying that if rich men have shined shoes, then poor men should shine their shoes to get rich.

Another study by Gilbert followed 6 students through 3 years of schooling, through fourth, fifth, and sixth grades. Each year the students were pretested, photographed while studying the pretested words, and posttested. Gilbert then compared the changes in eye movements from year to year. His conclusion was that there is a pattern of improvement in eye movements; students, as shown by their eye movements, learned better perceptual habits and word attack skills. The improvement in students' spelling is attributed by Gilbert to their improved perceptual habits.[201]

Last to be mentioned is the study by Luther C. Gilbert and Doris W. Gilbert. They wished to learn the "effects of teaching spelling by a method which places a premium on speed and accuracy of perception."[202] The Gilberts paired 100 fourth, fifth, and sixth graders to whom they gave a pretest on the

[199] Ethel M. Abernethy, "Photographic Records of Eye Movements in Studying Spelling," *Journal of Educational Psychology,* 20 (December 1929), 700–701.

[200] Luther C. Gilbert, "An Experimental Investigation of Eye Movements in Learning to Spell Words," *Psychological Monographs,* 43, 3 (1932), 77–79.

[201] Luther C. Gilbert, "A Genetic Study of Growth in Perceptual Habits in Spelling," *Elementary School Journal,* 40 (January 1940), 357.

[202] Luther C. Gilbert and Doris Wilcox Gilbert, "Training for Speed and Accuracy of Visual Perception in Learning to Spell," *University of California Publications in Education,* 7 (1942), 352.

160 words to be taught. The experimental period lasted for 8 weeks. The control group was taught by a method "generally approved in good school systems. . . which makes provision for pre-testing, directed study, independent study, individual checking of misspelled words, progress tests, reviews, a final test."[203] Visualization, dictionary work, syllabication, games, clarification of word meaning, and attention to hard spots were also part of the method employed. The experimental group used a specially prepared booklet with movable tabs to cover or uncover words. An initial trial showed the Gilberts that a word exposure of 7 seconds would be optional.

Students took a test every week on the words studied, and two weeks following the experimental period, all took a final, presumably a delayed recall, test. Students' eye movements were photographed just before the experimental period and 8 weeks later upon the conclusion of the experimental period.

The Gilberts found that "average scores of the experimental group were better than the average scores of the. . .control group at all grade levels both on the weekly and on the delayed spelling tests."[204] The photographs of eye movements showed that the experimental group had achieved better eye movements than had the control group.[205] The Gilberts' conclusion was that training in speed and accuracy can "effect an increase in rate and efficiency and can improve perceptual habits."[206]

What conclusions can be drawn from this accumulation of evidence? It may be possible, at least under laboratory conditions, to achieve an improvement in reading and spelling by giving students training to improve their eye movements. But evidence too good to be dismissed (Westover and Cason studies) points to a contrary conclusion. If the Morse study is correct, then one answer may be that students need to learn how to read or "attack" different kinds of reading (including spelling) tasks in ways which are more suitable and efficient. According to Miles A. Tinker, who in 1946 reviewed the research dealing with eye movements and reading (including spelling), "The improvement obtained by eye movement training, with or without elaborate apparatus, is no greater than that resulting from motivated reading alone."[207] Tinker's comment still seems to be a fair evaluation of the situation. It would appear not unlikely that reading and spelling are functions of the total personality and follow a course of development in relation to other aspects of the whole. Since it is impossible to undertake here a review of the literature in the field of human growth and development which deals with this matter, it may suffice to refer simply to one ingenious and,

[203] *Ibid.*, p. 356.
[204] *Ibid.*, p. 421.
[205] *Ibid.*, p. 422.
[206] *Loc. cit.*
[207] Miles A. Tinker, "The Study of Eye Movements in Reading," *Psychological Bulletin*, 43 (March 1946), 112; see also Tinker's "Eye Movements in Reading," *Journal of Educational Research*, 30 (December 1936), 241–277.

fortunately, accessible study by Willard C. Olson[208] and remark that the view just espoused is consonant with the findings of *gestalt* psychology.

Proofreading. "Check your spelling before handing in your paper" is familiar advice. Whether the advice, even when conscientiously heeded, does much good is the subject of several investigations.

Loyd S. Tireman, in 1924, reviewed two earlier studies and concluded that "in all the experiments cited. . .the children failed to detect correctly a large percent of the errors."[209] Children were poor proofreaders even when they were directed to scrutinize each word individually. Since teachers usually do not hold students to a rigid word-by-word proofreading procedure, Tireman set out to discover what would happen in a more "natural" experimental situation.

To 70 students in grades six through eight Tireman dictated a letter containing several key words of appropriate difficulty for the grade; then he supplied a hectographed copy of the same letter with the key words misspelled. Tireman also dictated a 20-word list containing 10 key words and then supplied a hectographed copy of the list with the key words misspelled. Students were directed to correct any misspellings they observed in the dictated and reproduced material and mark with a cross any words about which they were doubtful.

In the lists, the sixth graders overlooked 7.3 percent of the errors, the seventh graders overlooked 26.8 percent of the errors, and the eighth graders overlooked 19.4 percent of the errors. In the letters, the sixth graders overlooked 42.7 percent of the errors, the seventh graders overlooked 38.8 percent, and the eighth graders overlooked 29.6 percent.[210]

Tireman's results, so far as they go, support the contention that proofreading is an inefficient instructional device because students overlook many words they need to learn. Although the number of students involved in the experiment is small, it should be observed that the results are consistent with what Tireman's predecessors found.

James E. Goss's study, unlike Tireman's, investigated students' ability to proofread papers of their own composition as well as papers that had been previously prepared. Goss worked with 543 fifth graders in 16 classes located in "selected elementary schools in Tulsa, Oklahoma."[211] Eight classes served as a

[208] Willard C. Olson, "Reading Is a Function of the Total Growth of the Child," in W. S. Gray, ed., *Reading and Pupil Development,* Proceedings of the Conference in Reading at the University of Chicago. Supplementary Educational Monographs, No. 51 (Chicago: University of Chicago Press, 1940), pp. 233–237; summarized in Hunnicutt and Iverson, *Research in the Three R's,* pp. 39–43.

[209] Loyd Spencer Tireman, "The Determination of the Ability of a Group of Sixth, Seventh, and Eighth Grade Pupils to Proofread Their Written Work for Errors in Spelling" (Master's thesis, State University of Iowa, 1924), p. 4.

[210] *Ibid.,* p. 36.

[211] James E. Goss, "Analysis of Accuracy of Spelling in Written Compositions of Elementary School Children and the Effects of Proofreading Emphasis upon Accuracy" (Ed. D. dissertation, University of Oklahoma, 1959); in *Dissertation Abstracts,* 20, 3 (September 1959), 967.

control group, and 8 classes served as an experimental group. To the experimental group Goss's cooperating teachers gave "special instructions and experiences in proofreading for twelve weeks." The control group received no special help in proofreading. At the beginning and at the end of the experimental period, pupils in both groups were given two tests. The first was a proofreading exercise which had been previously prepared by Goss and was presented in the form of handwritten prose. The second was an exercise in which the pupil proofread his own composition.

As in previous experiments, the results are not encouraging. First, Goss found that his subjects were able to spell correctly only 55.4 percent of the words they had misspelled on their written compositions. Apparently, proofreading did not teach spelling very effectively. Second, although both experimental and control groups improved their ability to spot errors in their own compositions, neither group clearly excelled the other. Third, the experimental group was superior to the control group in its ability to proofread prepared exercises.

It would seem that proofreading is a difficult skill not only for elementary school youngsters. Forest O. Greenwood found that high school students are poor proofreaders. Preservice and inservice teachers are not good proofreaders either, according to studies by Martha L. Hays, Myrtle Morton, Eva A. Richardson, and Clarence Von Eschen.[212]

Although the last word has probably not been said on the subject of proofreading, the evidence so far seems sufficient to support several conclusions which may be defended in the absence of evidence to the contrary. The first is that proofreading has failed to show itself as an effective device for teaching spelling. The second (which should come as no shock even to professional writers) is that it is easier to proofread someone else's material than to proofread one's own. The third is that proofreading does not greatly increase the spelling accuracy of the work that has been proofread; students who have not proofread their papers will improve their spelling accuracy approximately to the same degree over the same period of time. The fourth and last conclusion (based entirely on Goss's study) is that specific instruction in proofreading does not confer a clear advantage.

---

[212] Forest O. Greenwood, "A Study of Spelling Difficulty on a High School Senior Level" (Master's thesis, State University of Iowa, 1924); Martha L. Hays, "The Spelling Ability of Normal Training Students in High School" (Master's thesis, State University of Iowa, 1930); Myrtle Morton, "A Study of the Preparation of Normal Training Students for Teaching Certain Basic Skills" (Master's thesis, State University of Iowa, 1936); Eva A. Richardson, "An Examination of the Spelling Ability of County Normal Students in Ohio" (Master's thesis, State University of Iowa, 1925); Clarence Von Eschen, "Teacher Performance on the Iowa Every-Pupil Test of Basic Skills in Reading and Language" (Master's thesis, State University of Iowa, 1936). All cited in Ernest Horn, "The Incidental Teaching of Spelling," *Elementary English Review,* 14 (January 1937), 5.

13. READING AND SPELLING

Some connection exists between reading ability and spelling ability. But to know the precise mechanism of that connection is to know the nature of perception itself, and this is one of the great unsolved problems in man's study of man. The information we do have is provided by studies such as the ones mentioned below.

Nellie L. Peake, in a purely statistical study, sought a relationship between spelling ability and one aspect of reading ability, namely, vocabulary knowledge. Using raw scores on the New Stanford Achievement Test (Form W) made by 355 children in grades four through eight, she calculated the coefficients of correlation and obtained an average figure for the whole group of .814 which, as she pointed out, is "fairly high."[213]

Luther C. Gilbert compared the ability of students to spell key words they had read in a prepared passage with the ability of the same students to spell key words they had not encountered in the same prepared passage. Three hundred forty-six students in ninth grade were involved in this portion of the study. (Another portion of the study, which need not be discussed, involved an additional 360 students.)

Gilbert's results achieved statistical significance with ease. He concluded that his students "tend to improve their spelling through reading even when attention is not directed toward spelling."[214]

In another experiment, quite similar to the first, Gilbert sought to identify the effect of reading on spelling among 380 university juniors and seniors and graduate students. First Gilbert established two matched 10-word lists of difficult words. Then he pretested students on both sets of words, gave a reading selection in which "were embedded the words of only one set," and posttested both sets "to compare the learning that had taken place."[215]

According to Gilbert, "college students improve their spelling through reading even when attention is not directed toward that end." Gilbert also noted in his conclusions that able spellers profit more from their reading than do poor spellers.[216]

Proceeding on the assumption that reading increases spelling power to some measurable extent, Luther C. Gilbert and Doris W. Gilbert sought clues to "the fundamental process involved in such incidental learning."[217] Using high scores

[213] Nellie L. Peake, "Relation between Spelling Ability and Reading Ability," *Journal of Experimental Education,* 9 (December 1940), 193.

[214] Luther C. Gilbert, "Effect of Reading on Spelling in the Ninth Grade," *School Review,* 42 (March 1934), 204.

[215] Luther C. Gilbert, "Study of the Effect of Reading on Spelling," *Journal of Educational Research,* 28 (April 1935), 570.

[216] *Ibid.,* p. 576.

[217] Luther C. Gilbert and Doris Wilcox Gilbert, "The Improvement of Spelling through Reading," *Journal of Educational Research*, 37 (February 1944), 458.

on a 50-word test as the means of selection, the Gilberts chose 23 "superior" spellers who were upperclass students at the University of California. Each of the 23 students was given a second 50-word test containing selected "critical" words. Then each student was asked to read a passage (containing critical words) at his customary rate in preparation for a true-false test on content to be given later. Then, after the reading, each student was asked to study 3 words while his eye movements were being photographed. Each student's eye movements were photographed again while he read a "prose passage in which some of the critical words were embedded" and while he studied "the spelling of other critical words in isolation." Finally, each student was tested to determine his spelling improvement and comprehension of the prose material.

The Gilberts recorded an average initial accuracy of 78 percent for the 10 critical words. After the students read the passage in which these words were embedded, the students achieved "a perfect gain. . .on 37 percent of these words." The initial accuracy of the words studied in isolation was 82 percent. After studying these words in isolation, the students achieved "a perfect gain of 44 percent."[218] Although these figures show a larger gain when words are studied in isolation, it is clear, according to these figures, that reading impressively improves students' spelling. Since eye fixations and regressions were fewest during the reading of the passage, the Gilberts concluded that it would be desirable to teach spelling "by a method which stresses accurate speed of perception."[219]

The Gilberts' study contains methodological problems. There is, of course, the problem of the size of the experimental group. More crucial, it would seem, is the possibility that the students, good spellers all, anticipated the experimental intent and, therefore, paid far more attention to spelling during the reading than they otherwise would have done. In fact, the Gilberts themselves reported that most of the students admitted during a post experiment interview that they recognized words in the reading which they previously had been asked to spell. Furthermore, one should be cautious about applying to children results obtained in an experiment with college upperclassmen, an adult population.

Regardless of the methodological problems, it must be conceded that the Gilberts' evidence agrees with evidence in other studies. Reading helps students to spell; especially it helps good spellers to spell better. As for the suggestion that spelling be taught in a way which increases speed of perception, this is more easily said than done, but no doubt it could be done and would be worth doing for students whose perception is slowed because of bad eye habits. But a remedy must be sought elsewhere whenever poor eye movements are found to be merely symptomatic of some more fundamental difficulty.

Even if fully accepted in every detail, the Gilberts' study cannot be used in support of the idea that reading is the preferable way to teach spelling. Greater

[218]*Ibid.*, p. 459.
[219]*Ibid.*, p. 463.

higher grades in their college course in writing than did students who had studied grammar but who had little work in writing.

Smith's study suggests that students will not be handicapped in their writing if they come to college unprepared in grammar. This is true, according to Smith's findings, if students have extensive writing experiences in place of work in grammar. What is more, the students with the writing background will be more successful, on the average, than those with a grammar background.

In interpreting Smith's study, it must be admitted that it is probably not entirely fair to judge the effect of grammar study when that study is divorced from its application in writing. However, the fact remains that when writing is divorced from grammar, writing does not appear to suffer. Perhaps grammar is indeed effective when taught within a writing context, but it hardly seems worthwhile to travel the grammar road when results as good or better can be obtained by concentrating directly upon writing.

Like Smith, Ray C. Maize compared a grammar approach with a writing approach. But Maize worked entirely with remedial freshmen, 149 in all, who were divided randomly into control and experimental groups. The control group used a traditional, workbook, drill method, and the experimental group used a method involving "multiple writing experiences and committee review of one another's manuscripts."[77] However, it should be noted that both groups did some writing. The control group wrote 14 themes, each about 250 words long, and the experimental group wrote 26 themes, each 250 words long, as well as a 1,500-3,000-word autobiography, a 3,000-word term paper, a social letter, and a letter of application.

Maize measured his results by means of tests, principally the Rinsland-Beck Natural Test of English Usage, and by averaging theme grades given by "two different English instructors after reading student manuscripts on an identical subject assigned before and after instruction."[78] He found "clear evidence of superiority on the part of the experimental group as the result of the methods of instruction."[79]

Nora Robinson, in 1960, reported her inquiry to "determine the degree of relationship between knowledge of grammar and ability in composition."[80] For this purpose she obtained a random sampling of 145 second and fourth year students in 4 English grammar schools. (These students may be considered as being equivalent to sophomores and seniors in a high school in the United States.) Each student took an intelligence test, 8 10-minute tests of grammatical knowledge, and a composition test consisting of 3 30-minute essays. Each com-

[77] Ray Charles Maize, "A Study of Two Methods of Teaching English Composition to Retarded College Freshmen" (Ph.D. Dissertation, Purdue University, 1952), p. 88.

[78] *Ibid.,* p. iii.

[79] *Ibid.,* p. 89.

[80] Nora Robinson, "The Relation between Knowledge of English Grammar and Ability in English Composition" (M.Ed. thesis, University of Manchester, 1959); reported in *British Journal of Educational Psychology,* 30, Part II (June 1960), 184.

position was graded for spelling, punctuation, and grammar; grammar alone; and general quality. The first two grades were calculated by means of a point system, the last, the grade for general quality, by the "method of general impression." A sample of 90 papers was regraded by 3 readers who had done the first grading. The resulting mark and re-mark correlations for the 3 30-minute compositions were rather high—.93, .88, and .89—showing that the readers were in substantial agreement with the grades as originally given.

With intelligence held constant, Robinson found that for all 145 students the correlation between grammatical knowledge and grammatical accuracy was only .25. The correlation between grammatical knowledge and general composition (spelling, punctuation, grammar) was .44. The correlation between grammatical knowledge and general composition quality was .49.[81] In other words, the correlation with grammatical knowledge improved as more nongrammatical elements of composition were included in the comparison. This is a paradoxical situation which should not, however, distract one from the basic point, namely, that grammatical knowledge was insufficiently reflected in the students' writing. In addition, Robinson found that students from schools where grammar was stressed did not write better than did students from other schools. She concluded that grammar study is ineffective.[82]

Richard Braddock and others have cited a study by Roland J. Harris as one of 5 especially worthy studies dealing with the teaching of writing. Although this study is not without problems, it does have strength where others are weak, and it has one intriguing methodological feature.[83] Harris, like Robinson and others previously mentioned, concluded that the "study of English grammatical terminology has a negligible or even a relatively harmful effect upon the correctness of children's writing. . . ."[84] How did Harris reach this conclusion, and to what extent is it a credible conclusion?

Harris set out to discover whether instruction in formal grammar would enable students to write better compositions. Harris began with a 3-month pilot study involving 2 classes. Instruction in both classes was the same except that one day each week one class was taught formal grammar whereas the other was taught functional grammar and usage. The formal grammar group used a logically organized traditional textbook, learned parts of speech, and used traditional grammatical terms in correcting compositions. The other group (which Harris called the Nongrammar group and Braddock called the Direct Method

---

[81]*Ibid.*, p. 185.

[82]*Ibid.*, p. 186.

[83]Roland J. Harris, "An Experimental Inquiry into the Functions and Value of Formal Grammar in the Teaching of English, with Special Reference to the Teaching of Correct Written English to Children Aged Twelve to Fourteen" (Ph.D. dissertation, University of London, 1962); a detailed summary, which was submitted to Harris to insure accuracy, appears in Richard Braddock, Richard Lloyd-Jones, and Lowell Schoer, *Research in Written Composition* (Champaign, Ill.: National Council of Teachers of English, 1963), pp. 70-83; references are to the Braddock summary.

[84]*Ibid.*, p. 83.

group) did not use a textbook, considered problems in sentence structure but avoided use of grammatical terms, concentrated on common errors which appeared in compositions, and learned inductively by way of example and imitation rather than deductively by seeking to apply a grammatical generalization. It would seem that the Direct Method resembles what is known as usage study and pattern practice.

During the pilot stage of the study, Harris refined his two tests which were both given before and after the experiment. One was a short answer test on formal grammar which required students to give grammatical labels to sentence elements and to explain in grammatical terms the errors in certain sentences. The other was a composition test. This test was unusual in that it sought to objectify an ordinarily subjective task by employing quantitative measures for certain features of writing style. This device has clear advantages over the familiar panel method of composition evaluation, and those who wish more detailed information about it are referred to Braddock's summary and to Harris' original study.

In his main experiment Harris used the tests he had developed during his pilot experiment. The main experiment lasted for 2 years and involved 2 classes in each of the 5 schools. One class in each school followed the Formal Grammar program and one the Direct Method program. There were 119 students in the Formal Grammar program and 109 in the Direct Method program. It was administratively impossible to match the two groups for intelligence, socioeconomic background, previous achievement, etc. However, both groups were heterogeneous to begin with and, by good fortune, were "roughly equivalent."[85] Unfortunately, the teacher variable was not controlled.[86]

In order to see how things were progressing, Harris gave his composition test in the ninth month to students in 3 schools. He obtained only "very inconclusive" results.[87] But after the full two years of the experiment had elapsed, the results on the composition test were significant and pointed to a clear advantage for the students in the Direct Method program. Of interest to future investigators is Harris' conclusion that one academic year is too short a time for instruction to bring about "stable changes" in students' use of language.[88]

Harris found no effective link between high scores on the grammar test and improvement on the composition test. Furthermore, only one class in the Formal Grammar program had more than half the answers correct on the grammar test. This fact, according to Harris, is major evidence for asserting the inadvisability of studying formal grammar in the early years of secondary school.[89] Harris also observed that the failure to benefit from instruction in

[85]*Ibid.,* p. 76.
[86]*Ibid.,* p. 78.
[87]*Ibid.,* p. 80.
[88]*Loc. cit.*
[89]*Ibid.,* p. 83.

formal grammar was not affected by students' social or economic or cultural backgrounds.

Of course, Harris' study tells nothing about the efficacy of other grammars in improving writing ability. The effects of methodological imperfections, such as failure to control the teacher variable and failure to match groups, seem either to have been minimal or nonexistent. For example, the Formal Grammar group had a slightly superior IQ, but the results of the study favor the Direct Method group. Another weakness is Harris' reliance upon only one administration of the composition test. A more generous sampling of writing would have strengthened this important part of the experiment. However, this deficiency would be more worrisome if the results of the composition test had not been so clear cut.

Studies like Harris' have been criticized for their hypothesis that knowledge of grammar relates to general quality of writing. The argument is that writing is a complex or synthesis of things called organization, intellectual content, style, and so forth, which could not possibly be influenced by the study and mastery of grammar. Therefore, according to this line of reasoning, the studies cannot reveal what they purport to reveal. Those who support studies like Harris' contend that the previous argument is *a priori* and a device for circumnavigating knowledge gained experimentally. As for the Harris study itself, it would seem that the criticism does not really apply because Harris judged the quality of his writing samples on points of structure which grammar study might be expected to affect.

Harris' experiment seems to be the best designed of the experiments on the grammar-composition issue. This is not to say that nothing better can be designed, but it is to say that the study is superior to its predecessors and good enough to be taken seriously. It is the largest of several buttresses supporting the contention that the study of formal grammar contributes little to students' skill in writing.

. . . . .

What meaning should one attach to the studies dealing with grammar and writing? Rarely does one find studies pointing so consistently in one direction. But, of course, consistency alone is meaningless, and, as Emerson observed long ago, consistency can be foolish. The path of error, no matter how often researchers tread it, leads to error. The really germane issue is whether the methods by which consistent conclusions are reached are defensible. Only then is one justified in attaching importance to the conclusions.

The studies which rely on correlation analysis, such as Boraas', show conclusively—but show only—that one condition (grammatical knowledge) is not accompanied by, or associated with, another condition (writing skill). Such research is static in that it deals with a preexisting, unmodified, nondeveloping situation, and such research shows only that under preexisting circumstances grammar and good writing have no special connection with each other. Correlation studies, therefore, supply clues to answers. They do not provide the answers themselves. They are important and, sometimes, indispensable preliminary maneuvers, and they lead (or should lead) to what Symonds called "the true test. . .the experimental test."

No doubt the experimental test is the true test, but even the experimental test can be less than conclusive because of loopholes in the experimental method. A perfect experiment is easier to speculate about than it is to design, and this is especially true of experiments involving human behavior conducted of necessity amid the exigencies of everyday life.

What makes the experiments recounted here worthy of consideration is that, in general and except as noted, they are well controlled, their variables are isolated, and their measuring instruments are designed with care. When a good study, like Frogner's, achieves an objective measurement by using a test, it is possible to complain that a test is a less direct measurement than might be obtained by substituting for it the act of writing itself. But such a substitution would increase the chances of a subjective evaluation—which illustrates another Emersonian dictum, namely, that for everything that is given something is taken.

To overlook the valid in a quest for the definitive is also foolish. These experiments, by various means and with such safeguards as could be devised, have come to similar conclusions. This is not the sort of consistency which is the consequence of a compounding or repetition of procedural errors. The research techniques do not appear to influence the results in any one direction. Nor are the techniques so crude that any result would be suspect. The research is of sufficient quality to warrant the conclusion that instruction in formal grammar is an ineffective and inefficient way to help students achieve proficiency in writing.

3. LINGUISTICS AND COMPOSITION

Like traditional grammar, linguistics seeks to reveal the way the language is put together, its structure, and the way the language works, its mechanism. Both deal with syntax. Beyond this point dissimilarity begins to loom large. The fundamental disagreement is over the issue of what a grammar, any grammar, should be and do. This is a philosophical issue. Traditional grammar has rightly been charged with purveying inaccuracies about the language, but if all such errors were miraculously purged in an instant, there would still remain a basic difference between traditional grammar and linguistics. Each elects for itself a different function founded on a different conception of its place in human affairs.[90]

Traditional grammar is prescriptive, and linguistics is descriptive. The one formulates rules based on assumptions about what English should be, and it propounds rules for speakers and writers to follow. The other derives prin-

---

[90] John C. Sherwood, "Dr. Kinsey and Professor Fries," *College English,* 21 (February 1960), 275-280.

ciples by which the language operates at a given time and place and in a given cultural environment. Broadly defined, it is a systematic study of language employing objective techniques for measurement and observation and avoiding value judgments about matters revealed by investigation. It seeks to fathom and describe and systematize what is; it does not pass judgment on whether whatever is is right. It is neutral; it is in quest of verifiable knowledge about language; it regards language as a form of human behavior; and it assumes a place for itself as a behavioral science. From a linguistic point of view, it is as foolish to speak of good or bad English (grammar) as it is to speak of good or bad histology —unless the reference is to the methods of investigation.

In its broad definition, linguistics includes old and new branches of language study—lexicography, philology, phonology, morphology, orthography, paleography, syntax, portions of the area of semantics, dialectology, linguistic geography, comparative linguistics, and historical linguistics. This introductory discussion is limited, however, to some observations about structural linguistics and generative-transformational grammar.

It is inaccurate to speak of a single linguistic grammar. Researches called linguistic have produced grammars distinctly different in detail and in concept. Advocates of these grammars have not always been cordial to each other. Even within structural linguistics, the first and most widely supported of the new grammatical systems, there is considerable variation. To illustrate this variation one need only compare C. C. Fries's *The Structure of English* with G. L. Trager and H. L. Smith's *An Outline of English Structure*—both originally published in 1951, which is a handy date to mark the rise of structuralism.

The method of the structuralist, whatever the details of his system, is strictly inductive. It is based on careful observation of the language in action, that is, in use. The spoken language is *the* language (the doctrine of the primacy of speech), and the written language is regarded as an adaptation of the spoken language which is only semisuccessful in its attempt to record what speech can accomplish with far greater subtlety. The structuralist sees himself as a scientist of human linguistic behavior. He identifies phonemes, which he defines as the smallest, indivisible, atomistic units of speech-sound. He distinguishes varieties of juncture, that is, gaps or pauses in the flow of sound. He notes the effects of differing patterns of stress or emphasis (usually four) and of pitch (again usually four). The structuralist is not primarily or immediately concerned with meaning. Of course, the structuralist recognizes that the ultimate significance of all language lies in its ability to communicate meaning; however, he fixes his sights as a language scientist upon the mechanisms of the language as a system in order to understand better the workings of the system. The meaning being communicated is not his first concern; rather, his first concern is to understand the systematic method employed in the language by which, as it happens, meaning is communicated. This separation between language system and language meaning is another tenet of the structuralist and distinguishes him from the traditional grammarian whose constructs sometimes involve meanings and sometimes do not; for example, meaning is at the heart of the definition of a sentence as a complete thought, but meaning is replaced by function in the definition of an adjective as a modifier of a noun.

In contrast to structuralism, generative-transformational grammar rejects what it regards as the inductive scientism of the structuralist and in its place offers a deductive procedure, a theory of kernel sentences, and a theory of intuition by which native speakers may achieve an understanding of the grammar of their language. Whereas structuralism utilizes inductive procedures to discover valid generalizations about language, generative-transformationalism employs a deduction procedure which tests or verifies whether generalizations or hypotheses about language will work. Since scientific method ordinarily employs both inductive and deductive procedures, the one to arrive at an hypothesis and the other to test it, both schools of linguistics can claim to share, at least in part, in the scientific method. But, to a structuralist, a generative-transformationalist is less than scientific because he starts with a generalization and works downward, deductively, without first scrutinizing the particulars.

Both the structuralist and the generative-transformationalist subscribe to the doctrine of the primacy of speech, but the work on the subject has thus far been done by the structuralist. Regarding the role of meaning in linguistic analysis, the generative-transformationalist, unlike the structuralist, maintains that structural relationships cannot be understood apart from meaning, and, indeed, that meaning must be known before grammatical relationships can be explored.

Generative-transformations posit the existence of kernel sentences which are simple, declarative, active sentences modifiable in various ways to produce or generate new sentences. It is intuition, according to the generative-transformationalists, which enables even youngsters of no special talent to create new sentences out of combinations and permutations of kernel sentences.

What all the grammars mentioned have in common is an intent to formulate a systematic analysis of the language. Where they differ is in their motive for system-making and in their method. Traditional grammar seeks to explain and to regulate according to precepts which, sometimes, are external to the language itself and in opposition to the facts of language use. (For theological influences upon traditional grammar, see the introductory section to the chapter on sentence diagraming.) Linguistic grammars, however, derive from the language itself, either originally by inductive observation leading to the formulation of generalizations or ultimately by a deductive process in which generalizations must square with the language.

The details of the several grammars are beyond the scope of this work, but anyone wishing to inquire further would do well to consult H. A. Gleason's annotated bibliography.[91] Andrew Schiller has written a popularized, adequate,

[91] H. A. Gleason, Jr., *Linguistics and English Grammar* (New York: Holt, Rinehart and Winston, Inc., 1965), pp. 501 ff.

brief exposition of structural linguistics based on the work of Trager and Smith.[92]

One issue is whether a linguistically oriented approach to language instruction gets better results than some other approach. Another issue is whether linguistics should be studied for its own sake without regard for its application to writing or speech. For opinions on these matters, one may go to the professional journals.

In 1959, for example, Robert D. Williams defended linguistic study in the schools on the grounds that it investigates the "activity which most clearly distinguishes man from the beast,"[93] and he attacked Robert C. Pooley and others for believing that grammar instruction in the schools can be justified only to the extent that it helps students to use the language more effectively. In 1960, Paul Roberts expressed his doubt about a connection between ability to analyze a sentence and ability to write a sentence. He said he thought the language should be studied in school "objectively and dispassionately, and for its own sake."[94] Also in 1960, J. J. Lamberts asserted that studying language "scientifically" is justifiable because "English is our language and. . .language is our most important day-to-day activity. . . ."[95] In other words, linguistics should be studied for its own sake. In 1961, Robert M. Gorrell stated flatly that "We do not need to justify the study of language by proving that it corrects usage or improves writing."[96] In 1962, W. Nelson Francis urged linguistic study as part of a person's liberal education.[97] In 1963, Harold B. Allen said he was prepared to assume, in the absence of evidence to the contrary, that "pedagogically sound," i.e., linguistically sound, techniques for teaching the English language will produce better results.[98]

Again in 1963, Paul Roberts, who was quoted earlier, affirmed his belief that linguistics is worth studying for its own sake. According to Roberts, the English language, like English literature, should be taught because "it is a good thing to know."[99] Yet again in 1963, Robert B. Lees, one of the principal figures among generative-transformationalists, doubted that the "study or teaching

[92] Andrew Schiller, "The Coming Revolution in Teaching English," *Harper's Magazine,* 229 (October 1964), 82–92.

[93] Robert D. Williams, "Linguistics and Grammar," *English Journal,* 48 (October 1959), 388–389.

[94] Paul Roberts, "The Relation of Linguistics to the Teaching of English," *College English,* 22 (October 1960), 7–8.

[95] J. J. Lamberts, "Basic Concepts for Teaching from Structural Linguistics," *English Journal,* 49 (March 1960), 176.

[96] Robert M. Gorrell, "Giggles of Geese and a Pure of Meadowlarks," *College English,* 22 (May 1961), 556.

[97] W. Nelson Francis, "New Perspectives on Teaching Language," *College English,* 23 (March 1962), 437.

[98] Harold B. Allen, "Linguistics and Written Composition," *Language, Linguistics, and School Programs,* Proceedings of the Spring Institutes, 1963, of the National Council of Teachers of English (Champaign, Ill.: National Council of Teachers of English, 1963), p. 87.

[99] Paul Roberts, "Linguistics and the Teaching of Composition," *English Journal,* 52 (May 1963), 333.

of English grammar is very helpful in training children to write. . . ." In Lees' view, linguistics "belongs in. . .science and general education along with psychology and anthropology."[100] In 1965, Harold B. Allen affirmed in stronger language his conviction that linguistics will provide "substantial" help to the teacher of composition.[101] In sum, there are those who believe that linguistics can improve the teaching of language and those who prefer to say about linguistics what Emerson said about Beauty, that it is its own excuse for being. In this latter group, some appear to think of linguistics as a science and some appear to think of it as one of the humanities; all in this group eschew practical claims.

The practical value, if any, of instruction in linguistics will have to be decided experimentally, and experimental studies are only now beginning to appear. Before examining the experimental evidence, it may be permissible to editorialize briefly about the debate over the value of linguistics, the nature of which debate is suggested by the views reported in the preceding paragraphs.

Any bid for time in the crowded educational program should be scrutinized. Whether the study of linguistics deserves an allotment of valuable educational time should be determined after an open assessment of the experimental evidence and a clear presentation of the aims of instruction to those who pay the bills and whose children the profession serves. This is not to say that professional decisions should be left to the lay community, but it is to say that the educational institution, like any institution, is ultimately responsible to society and that important decisions should not be made silently or capriciously and without laying bare the reasons. In time, these reasons may prove foolish and the decisions unwise, but at any given moment of decision, the reasons for it should be clear and a popular consensus or (at least) acquiescence should be obtained.

To date, there has been very little clarification of the whys and wherefores of linguistics, either among members of the scholarly and teaching profession or (especially) between the profession and the public. The assertion that linguistics should be taught for its own sake is a particularly troublesome bit of ambiguous scuffling. To say that linguistics should be taught for its own sake is to say that linguistics should be taught because linguistics should be taught. A dog, not an argument, is permitted to chase its tail. What is worse, such an argument implies that no better argument is possible.

Art, literature, anthropology, and linguistics—to name but a few subjects— have their reasons for being. Literature, for example, enlarges experience vicariously and in a controlled manner that firsthand experience cannot match. Not only does it enlarge or widen experience (in time and place) but it is also an exploration of the mind and spirit of man and of his relationship to himself, to society, and to nature. Looked at in this way, literature is not impractical and

---

[100] Robert B. Lees, "The Promise of Transformational Grammar," *English Journal,* 52 (May 1963), 345.
[101] Harold B. Allen, "From Prairies to Mountains," *College English,* 26 (January 1965), 265.

need not be defended weakly as its own justification. Of course, nobody knows precisely and measurably what impact literature has upon readers, but literature orders experience and it explores the human condition even though the impact of that ordering and exploring is as yet imperfectly known. Herein lies the claim to "practicality." Literature deals with matters which are important and potentially consequential and which are referred to by such terms as self-knowledge, values, and aesthetics. It is ironic in these times to encounter statements by responsible people which assume the impracticality of subjects which as much as any obey the injunction that the proper study of mankind is man.

It would be a great boon if linguistics also enabled teachers to do a better job of teaching writing. But whether it does or not, the people who urge its inclusion in the course of study will have to be very certain in their own minds about why they want it included, and they should be prepared for questioners who are unwilling to accept a reason such as "because it is true." Truths are more numerous than the curriculum is capacious. Many truths are not, and need not be, included in the curriculum. It remains to be seen whether linguistics will be one of them.

. . . . .

The first eight studies to be discussed inquire into whether writing will be improved more by a linguistic method than by a traditional method (studies by Suggs, Zidonis, Johnson, O'Donnell, Link and Schuster, Miller, Blake, and Weinfeld). A ninth study, Zais's, attacks the problem of the practicality of linguistics in a novel way by investigating whether the linguistic characteristics of punctuation symbols influence the ways these symbols should be taught. A tenth study by De Lancey, which deals with reading, is presented as a bare indication of the practical value of a linguistic approach to a related, albeit nonwriting, area of language skill. Finally, three studies (by Mellon, Raub, and Ney) examine whether the use of a technique associated with transformational grammar will increase ability to compose sentences. The studies will be described and interpreted in the light of the methods employed. The presentation of the studies will be followed by a general assessment of what, at present, is known about the contribution of linguistics to the improvement of writing.

In the experiment by Lena R. Suggs (1961), eleventh graders in a Florida high school were divided into two groups of "approximately alike" achievement as determined by past performance. Suggs acknowledged that matching by this method "is far from scientific"; nevertheless, she felt the groups were enough alike to suit her purposes.[102] The structural group used an inductive, pattern approach; the traditional group used a deductive, analytical, rule approach. The effect of instruction was measured by the STEP Test (Form 2A) given in January and the Cooperative English Test—Test B1: Effectiveness of Expression given in May.

[102] Lena Reddick Suggs, "Structural Grammar Versus Traditional Grammar in Influencing Writing," *English Journal,* 50 (March 1961), 175.

Aside from the question of her method of equating her groups and aside from the question of whether the Cooperative English Test is the most suitable measuring device for her purposes, there is a further and serious question about the experimental conditions of the study. Mrs. Suggs observed the "chagrin of many of the brightest pupils"[103] in her traditional group when they discovered they were not placed in the experimental, structural group. She mentioned, also, that the students in the structural group "were stimulated by the newness of the subject matter."[104] That the so-called Hawthorne Effect influenced the results is a distinct possibility.[105] The results should be regarded with more caution than Mrs. Suggs displayed when she referred to them as lending "definite proof" of the superiority of her linguistic method.

Methodologically superior to Suggs's study is the study by Frank J. Zidonis (1965) which compared instruction in generative grammar with "regular" instruction in order to discover which would lead to a greater improvement in writing. Two teachers and 50 ninth graders (divided into two classes by random selection) participated in the study. The published report of the study does not mention any attempt to discover the language aptitudes or achievement of the two groups. For two years the classes studied the same curriculum except that the experimental class "was exposed to materials especially adapted from the area of generative grammar" and the control class received the language instruction customarily given in the school.[106] Zidonis did not describe this regular or customary instruction, but, apparently, it consisted of formal grammar; otherwise it would not have been necessary for him to mention that neither group had received instruction in formal grammar during their two immediately preceding years in elementary school.[107]

Compositions written during the first and last 3 months of the experimental period were collected and analyzed for grammatical quality. Zidonis calculated the (1) proportion of well-formed sentences—PWF, (2) structural complexity score—SCS, and (3) error change score—ECS. By comparing the calculations based on the papers written at the start of the experiment with the calculations based on the papers written at the end, Zidonis planned to show whether generative grammar enabled students to improve their writing.

[103] *Loc. cit.*

[104] *Loc. cit.*

[105] Desmond L. Cook, "The Hawthorne Effect in Educational Research," *Phi Delta Kappan,* 44 (December 1962), 116–122; see the chapter on spelling, section 12, for a brief explanation of the Hawthorne Effect.

[106] Frank J. Zidonis, "Generative Grammar: A Report of Research," *English Journal,* 54 (May 1965), 405. See also the original report by Donald R. Bateman and Frank J. Zidonis, *The Effect of a Knowledge of Generative Grammar upon the Growth of Language Complexity,* United States Office of Education Cooperative Research Project No. 1746 (Columbus: Ohio State University Research Foundation, 1964); and Donald R. Bateman and Frank J. Zidonis, *The Effect of a Study of Transformational Grammar on the Writing of Ninth and Tenth Graders,* NCTE Research Report No. 6 (Champaign, Ill.: National Council of Teachers of English, 1966).

[107] *Loc. cit.*

With respect to well-formed sentences, Zidonis found that his experimental group achieved a statistically significant improvement. But analysis of structural complexity scores failed to show a statistically significant difference between the control and experimental groups.[108]

Regarding the error change scores for 5 classes of errors, Zidonis found that only Class 1 Errors ("Misapplication of a transformational operation") and Class 5 Errors ("Co-occurrence errors: the use of mutually exclusive grammatical elements in kernel sentences or in kernel sentences underlying complex sentences") occurred sufficiently often to warrant analysis. The statistical analysis of Class 1 Errors in part supported and in part did not support the claim that generative grammar helped students to improve their writing. The statistical analysis of Class 5 Errors led Zidonis to observe that the "study of grammar is more directly related to the reduction of Class 1 Errors" and that "Class 5 Errors apparently include pre-grammatical mis-operations that lie outside the scope of grammar."[109] In short, of the 3 measures employed in this study (PWF, SCS, and ECS), one (PWF) indicated to a statistically significant degree that generative grammar helps students to improve their writing.

Undoubtedly the Zidonis study buttresses the case for generative grammar as an aid in teaching writing. However, the buttressing would be stronger if Zidonis had been more explicit about the methods and content with which the teaching of generative grammar had been compared. As reported in the *English Journal,* the study does not reveal whether generative grammar works better than structural grammar or usage instruction or something else. According to the report, it does work a bit better than something called "regular" instruction, which would ordinarily mean instruction in traditional grammar with its eight parts of speech, prescriptive assumptions, and deductive instructional techniques. If traditional grammar is as poor a method as several studies would have us believe, then the slight superiority of generative grammar over traditional grammar is nothing to get excited about. It is a contest between pygmies in which a small victor won a small victory.

Falk S. Johnson's study (1960) involved 150 remedial freshmen and 100 regular freshmen during a 3-year period. The inclusion of remedial students was intended to provide the approaches being compared with the "severest possible test." The remedial group was divided into 6 classes of which 3 were taught by a structural method and 3 by a traditional method. Similarly, the regular group was divided into 6 classes of which 3 were taught structurally and 3 traditionally. Chance determined whether a student was assigned to a structural or to a traditional program. Each of the 6 teachers involved taught two classes—one structural and one traditional. This plan was designed to minimize the effects of the teacher variable.

The traditional instruction included teaching many rules and assigning exer-

[108]*Ibid.,* pp. 406–407.
[109]*Ibid.,* p. 407.

cises. Students used the *Macmillan Handbook* or the *Harbrace Handbook.* Students in the structural program used oral drills and studied patterns. Their textbook was Lloyd and Warfel's *American English in Its Cultural Setting.* All students were given an academic inventory test, an aptitude test, and a short-answer test (on vocabulary, spelling, and grammar). But the crucial evaluative instruments were the impromptu themes written before instruction and afterward. Reasonable precautions were taken during the grading of the themes. The results? On all objective tests and on the themes, both groups showed equal improvement; that is, both improved to the extent of one letter grade or the equivalent. The study, therefore, concluded that "neither approach offered any statistically significant advantage over the other."[110]

Another study, by O'Donnell (1963), sought to discover whether writers could be helped more by a linguistic than by a traditional approach. However, unlike the researchers just mentioned, O'Donnell chose to attack the problem from another angle. What he did was to examine whether the correlation between ability in composition and awareness of linguistically determined syntactic relationships is different from the correlation between ability in composition and ability to verbalize the rules and terms of traditional grammar. He reasoned that if traditional grammar inadequately describes the actual structure of English, then the mastery of traditional grammar should not correlate well with ability in composition (as other studies have shown; see preceding section 2). He reasoned, further, that if linguistically determined syntax were a truly accurate description of the language, then it might, as some of its advocates claim, correlate closely with ability in composition. If the correlation between knowledge of a linguistic syntax and skill in composition were significantly higher than the correlation between knowledge of traditional grammar and skill in composition, then, O'Donnell believed, this would be strong evidence in support of linguistics as a means of improving writing skill.

To freshmen entering Mount Olive College, North Carolina, in 1961 and 1962 (201 students in all), O'Donnell gave the Iowa Grammar Information Test, the STEP Essay Test, and a Test of Recognition of Structural Relationships in English which was constructed by O'Donnell and designed to measure "ability to recognize various structural relationships of words in English sentences without use of grammatical terminology."[111] O'Donnell's investigation did not involve teaching or control and experimental groups. The study did involve testing and correlation analysis. It resembles, therefore, some of the studies (like Boraas') mentioned earlier (see section 2). Being "static" and statistical rather than experimental, the study cannot, by its nature, supply a final answer; it is capable, however, of supplying circumstantial evidence which may point to an answer

---

[110] Falk S. Johnson, "Structural Versus Non-structural Teaching," *College Composition and Communication,* 11 (December 1960), 215.

[111] Roy C. O'Donnell, *The Correlation of Awareness of Structural Relationships in English and Ability in Written Composition,* United States Office of Education Cooperative Research Project No. 1524 (Mount Olive, N.C.: Mount Olive College, 1963), p. 13.

which, later, must be verified experimentally before it can be accepted as a reliable truth. What circumstantial evidence, then, does the O'Donnell study reveal?

After analyzing his data, O'Donnell found that in no case was the "degree of correlation. . .sufficiently high to provide a basis for the assumption that either knowledge of traditional grammar or awareness of basic structural relationships in English will be regularly accompanied by excellence in written composition."[112] O'Donnell's evidence (with its limitations in mind) suggests that knowledge of linguistic structure and a knowledge of traditional grammar are equally unlikely to affect a student's ability to write.

O'Donnell's discussion of the implications of his findings seems to betray a desire to contradict his own results. At one point he observed that "It seems impossible that a student who is unaware of the basic grammatical relationships. . . could master the most elementary writing skills."[113] He wondered why statistical studies do not discover high correlation between writing and grammatical knowledge, and he suggested that the reason may be found in the "nature of the tests" being used.[114] After enumerating the possible flaws in his tests, O'Donnell observed that his findings should *not* be interpreted as proof that a relationship between writing and grammatical knowledge does *not* exist. Then he added daringly that 'it seems evident that awareness of basic structure is essential to elementary written composition."[115] Here, then, is a three-page odyssey in which O'Donnell began by expressing incredulity that a grammar-composition link should be doubted, proceeded to a questioning of his tests, continued to a suggestion that what he did not find might still exist, and, finally, concluded with a statement that what he did not find must be "essential to. . .composition." The journey carried O'Donnell from a negative finding to a positive statement of faith.

It is true that O'Donnell's tests are deficient in some ways. It is true that the STEP Essay Tests, for example, give an 80 percent weight to thought and style and only a 20 percent weight to structural matters with which O'Donnell's other tests are primarily concerned. But O'Donnell's objections to his own "Test of Recognition of Structural Relationships in English" seem unduly severe and based in part upon a semantic confusion. Since the test was supposed to test the student's knowledge of structural relationships, it does not matter if the student uses "traditional grammatical terminology in his reasoning as he attempts to find a correct response."[116] It is not "terminology" but a linguistically valid conception of relationships that is important. That is what the test was supposed to test, and that is what it may indeed test in spite of O'Donnell's doubts.

Paradoxically, what O'Donnell and Suggs have in common are opposite find-

---

[112]*Ibid.*, p. 23.
[113]*Ibid.*, p. 24.
[114]*Loc. cit.*
[115]*Ibid.*, pp. 24–26.
[116]*Ibid.*, p. 25.

ings and attitudes toward their findings which err in opposite directions—Suggs's being too accepting and O'Donnell's being too critical. Since O'Donnell's study is probably neither so imperfect as he would have us believe nor so sound as we would prefer it to be, it would appear best to recommend that the results be accepted tentatively. This means that the search for verifying evidence should continue. The most positive statement which can be made about O'Donnell's findings is that the findings point toward a conclusion which is theoretically possible.

Another relevant study was reported twice, once by Edgar H. Schuster in 1961[117] and once by Frances R. Link and Edgar H. Schuster in 1962.[118] The Schuster version appears to be a preliminary report, and the Link-Schuster version appears to be an attempt to report the complete experiment. Unfortunately, the reports do not agree in all details.

There were two experiments. The first (in 1959-1960) involved 4 classes of which one served as a control group. (Which one served as the control is uncertain from the published reports.) The experimental classes studied Roberts' *Patterns of English,* and the control classes used the *Century Handbook* and supplemental material of a traditional sort. A shortage of the Roberts book prevented all experimental classes from studying at the same time. No mention was made in either report of any attempt to equate the groups involved.

The STEP Writing Test and the Cooperative English Test, Effectiveness of Expression were administered, but both were not administered to all groups. This is an important experimental detail which might have been more fully and precisely explained in the two published accounts. The researchers also devised 3 other tests. One was intended to measure student attitudes by means of objective questions and an unsigned essay. The second, an objective test, was intended to measure grammatical knowledge and included questions on punctuation and usage. The third, also objective, was intended to measure "knowledge of the relationships of the parts of the sentence to each other and to the sentence as a whole."[119]

Essentially the same experiment was repeated the following year (1960-1961). Both reports claimed that students preferred a linguistic approach to a traditional approach. Neither the Schuster[120] nor the Link-Schuster[121] article gives evidence that the study of linguistics improved students' writing. To his credit, Schuster's interpretation was consistent with his findings. He said he was "inclined to agree with those linguists who believe that the study of grammar will do little to help improve writing skill."[122] However, Link and Schuster, though admitting the existence of "very little evidence that. . .new or traditional

[117]Edgar H. Schuster, "How Good Is the New Grammar?" *English Journal,* 50 (September 1961), 392–397.

[118]Frances R. Link and Edgar H. Schuster, "Linguistics in High School," *Educational Leadership,* 19 (February 1962), 294–299.

[119]Schuster, "How Good Is the New Grammar?" *English Journal,* p. 393.

[120]*Loc. cit.*

[121]Link and Schuster, "Linguistics in High School," *Educational Leadership,* p. 297.

[122]Schuster, "How Good Is the New Grammar?" *English Journal,* p. 397.

grammar improves. . .writing,"[123] nevertheless asserted that "linguistic science will affect profoundly. . .the teaching of composition."[124] Perhaps the attitude to take toward this study (in its two reports) is that it is too weak in method, too unclear in detail, and too inconclusive to warrant serious consideration in any attempt to assess the present state of knowledge on the subject.

The study by Frances Miller (1962) may or may not compare a linguistic method with traditional grammar. What Miller reported is less an experiment than a record of what she did with her classes and of her impressions of the worth of what she did. According to the editor's brief prefatory note to the article, Miller performed some "informal experiments." The emphasis should be on *informal* because (for example) there was no provision for checking the evaluations of student writing.

For 3 months, Miller taught structural grammar to 3 seventh grade classes. A fourth served as a control group and was taught a "standard" method which was not explained. In all, 118 students participated. What Group B did and why it did it was not explained, and the scores or grades were not reported. However, Miller felt herself able to conclude that the study of structure "can be intellectually stimulating"[125] and that the "structural approach produces a greater relationship between analyzing a sentence and writing one."[126]

It is easy to be critical of this study. But, then again, it probably should not be judged as though it were a formal experiment. It does contain one keen observation. Miller recorded that her least able students were better at talking about language than they were at writing the language.[127] Here, at least, is an implied caution worthy of any language teacher's notice.

Robert W. Blake, in his study (1964), used punctuation lessons to discover the comparative worth of the structural and traditional approaches. He randomly assigned 130 tenth grade students to experimental (structural) or control (traditional) groups. An analysis of the verbal scores of these students on the Lorge-Thorndike Intelligence Test indicated that there was "no significant difference between the two groups." Blake adapted his linguistic units from Paul Roberts' *English Sentences* and devised traditional units to cover the same material. These units were field tested. All were self-study units because Blake hoped by this means to avoid complications introduced by the teacher variable. Blake's pretest and posttest were Forms OM and PM of the Cooperative English Test (section 2: Punctuation). He also devised and field tested a punctuation test. Blake devised another test to measure students' attitudes toward their course of study; this instrument was not, apparently, field tested.

Blake found that (1) students did not prefer the linguistic approach and

[123] Link and Schuster, "Linguistics in High School," *Educational Leadership,* p. 297.
[124] *Ibid.,* p. 294.
[125] Frances Miller, "Structural Plotting for Understanding," *English Journal,* 51 (December 1962), 639.
[126] *Loc. cit.*
[127] *Ibid.,* p. 633.

(2) students preferred teacher-taught lessons to self-study lessons. In addition to these student opinions (the first of which is distinctly unusual), Blake found "no significant difference in knowledge of punctuation" as revealed by the Cooperative English Test, although both the linguistic and the traditional groups profited from their self-instruction lessons.[128]

Although Blake did not explicitly state the length of his experiment, it would appear that it lasted for 18 school days and consisted of 18 15-minute lessons. If this deduction is indeed correct, then the experiment was rather too brief for comfort. Also, the study did not investigate retention. Nor did it examine students' ability to punctuate ordinary expository writing such as could be obtained by assigning impromptu and home-written themes. Admittedly, themes are exceedingly difficult to evaluate and the evaluation exceedingly difficult to convert into meaningful scores; nevertheless, themes provide the acid test of ability to punctuate. Even a crude measure of skill in punctuating themes would be a valuable addition to the data provided by the Cooperative English Test.

It seems fair to say that Blake's study did not probe deeply. At most, its findings are indicative or exploratory. Blake's and Johnson's studies point in the same direction, and neither supports Suggs's and Zidonis's findings.

Frederic D. Weinfeld's dissertation investigated whether what students learned by 3 methods would transfer and thereby improve the students' writing. Although essentially a study in "transfer of training," it also is a study which speaks to the linguistics-composition issue. Weinfeld worked with ninth graders who used a Verbal Fluency method, tenth graders who used a Structural Grammar method, and eleventh graders who used a Logical Structure method. The premise of the Verbal Fluency method was that students learn writing by writing and not by studying grammatical rules or by doing grammatical drills. The Structural Grammar method taught functional linguistic patterns, structural groups, form classes; the assumption was that students with a better understanding of the dynamics of English would be able to apply this knowledge in their writing. The assumption underlying the Logical Structure method was that training in logic, reasoning, clear thinking, and organization would benefit writing. Each teacher taught by one of these 3 experimental methods and also by a control method, that is, by a "regular" or conventional method which included traditional grammar. Weinfeld's analysis revealed, among other things, that the "Structural Grammar and Logical Structure methods were not superior to a conventional method of teaching English composition. ..."[129] Like other studies previously mentioned, Weinfeld's supports the contention that grammatical

---

[128] Robert W. Blake, "Linguistics and Punctuation," *English Record,* 15 (October 1964), 12–13.

[129] Frederic David Weinfeld, "A Factor Analytic Approach to the Measurement of Differential Effects of Training: An Evaluation of Three Methods of Teaching English Composition" (Ed.D. dissertation, Graduate School of Education, Harvard University, 1959), p. 192.

study *per se*, whether traditional, structural, or some other, does not appear to be a preferable way to teach writing.

Robert S. Zais, in another study involving punctuation, set out to discover whether the "characteristic features ascribed to punctuation symbols by linguistic scientists influenced the effectiveness of the method used to teach these symbols."[130] Zais reasoned that if some punctuation symbols are phonemic or orthographic or grammatical, then a different method should be used to teach each type. For example, an orthographic punctuation (the possessive apostrophe) might best be taught by methods that have proved successful for teaching spelling.

In order to test this idea, Zais conducted a 3-month experiment with 50 "average" eleventh graders in the Hope High School, Providence, Rhode Island. Each student was given a diagnostic punctuation test and a diagnostic theme to obtain a measure of his performance prior to instruction. Then students were taught according to the "Hope method" which discouraged memorization of rules and aimed instead at (1) conveying an understanding of logical principles, or rules, and (2) applying the principles during the act of writing.

In order to measure students' understanding of punctuation principles, Zais gave 5 tests in which students were asked to correct some incorrectly punctuated sentences. Students were permitted to consult a rule sheet because Zais felt that this procedure would be a better test of understanding and would discourage rote memorization. In order to measure students' ability to apply their understanding during the act of writing, Zais assigned 5 themes. He first counted the opportunities in each theme for violations of a punctuation rule and then counted the actual violations of the rule. Finally, he obtained an error quotient by dividing the number of errors by the number of possible errors.

Zais found "no correspondence. . .between a punctuation symbol's characteristics and the effectiveness of the method used to teach the principle which governs its use."[131] For example, the rule that was learned most effectively and the one learned least effectively were orthographic rules; both were taught by the same Hope method to the same students. Why one was learned well and the other was not is unknown. But the fact that both rules were orthographic in nature had, apparently, no influence upon what was learned.

Zais found a similar situation with respect to students' ability to apply rules in their writing. In Zais' words, ". . . pupils' error quotients. . .vary considerably for each rule with no apparent correspondence between rules with similar linguistic characteristics and rules with similar percentage decreases (or increases)."[132]

Zais' study is ingenious. It avoids matching groups, the problem of the teacher variable, and other experimental difficulties. But it is a small-scale study,

[130]Robert S. Zais, "The Linguistic Characteristics of Punctuation Symbols and the Teaching of Punctuation Skills," *English Journal*, 52 (December 1963), 678.
[131]*Ibid.*, p. 680.
[132]*Loc. cit.*

and, besides, there is the chance that its results are what they are because the Hope method of instruction was inadequate in some way. Maybe the easy rules were learned, and the harder or more complex or more obscurely stated rules were not learned quite so well. The operating factor, then, would be more the quality of the Hope method and less the linguistic nature of the punctuation principles. This speculation is not offered as an indictment of the study. The point is only that the findings need additional experimental confirmation.

A study by Robert W. De Lancey (1962) involved 316 fifth graders and 261 ninth graders who were tested to see to what degree their awareness of form classes would affect their reading comprehension. De Lancey constructed a test which used "nonsense syllables to minimize the effect of vocabulary knowledge, to measure the ability to recognize the four major form classes—nouns, verbs, adjectives, and adverbs—from the structural clues of position, inflection, derivational affixes, and structure words."[133] To all students De Lancey also administered the Iowa Test of Basic Skills, the Iowa Test of Educational Development, and the California Test of Mental Maturity. The study, thus, consisted of statistical analyses of the data obtained from the tests; no teaching and no measurement of the effects of teaching were involved.

De Lancey found a high correlation at both fifth and sixth grade levels between ability to recognize form classes and all variables except one. For example, intelligence and arithmetical ability correlated with students' awareness of form classes. However, De Lancey also found that although "ability to recognize form classes from structural clues is a factor in reading, knowledge of vocabulary contributes far more to the variance in reading comprehension test scores."[134] In other words, reading comprehension correlates well with certain other abilities. But it correlates less well (though positively) with ability to recognize form classes. Furthermore, reading comprehension appears to be less closely related to knowledge of form classes than it is to knowledge of vocabulary. It would seem from this that it is more important for a student to be intelligent and to have a good vocabulary (two factors which are themselves related) than it is for him to be able to recognize form classes. No one of these elements, according to De Lancey, seems to be unrelated to reading comprehension; it just so happens that recognition of form classes is least closely related to reading comprehension.

Like other purely statistical studies, this study is static rather than active and experimental. Therefore, it is productive of indications and of hypotheses, even strong hypotheses, but not of demonstrable truth. To be sure, absolute experimental proof is very hard to come by. Until it comes, if it ever does, informed people must in the meantime be guided by whatever is known short of proof. Such interim knowledge is especially subject to interpretation. In this case the proffered interpretation is that the results do not greatly strengthen the case of the advocates of the efficacy of a linguistic approach to language teach-

---

[133] Robert W. De Lancey, "Awareness of Form Class as a Factor in Reading Comprehension," *Dissertation Abstracts*, 23, 8 (February 1963), 2975.
    [134] *Loc. cit.*

ing. All the De Lancey study can claim is that certain linguistic knowledge is less positively related to reading comprehension than some other knowledge. This makes a minor virtue out of linguistic knowledge. This is snaring a mouse on a lion hunt.

Three studies (by John C. Mellon, Donna Kay Raub, and James W. Ney) test some version of transformational sentence-combining. All find it to be a promising means for increasing students' writing skills, but only Mellon provides substantial evidence for that promise.

In transformational sentence-combining, kernel sentences are combined into more informative and complex structures. For example,

The girl drank coconut milk.

The girl was thirsty.

These kernel sentences may be combined to produce:

The girl drank coconut milk because she was thirsty.

The girl who was thirsty drank coconut milk.

The thirsty girl drank coconut milk.

These sentences illustrate the basic sentence-combining process. There are, of course, variations in form and far more complex examples.

Mellon addressed his study to teachers and to everyone concerned with the English curriculum, which suggests that his study had a practical purpose. However, he disclaimed any intention to "rule on the question whether grammar should...be taught in the schools, since...this question must be argued on grounds considerably more general than those of a narrowly immediate and often fancied pragmatism."[135] Instead, Mellon determined to discover whether "specially structured but a-rhetorical activities germane only to the study of grammar may yield fortuitous and quite naturalistic by-products observable in student performances in the composition class."[136] In other words, Mellon's study does not investigate the practical worth of instruction in grammar as such, the details of grammar, but does investigate whether activities "germane" or closely akin to grammar study will have a desirable influence upon students' ability to compose sentences. The activity referred to is transformational sentence-combining practice which is a refinement of exercises long in use in grammar textbooks.[137]

Mellon's experiment did not attempt to relate sentence-combining practice to composition. Sentence-combining was treated as an "integral part of the student's work in grammar." The object was to discover whether when the student writes he would, "as a natural result of prior sentence-combining practice, pro-

---

[135] John C. Mellon, *Transformational Sentence-Combining: A Method for Enhancing the Development of Syntactic Fluency in English Composition,* United States Office of Education Cooperative Research Project No. 5-8418 (Cambridge, Mass.: Graduate School of Education, Harvard University, 1967), pp. 1–2.

[136] *Ibid.,* pp. 2–3.

[137] See, for example, N. Foerster, J. M. Steadman, Jr., and J. B. McMillan, *Writing and Thinking* (Boston: Houghton Mifflin Company, 1952), pp. 14–15; F. N. Scott and J. V. Denney, *Elementary English Composition* (Boston: Allyn & Bacon, Inc., 1900), pp. 64–65.

duce sentences whose structures would be more mature than those of sentences he would otherwise have written."[138] All of the work in grammar, including sentence-combining practice, was presented to students as a problem in "describing the language competence they and all other speakers already possess."[139] The work was not presented as a means for improving usage.

The subjects of the experiment were 247 seventh graders attending one of 4 schools. The schools were selected to "represent urban, suburban, and private education serving a clientele ranging from upper-middle to lower-middle class students."[140] The students were divided into 3 groups and spent one third of their time in activities related to the experiment. The first group, the experimental group (100 students), studied lessons in transformational grammar prepared by Mellon. From September through December, this group learned the basics of transformational grammar. This included some work in which basic sentences were rewritten in their alternate forms; however, it was during the remaining 5 months, through May, that problems in sentence-combining were stressed. For the experimental group, therefore, the experimental period was really only 5 months long.

The second group, the control group (100 students), studied the grammar and usage sections in their textbook and completed all the exercises. One school used Warriner and Blumenthal's *English Workshop, New Series, Grade Nine* (Harcourt, 1955) and the other 3 schools used Warriner, Treanor, and Naas' *English Grammar and Composition: Grade 7* (Harcourt, 1959). Students worked out sentence diagrams, identified or labeled elements in sample sentences, and selected appropriate answers to fill in blanks in sample sentences. Mellon complained that the exercises "represented immature. . .puerile sentence types."[141]

The third group, the placebo group (47 students) did not study any formal grammar, although this group had previously learned some grammatical terms. The placebo group wrote compositions, completed "direct-method usage exercises," and did additional work in literature. Even the composition lessons "consisted of a series of direct-method presentations of ways to vary sentence structure through use of inversions, post-noun adjective pairs, questions, novel vocabulary, and introductory constructions such as direct objects, adverbs, preposition phrases, and participle phrases—all represented by example only."[142] The placebo group was included in the experiment in order to discover whether the sentence-combining technique really encourages writing maturity or whether it merely seems efficacious in comparison with a conventional grammar which, by being a poor technique, makes the experimental technique appear better than it actually is.

Before the experiment began, all students took the STEP Writing Test

[138] Mellon, *Transformational Sentence-Combining*, p. 37.
[139] *Ibid.*, p. 40.
[140] *Ibid.*, p. 46.
[141] *Ibid.*, pp. 57–58.
[142] *Ibid.*, pp. 56–57.

(Form 3A). This enabled Mellon to identify each student's ability level. Also, during the first 4 weeks, students wrote 9 one-hour compositions under teacher supervision. During the last 4 weeks of the year, students wrote 9 more compositions. An attempt was made to suit topics to a student's level of ability. An attempt was also made to prepare parallel topics so that initial and concluding writing tests taken by each student would provide similar stimuli. The effect of instruction was measured by comparing changes in the number and kind of sentence structures used by students in their writing.

According to Mellon, "The experimental subjects as a group underwent the growth hypothesized for them. This growth was significantly greater than that observed in the control and placebo groups, whose final standings were mutually indistinguishable."[143] Mellon observed at another point: "In general, two conclusions seem warranted. First, the growth produced by sentence-combining treatment represents a significant enhancement of normal growth, regardless of whether the latter is defined in a curriculum environment featuring conventional grammar, or in one with no grammar study of any kind. Second, conventional grammar is in fact a kind of placebo treatment itself, in that the effects which it produces do not differ significantly from those observed in a no-grammar environment."[144]

Mellon enumerated several "reservations" which may persuade some readers to forego accepting his data. For example, he mentioned that a "longer-term experiment including a mid-test measure would obviously have been more convincing. . . ." A final test based on writing "produced under ordinary and wholly unstructured conditions" would have been a far better, indeed "crucial," test of the experimental method. Also, it would have been desirable to give a delayed recall test to discover the extent to which skills learned at the conclusion of the experimental period are retained.[145] In spite of any shortcoming, however, it does seem that Mellon's study is, if not definitive, at least secure in the absence of equally good evidence to the contrary. The significance of his findings will be discussed after a review of the studies by Raub and Ney.

Raub's experiment lasted for 8 weeks and involved 12 students in an experimental group and 25 in a control group. All were seventh graders in the Demonstration School of George Peabody College. All were given a pretest and a posttest. Seven students in the experimental groups were matched with 7 in the control group.

The experimental group practiced transformational sentence-combining by means of oral drills. The vocabulary and ideas in the drill sentences were based upon the reading assignments in John Steinbeck's *The Pearl* and *The Red Pony*. Both stories were read aloud in class by the teacher or by a student. The class would repeat in unison what had been read. Unfamiliar words and expressions were written on the blackboard and discussed. Students analyzed sentences by

[143]*Ibid.*, p. 107.
[144]*Ibid.*, p. 93.
[145]*Ibid.*, pp. 108–109.

identifying kernel constituents and by combining kernel sentences into pattern sentences.[146]

The control group spent its time writing sentences and paragraphs. Students wrote single sentences intended to convey, for example, an impression of October. They were encouraged to expand simple sentences like "The auditorium was empty." Students used Warriner's *English Grammar and Composition* to help them correct choppy, run-on, or fragmentary sentences. They classified sentences as simple, compound, complex, interrogative, etc. Students in the control group also read the Steinbeck stories. They discussed character, style, and theme; and they wrote 5 short papers answering questions about the stories. In addition to doing vocabulary work based on the stories, the students used Ward and Miller's *Word Wealth Junior.*[147]

In order to determine the effects of instruction, Raub compared the results of the pretest and posttest. These tests (really one test which was repeated at the end of the experiment) consisted of two films about which students were asked to answer questions in writing. These responses were analyzed by counting and comparing T-units, a T-unit being "a single independent predication with all of the modifications. . .grammatically attached to it."[148] Although the results were not uniformly definite, Raub was able to support a claim that the audio-lingual method of sentence-combining "did a superior job in improving sentence length and in improving complexity."[149] Teaching vocabulary in conjunction with the method also proved successful.[150]

Raub's experiment, which preceded Mellon's, is far less impressive than Mellon's in both scope and conception. Raub frankly stated that her study was handicapped by inexperienced teaching, too small an experimental group, and "poor physical surroundings." Her results, nevertheless, point in the same direction as Mellon's.

In Ney's experiment, as in Raub's, students orally practiced transformational sentence-combining. These "audio-lingual drills" were based on Stephen Crane's "The Open Boat." Although the students read the story sentence by sentence in unison, that is, orally, after hearing the instructor's reading, this device was "not basic to the experimental methodology; it merely provided diversion. . ., a relief from the routine of practicing audio-lingual drills."[151] However, Ney thought the choral reading reinforced the effect of the drills and provided a kind of "linguistic context" which prevented the drills from becoming "meaningless and unrelated."[152]

[146] Donna Kay Raub, "The Audio-Lingual Drill Technique: An Approach to Teaching Composition" (Master's thesis, George Peabody College for Teachers, 1966), pp. 17–21.
[147]*Ibid.,* pp. 21–22.
[148]*Ibid.,* p. 9.
[149]*Ibid.,* p. 31.
[150]*Ibid.,* p. 32.
[151] James W. Ney, "Applied Linguistics in the Seventh Grade," *English Journal,* 55 (October 1966), 895–896.
[152]*Ibid.,* p. 896.

Nineteen students participated. They were sixth, seventh, and eighth graders who were underperformers and who had come to the Demonstration School of George Peabody College to take "extra work" in composition. The class met daily for one month.

Each day the instructor put one pair of cue (or kernel) sentences on the blackboard and showed how the sentences could be combined. Then he read between 10 and 15 pairs of sentences, pair by pair, and asked one student at a time to combine the cues into an appropriate sentence. The class repeated correct answers in unison. When an answer was incorrect, the teacher supplied a proper response which the class repeated in unison. Also, each day the students wrote answers to 5 sentence-combining problems which were read to them. These papers were graded for sentence-combining and for spelling. Previously, unfamiliar words had been written on the blackboard. Students in doubt about the spelling of any word in the 5-question written exercise were permitted to ask for the proper spelling.

Students took an identical pretest and posttest which consisted of written reactions to a silent film. The effect of instruction was measured by counting the "difference in the number of drilled structures between pre-test and post-test."[153] For the class as a whole, the results showed a clear gain from pretest to posttest. However, 6 of the 19 students contributed disproportionately to the gain, thereby inflating the group-gain figure and creating the illusion that the group fared better than it did. Nevertheless, Ney concluded that the experiment "did demonstrate that. . .linguistic behavior. . .can be changed through the use of audio-lingual drills"[154] and that spelling can be taught "without depending on the negative approach of merely correcting. . .errors. . . ."[155]

Ney referred to his experiment as a pilot project.[156] Certainly the experiment is sharply limited by its size, the complete absence of controls, and elementary handling of statistics. Of the 3 sentence-combining studies mentioned, this one is most innocent in design, and its results are least definite, least searchingly analyzed, and least convincing. The principal finding, namely, that 6 students of 19 were helped, is no more than a weak indication that the problem deserves further investigation.

. . . . .

It is necessary to be cautious in assessing what is, at present, known about the contribution of linguistics to the improvement of writing. The research is all quite recent, and researchers are still maneuvering for the best way to come to grips with the problem. The complexities of the task are increased by the fact that linguistics is itself not a single and readily definable subject or method. In

[153]*Ibid.*, p. 897.
[154]*Loc. cit.*
[155]*Ibid.*, p. 902.
[156]*Ibid.*, p. 895.

assessing the present state of knowledge it would be imprudent to imply very much about the future. But with all present uncertainties and limitations in mind, it is nevertheless worth asking what we know so far.

How should the transformational sentence-combining experiments be interpreted? The Raub and Ney experiments are bare indicators of tendencies better revealed in Mellon's study. At this time, the case for sentence-combining rests upon Mellon's study. What do Mellon's findings at face value mean?

Anticipating the misinterpretation of his findings, Mellon declared that his experiment should not be cited as proof that grammar should retain a place in the curriculum.[157] Although his reasons may provoke more rather than less argument, it is true that his results were obtained with a minimum investment in grammatical preparation. The case for the thorough study of the details of grammar, transformational or any other, cannot be supported by a study which obtained positive results with relatively little study of grammar *per se.*

An important and still unanswered question is whether the results were obtained because sentence-combining is effective or because transformational sentence-combining is effective. If it should turn out that plain, old-fashioned, sentence-combining exercises are equally effective, then the technique is stripped of its modest connection with grammar. This question deserves to be investigated.

As it is described in all three studies, transformational sentence-combining, whether or not associated with oral (audiolingual) exercises, is essentially a device for structuring the process of composing a sentence. In other words, it appears to be less a grammar-related device than a device for teaching writing by providing controlled experience with writing. If someone would do a good writing-to-teach-writing experiment (like McColly's, discussed in the fourth section of this chapter) and include an experimental comparison with both plain and transformational sentence-combining, then it would be possible to judge what is operating in this situation. All one can say now is that transformational sentence-combining is a promising way to help students toward greater skill in writing.

Eight studies compared a linguistic approach to a traditional grammatical approach. Of these, the ones by Suggs, Link-Schuster, and Miller are too uncertain in their research technique to be included in any reckoning. Of the remaining five studies, one, by Zidonis, found a small advantage for generative grammar; a second, by Johnson, found structural linguistics and traditional grammar to be about equally effective in improving students' themes; a third, by Blake, found structural linguistics and traditional grammar to be about equally effective in improving students' use of punctuation (as determined by a test). A fourth study, by Weinfeld, found only insignificant differences between gains scores of students who had studied structural linguistics and those who had studied traditional grammar. A fifth study, by O'Donnell, a correlative analysis,

---

[157]Mellon, *Transformational Sentence-Combining,* p. 113.

could find no special advantage for students who knew linguistics or for those who knew traditional grammar.

Zais tested the hypothesis that the linguistic characteristics of punctuation symbols influence the ways these symbols should be taught. Zais's data did not support his hypothesis. A statistical study by De Lancey inquired into whether a knowledge of form classes would affect students' reading comprehension. De Lancey found a positive correlation between a knowledge of form classes and reading comprehension, but he also found that reading comprehension is more closely related to a knowledge of vocabulary than it is to a knowledge of form classes. Thus it would seem that De Lancey's evidence would not encourage the study of form classes (or, by extension, the study of linguistics).

In short, most of the studies examined which appear to have any merit do not encourage the belief that a linguistic approach or linguistic knowledge is more effective than a grammatical approach or grammatical knowledge. Nor does the evidence, in sum, support the contention that linguistics is especially efficacious in the areas of reading or punctuation. It is obviously too soon to pass judgment on the matter, but certainly it can be said that the case for linguistics remains to be proved and that the investigations to date do not justify mass conversion to any linguistic method on the grounds that such a conversion will improve writing. The situation calls for more and better experimentation.

4. DOES WRITING TEACH WRITING?

Just as there are many loyal supporters of the doctrine that grammar study will improve students' writing, so there are those who maintain that the act of writing teaches students to write. This latter group, whose position has been ably presented by Lou La Brant, holds that "persistent practice"[158] in writing on a subject of interest is a far more effective way to teach than providing drill in grammar or in supplying exercises for correction. The argument is attractive because indirect attacks upon the writing problem, such as teaching grammar and sentence diagraming, have not so far been shown to be worthwhile. Would not a direct attack in which students repeatedly engage in the act of composition be successful?

In an amusing parable, William D. Baker tells of a high school swimming coach who kept his swimmers out of the water and busy memorizing the names of the bones in the human body so that they would understand him when he criticized their strokes during the few times each semester when he permitted them to swim. The coach was also the head of the English department.[159] Assuming that the "way to teach swimming is to have students swim most of the time," is it also correct to assume that the way to teach writing is to have

[158] Lou La Brant, "Writing Is Learned by Writing," *English Journal*, 30 (November 1953), 417.
[159] William D. Baker, "The Swimming Coach," *English Journal*, 56 (January 1957), 41.

students write most of the time? Should writing be "corrected" intensively, that is, with painstaking attention to detail?

For the most part, the research on the subject deals with quantity of assignments and intensity of correction. Occasionally, a finding will seem to suggest that writing can be taught by reading rather than by writing, but this possibility is never presented by the writers as a serious alternative. Admittedly, the evidence for a reading solution to the writing problem is skimpy. The general conclusion of the body of research on writing-to-teach-writing is that merely increasing the number of assignments will not improve the quality of writing and that intensive correction, similarly, will fail to achieve the intended result. This conclusion will be discussed following a review of the studies.

. . . . .

John Fellows set out to discover whether the practice of assigning themes and correcting them is successful in eliminating selected errors in spelling, capitalization, punctuation, and grammar. For 12 weeks, each of 12 teachers taught two ninth grade classes. Each taught his class in an identical manner, and each class wrote a composition a week for 11 weeks. However, one class taught by each teacher wrote themes in which errors were carefully indicated and for which a grade was assigned. Students in this class were required to rewrite and return their compositions. The other class also wrote themes which were given a grade, but the teacher did not indicate errors and did not require rewriting.

Initially, each student was tested in mechanics and grammar and was required to write 3 compositions on different subjects. After the experimental period, each student was again tested on the same subjects and was again required to write 3 compositions on 3 new topics.

Apparently for administrative reasons, Fellows was obliged to forego any "scientific" attempt to match his "theme-correction group" and his "non-theme-correction group." He had to rely instead upon previous marks as an indication of English ability. The groups were evenly divided according to sex and number.

Fellows found that the theme-correction group made "slightly greater gains" than did the non-theme-correction group. Though "not. . .strictly statistically significant," the improvement was, according to Fellows, "large enough to warrant the assumption that this difference was not entirely due to. . . chance."[160] However, Fellows went on to say that he thought the theme-correction procedure to be "highly questionable" and that he believed the "burden of proof must surely lie in the hands of the teacher employing it."[161] His reason for doubting the worth of the procedure is not explicitly stated. Perhaps he thought it excessive that a mountain should labor to bring forth a mouse.

[160] John Ernest Fellows, "The Influence of Theme-Reading and Theme-Correction on Eliminating Technical Errors in Ninth Grade Pupils," *University of Iowa Studies in Education*, 7 (1932), 42.
[161] *Ibid.*, p. 43.

The purpose of an experiment by Virgil Lokke and George Wykoff "was to discover what results would be obtained when freshmen students did twice the amount of assigned writing that composition students usually do."[162] Lokke and Wykoff's experimental group consisted of two classes enrolling a total of 20 Purdue University freshmen. There were two control groups in each of which a student was paired with a student in the experimental group. Both groups took the same course of study. But each student in the control group wrote 16 themes during the semester, and each student in the experimental group wrote from 32 to 34 themes during the semester.

Each student took an English placement test and an intelligence test. Gains were determined by comparing scores on grammar, punctuation, and spelling tests and by comparing theme grades and semester grades.

Lokke and Wykoff found that students in the experimental (double-writing) group had 66 percent fewer failures. They found, also, that "student improvement, judged by the final semester grade, can be increased 60 percent." However, 40 percent of the students, according to Lokke and Wykoff, reached the "level of achievement by the end of a writing period of 12 to 15 themes. . . ."[163]

One handicap of the study, as the researchers themselves acknowledged, is the very small size of the experimental group. Another weakness, at least as important, is the absence of safeguards built into the method of computing gains; even a small but consistent misjudgment in the awarding of theme grades could easily have affected the final results.

The Lokke-Wykoff study has been analyzed by William McColly, whose own study will be discussed later. McColly reanalyzed Lokke and Wykoff's data and found that "they really show. . .that the difference between the control and experimental groups' grades can be expected to occur 9 out of 10 times simply by chance." McColly pointed, also, to several other flaws—a "lesson learning effect" in which students learn to do what the teacher wants, a "halo effect" in which a teacher is deceived into reporting precisely the results he had been seeking, a "Hawthorne effect" by which the experimental group achieves a motivational advantage over the control group, and, finally, a possible "matching error factor." In view of all of this, it is possible to conclude with McColly that the experiment should be interpreted "as really confirming the null hypothesis about doubling writing. . . ." That is, Lokke and Wykoff thought they found a difference when they doubled writing, but they really found no difference at all.[164]

Results quite the opposite to Lokke and Wykoff's were obtained by Paul Dressel, John Schmid, and Gerald Kincaid. Having observed Lokke and Wykoff's

[162] Virgil L. Lokke and George S. Wykoff, "'Double Writing' in Freshman Composition—An Experiment," *School and Society,* 68 (December 18, 1948), 437.

[163] *Ibid.,* p. 438.

[164] William McColly, *Comparative Effectiveness of Composition Skills Learning Activities in the Secondary School,* United States Office of Education Cooperative Research Project 1528 (Madison: University of Wisconsin, 1963), pp. 9–10.

findings, Dressel and Schmid and Kincaid sought to discover whether additional writing assignments would also improve the performance of their students at Michigan State College (now Michigan State University). Rather than add another writing course or increase the writing assignments in the freshman communication course already required, they chose instead to examine the effect of an increase in the writing required in academic and professional courses. They hypothesized that "if students were given sufficient opportunity to exercise. . . writing skills, developed, in part, in their communication skills course, then improvement of expression might be a natural consequent, even though no formal attempt is made by the teaching staff to point out poor expression."[165]

Two thousand four hundred freshmen reported on a questionnaire how much assigned essay-type writing they had done during their freshman year. The 99 students reporting the greatest number of completed writing assignments (average of 131 hours) were compared with the 99 reporting the fewest number of writing assignments (average of 4 hours). Writing done in the freshman communication course, since it was the same for all, was not included in the calculation of average hours of writing.

Each student wrote a theme on an assigned topic at the beginning of the year and another at the end. These were graded by two faculty members who used a rating scale. Any "discrepancy" between the two ratings of a paper caused the paper to be referred to a third reader. As a further safeguard, students' names were removed from the standardized booklets in which they wrote their themes.

Dressel, Schmid, and Kincaid found that "mere frequency of writing essay material in courses other than English is insufficient to improve the quality of the students' written expression."[166] However, they did not interpret this finding to mean that frequent writing is valueless. Instead, they expressed the belief that frequent writing failed to benefit the students because teachers did not hold the students responsible for the quality of their writing in other courses and because many of the topics upon which students wrote were either too complex or ambiguous.

One finding of this study seems secure. The mere act of writing does not in itself improve writing; merely increasing writing activity will not improve writing. But is writing better taught with frequent assignments accompanied by instruction and motivation for quality? This question is not answered by this study, yet this is the really practical question to which an answer needs to be found. Studies by Buxton and McColly, discussed later, deal with this question.

It may be recalled that studies by Rosemary Smith, I. O. Ash, and Ray Maize, which were discussed in the preceding section, found that experience in writing is more likely to improve writing quality than is the study of grammar.

[165] Paul Dressel, John Schmid, and Gerald Kincaid, "The Effect of Writing Frequency upon Essay-type Writing Proficiency at the College Level," *Journal of Educational Research,* 46 (December 1952), 287.
[166] *Ibid.,* p. 292.

Although these studies show that writing teaches writing better than grammar teaches writing, they do not reveal whether the situation is the result of the strength of the writing approach or the weakness of the grammar approach. All that these studies reveal is the effectiveness of two approaches relative to each other. The question remains as to whether increasing motivated writing and including classroom discussion of the writing will improve the quality of writing to a significant and worthwhile extent.

Earl Buxton reported an experiment which shed some light upon the question just stated. In September 1957 Buxton gave the Cooperative English Test (Mechanics and Effectiveness of Expression) to 257 college freshmen. He also gave an initial impromptu theme. As a final test in March 1958 he administered another form of the Cooperative English Test and gave another impromptu theme. Buxton set up 3 randomly selected groups with 86, 86, and 85 students in each. One group served as a control and did no writing. The second wrote a theme a week for 16 weeks; these students' papers were corrected, graded, commented upon by the instructor, and returned without further comment or discussion. The third group also wrote a theme a week; these students' papers were also corrected, graded, and returned with comments, but this time the students had the benefit of "thirty to fifty minutes of class time devoted to discussion and revision."[167]

The initial and final essay tests were marked by "two well-trained, experienced" teachers who used a rating scale and who "worked independently" of each other. The correlation of their grades was very high (.90)—indicating that they were inclined to give a theme the same grade.

All 3 groups fared about equally on the mechanics of expression tests. The writing and revision groups surpassed the control group on effectiveness of expression tests. The revision group surpassed the other two on the essay test. This achievement by the revision group was made possible by large gains in such matters as diction, fluency, and variety; the revision group did not exceed the others in such matters as critical thinking, originality, or organization. Buxton concluded that regular writing assignments alone will not result in significantly improved essay writing but that regular writing assignments accompanied by discussion, criticism, and revision will improve essay writing. In short, Buxton's evidence supports the contention that writing plus teaching writing equals improvement in writing. Omit the teaching and the results are disappointing.

Studies since Buxton's have come to similar conclusions. These—by Frank Heys, William McColly, Dwight Burton and Lois Arnold, and Mark Christiansen—will be discussed in their order of publication.

Frank Heys, Jr., tested what he called the "theme-a-week assumption." Participating in his study were 8 classes in the Lincoln-Sudbury High School in

---

[167]Earl William Buxton, "An Experiment to Test the Effects of Writing Frequency and Guided Practice upon Students' Skill in Written Expression" (Ph.D. dissertation, Stanford University, 1958); in *Dissertation Abstracts,* 19, 4 (October 1958), 709.

Massachusetts—two classes in each grade from nine through twelve. The two classes at each grade were taught by the same teacher. One class was a writing class in which students wrote a theme a week; these themes were carefully corrected by the teacher who strictly required whatever revision or rewriting might be needed. The second class taught by the same teacher was a reading class in which students spent one period a week reading books they had chosen and brought to class. Students in the reading class wrote approximately one theme every 3 weeks. "The experiment thus consisted of giving students in two classes in each of four grades a year's experience that differed in but one respect: the amount of reading and writing done."[168]

To evaluate the two courses of study, Heys gave the STEP Writing Test, Form 2A, in the fall and Form 2B in the spring. So as to avoid a purely objective, test-type, measure of writing, Heys gave an initial composition test in the fall and a final composition test in the spring. These compositions were assigned code numbers to disguise the authors' identity and the sequence of composition. Three experienced readers of the College Board's English Achievement Test were employed to evaluate these compositions.

After analyzing the data in a variety of ways, Heys found that "except for seniors (but not all) and except for some low groups (but not all) and except for the area of content and organization (but not always), we got consistently better results from those students in the reading classes."[169] Heys and his associates at the Lincoln-Sudbury school concluded that the "claim that 'the way to learn to write is to write' is not substantiated by this experiment." They further concluded that the claim that writing ability "is related to the amount of writing done is not substantiated by this experiment."[170]

A year after the Heys experiment, in 1963, William McColly reported his experiment to determine which of the several kinds of composition learning activities are effective and which are not. Specifically, McColly sought to identify the worth of the following teaching activities: (1) writing *per se* ("mere writing"); (2) group discussion; (3) self-instruction (such as revising, rewriting, editing, correcting); (4) practical instruction (as distinct from theoretical instruction) in which teachers give explanations and students practice on points of usage, spelling, punctuation, organization, sentence structure; (5) conventional theme correction, and (6) tutoring in which the student receives an immediate response from the teacher *during* the process of composition ("Immediate feedback tutoring").[171]

At each grade from eight through twelve, McColly set up a control group and one or two experimental groups depending upon the number of variables to

---

[168] Frank Heys, Jr., "The Theme-a-Week Assumption: A Report of an Experiment," *English Journal*, 51 (May 1962), 321.

[169] *Ibid.*, p. 322.

[170] *Loc. cit.*

[171] McColly, *Comparative Effectiveness of Composition Skills Learning Activities*, pp. 1, 16.

be examined at that grade level. It was possible to assign students to some groups in a random fashion. But when a completely random procedure could not be followed owing to scheduling difficulties, McColly used a statistical means to "remove bias and to increase the precision of the analysis."[172] Two hundred eighty-three of an original 295 students completed the experiment which lasted throughout the academic year 1962–1963.

Before the start of the experiment, each student was tested for general ability, reading ability, correctness and appropriateness of expression, and ability to interpret literature. Each student, also, wrote two impromptu compositions. Finally, a cumulative average and an English average were recorded for each student. This preliminary testing program enabled McColly to assess the status of the students prior to the experiment and provided him, also, with a means for predicting their success and for comparing their predicted success with their actual success. With such preliminary information at hand, McColly was able to equalize his groups, that is, make statistical adjustments to minimize the effects of initial advantages or disadvantages which members of each group possessed.

Of particular interest here is that portion of McColly's experiment which tested the "Hypothesis That More Writing Alone Means Better Writing." To all eighth and ninth graders in the control and experimental groups, McColly gave an equal amount of the same kind of instruction. Only the amount of the writing for the experimental groups differed. They received 4 times as many writing assignments as the control group received.

Upon the conclusion of the experimental period of one year, McColly obtained two samples of student writing, two period-long impromptu themes. These two impromptu themes and the initial two impromptu themes were graded by 4 teams each of which contained a male and female college teacher and a male and female high school teacher—all randomly chosen from the membership lists of the Wisconsin Council of Teachers of English. Each team attended an orientation meeting and read themes the following day. The themes were randomly selected in such a way that each team read equal numbers of themes written by boys and girls. Each theme was read by 4 readers and rated by each reader for general merit on a 4-point scale. In addition, the two final themes were measured "objectively" by a number of teaching assistants in the University of Wisconsin English department who counted such errors as comma faults, run-on sentences, misspellings, and errors in agreement. In this way McColly obtained what he believed to be a satisfactory "index of difference in the ability to use standard mechanics of writing."[173]

The rationale for the procedures described here (and others unmentioned for the sake of brevity) are given in full in the study and will repay a careful reading. Indeed, the study is painstaking, resourceful, and as convincing as any

[172]*Ibid.*, p. 23.
[173]*Ibid.*, p. 47.

mentioned in any portion of this work. What McColly found should be a challenge to those who subscribe to the "popular belief that more writing alone means better writing. . . ." This belief, McColly concluded, "is untenable, at least for the junior and senior high schools."[174]

> The activity of writing in and of itself is fruitless. The activity of tutoring, even where immediate feedback is possible, either is negative, or ineffective, or does not increase the effectiveness of. . .feasible functional activities, or to be effective must be given in such great amounts as to be unfeasible. . . .
>
> What are the implications. . .for English teachers. . . ? First, they should not assign or elicit any writing. . .unless this writing becomes the vehicle for functional instruction. Second, they can reduce greatly the time they spend in "tutoring" writing and conferring. . .if they give adequate functional composition instruction in the classroom.
>
> But what is the adequate amount of these functional activities? It can be inferred in part from the facts that writing per se is ineffective and functional instruction for about half the time spent in English is significantly more effective than one-fourth that amount. Until more is known, the best inference seems to be that to teach composition effectively, teachers should give a weekly writing task on which they base about 2 and ½ days of practical explanation, student practice, discussion, revising, rewriting, etc.[175]

Like McColly, Dwight Burton and Lois Arnold investigated whether frequent writing is more effective than infrequent writing. In addition, Burton and Arnold sought to discover whether intensive evaluation, that is, the "marking of every error and the writing of detailed comments," is more effective than moderate evaluation, that is, "marking in which the teacher selects only an occasional paper to grade or corrects only those errors pertaining to skills which students are studying at a particular time."[176]

Their findings were based on data supplied by 137 tenth graders in two similar high schools who were taught by two different teachers. All students participating in the study had been placed by their schools in the "average" group, but Burton and Arnold were able to distinguish "high," "middle," and "low" levels within this classification by means of the Differential Aptitude Test—Verbal Reasoning.

Early in the experimental period, which lasted for one academic year, Burton and Arnold administered the STEP Essay Test and the STEP Writing Test. Alternate forms of these tests were given at the conclusion of the experi-

[174]*Ibid.*, p. 62.
[175]*Ibid.*, pp. 64–65.
[176]Dwight L. Burton and Lois V. Arnold, *Effects of Frequency of Writing and Intensity of Evaluation upon High School Students' Performance in Written Composition,* United States Office of Education Cooperative Research Project 1523 (Tallahassee: Florida State University, 1963), p. 28. A more readily obtainable but less detailed account is Lois Arnold, "Writer's Cramp and Eyestrain—Are They Paying Off?" *English Journal,* 53 (January 1964), 10–15.

mental period. Each teacher used one of the following 4 procedures in one of her classes:

   infrequent writing (250 words three times a semester) and moderate
     evaluation;

   frequent writing (writing 4 days a week ranging in length from two
     sentences to two or more pages) and moderate evaluation;

   infrequent writing and intensive evaluation;

   frequent writing and intensive evaluation.

In an attempt to achieve a larger measure of consistency and objectivity in the evaluation of student writing, the teachers used the scales prepared by the California Association of Teachers of English (*A Scale for Evaluation of High School Student Essays* [Champaign, Ill.: NCTE, 1960]) and by the Association of English Teachers of Western Pennsylvania (*Suggestions for Evaluating Junior High School Writing* [Champaign, Ill.: NCTE, n.d.]). Students were informed of the standards by which their papers were to be evaluated.

Except for the difference previously noted in writing frequency and intensity of evaluation, all classes received substantially the same instruction. The textbook used was John E. Warriner's handbook (*English Grammar and Composition: Grade 10* [New York: Harcourt, Brace & World, Inc., 1958]). The use of the Warriner book would suggest that instruction in writing was strongly grammatical and that the grammar was traditional and prescriptive.

Burton and Arnold found that the data revealed "no differences in group performance resulting from writing practice or intensity of evaluation."[177] In other words, Burton and Arnold concluded that frequency of writing is not "in itself a means of improving writing" and that the different intensities of grading do not significantly affect the quality of student writing.

Burton and Arnold's results resemble McColly's and would ordinarily reinforce doubts about the value of frequent writing as a means for teaching writing. However, Burton and Arnold's negative results could have been obtained because both methods being compared were insufficient to overcome the handicap of a traditional, prescriptive, grammatical approach to writing, an approach which research recounted earlier has shown to be unrewarding.

Last to be mentioned is a study by Mark A. Christiansen which produced results similar to Burton and Arnold's, McColly's, and Heys'. One hundred forty-eight college freshmen were enrolled by a random procedure in classes which were either control or experimental. Three teachers, including Christiansen, taught "an equal number of experimental and control classes,"[178] presumably one class of each kind. (The report of the experiment is not specific about these arrangements.) During the experimental period of one semester, the control group wrote 8 themes and read prose selections from a "regular freshman

[177]*Ibid.*, p. 62.
[178]Mark A. Christiansen, "Tripling Writing and Omitting Readings in Freshman English: An Experiment," *College Composition and Communication*, 16 (May 1965), 123.

reader." The experimental group wrote 24 themes, 3 times the number written by their coevals in the control group, and did not read prose selections. Except as just mentioned, both groups received the same instruction.

Apparently with the Hawthorne Effect in mind, Christiansen did not tell his students that they were taking part in an experiment. As a further safeguard, Christiansen used a numbering scheme to disguise the authorship of a paper and to obscure whether the paper was written by a student in the control or experimental group. Also, by obtaining the services of two "competent" teachers to supplement his own efforts, Christiansen hoped to minimize the effects of any prejudice he might have which might influence the results. Assigning each teacher both an experimental and a control class was another device designed to minimize the influence of the teacher variable. The report mentions no steps taken to objectify or regularize the teachers' evaluations of themes, no staff training, conferences on evaluation, statistical checks on the consistency of grading, or formal rating scales. However, the grading process was structured somewhat by requiring teachers to consider "central idea. . . , supporting material, organization, expression (diction and sentence style), literacy (grammar and mechanics)."[179]

In order to obtain an initial measure of students' ability, Christiansen gave the Cooperative School and College Ability Test (SCAT), the writing part of the Sequential Test of Educational Progress (STEP), the New Purdue Placement Test in English, and the Measurement Test (covering style and rhetoric) prepared by the Department of English of the University of Kansas. The Purdue and Kansas tests were given again at the end of the semester to see if the students had improved in reading and vocabulary. Improvement in writing was measured by comparing the initial and the final theme.

Christiansen found that both experimental and control groups made a statistically significant improvement in their writing; however, both groups improved approximately to the same extent, and any small differences between them were not statistically significant. In short, tripling writing did not pay off.

Christiansen also found that the control group, which read prose selections, improved in reading ability just as much as the experimental group, which did not read prose selections. This finding suggested to Christiansen that "apparently the reading done in the control classes did as much to promote growth in writing as did the writing of 16 extra themes in the experimental classes."[180]

Christiansen's observation about the value of reading is, after all, an interpretation based upon his data, and it is not a demonstrable conclusion inescapably derived from his experiment. The matter might well be investigated in a separate study. In fact, it is regrettable that Christiansen introduced reading as a second variable. Had the difference between the two groups been only quantity of writing, it would at least be possible to tell what difference quantity of writing would make. Now, all that is known is that both groups did equally well

[179]*Ibid.*, p. 122.
[180]*Ibid.*, p. 124.

and that the control group might have improved its performance because of some advantage that reading might have conferred. This study would have been more informative if Christiansen had limited himself to one problem. Even St. George was content to slay one dragon at a time.

. . . . .

The conscientious teacher who brings, say, 150 compositions home each week to grade with great care and in great detail may be making a magnificently heroic contribution to his students' language skills, or he may be merely a victim of an educational delusion. Research has not charted a sure passage to improved writing. Nor has it charted an easy passage unencumbered by heavy bundles of papers. One point stands out clearly. As Dressel, Schmid, and Kincaid expressed it, "mere frequency of writing. . .is insufficient. . . ." Quantity of writing alone will not achieve the desired result. The Lokke-Wykoff study, which contradicts this conclusion, is probably too faulty to be counted on either side of the issue, and all the other studies mentioned here support this conclusion. However, the conclusion should not be misinterpreted or overstated.

It is significant that none of the researchers who have questioned the quantity approach to writing have interpreted their findings to mean that students can learn to write without actually engaging in the act of composition. Even Heys hesitated to draw this conclusion, although his composition test showed his reading group to be superior to his writing group and the STEP Writing Tests showed both groups to be about equally adept. Christiansen, too, hesitated to conclude that writing can be learned without writing, although he interpreted his data to mean that reading essays was as efficacious as the writing of 16 extra compositions.

Most likely Heys' and Christiansen's caution is justified. It may be that teaching writing resembles watering a lawn to the extent that pouring on a double or triple dose in a given length of time adds only to the run-off. There should be a balance between the amount being applied and the ability to absorb. Support for this point of view may be found in some likely and unlikely places. Lokke and Wykoff, whose study favors the quantity approach, observed (on page 138) that 40 percent of their students reached "their limit of achievement" after writing 12 to 15 themes. But even if this evidence be disallowed, as perhaps it should, there is still McColly's finding that the quantity approach alone is "fruitless." According to McColly, when functional activities were "increased from 1/8 to 1/2 of the total instructional time," writing improved significantly. What this means, then, is that writing activities produce desired results when proper steps are taken ("functional activities") to facilitate the absorption, so to speak, of the experience. This conclusion is supported by Buxton who, it may be recalled, found that quantity of writing alone is less effective than "guided practice" which includes discussion, criticism, and revision. Within the limits imposed by its method, the Burton-Arnold study also suggests the ineffectiveness of the quantity approach.

Judging from the studies, intensive marking is no more defensible than multiplying writing assignments. Fellows found only a slight advantage in minute correction by the teacher and revision by the student, an advantage insufficient to justify the effort and time expended. Papers written by Heys' experimental group were carefully marked by the teacher and revised by the students, yet Heys could detect no special benefits from these activities. Neither did Burton and Arnold find that intensive evaluation significantly affected student writing. This conclusion, too, should not be misinterpreted.

Intensive evaluation means painstaking attention to the many details of writing, such as punctuation and spelling, and to matters of broader scope, such as sentence and paragraph development, unity, and coherence. If intensive evaluation, which is so costly in time and effort, does not pay dividends, are we to conclude that teachers should stop reading and evaluating papers?

Even from a purely theoretical point of view, intensive evaluation is not a promising technique. It submerges the student in a sea of particulars. It forces him to attend to all his missteps at once. No self-respecting swimming coach would teach in this way. He would have his students learn one movement of a stroke (or part, as it is technically known) and then another. Next, he would coordinate the two; next, teach a third; next, add the third to the previous two; and so forth. All the while he would be reviewing until he succeeded in assembling a coordinated pattern of movements. The learning theory underlying this procedure is widely known and has been in use for a long time. Its most recent application is in programed learning. Briefly stated, it holds that learning takes place more efficiently when it proceeds one step at a time in an orderly, progressive, cumulative way toward the attainment of a previously selected goal.

5. SUMMARY AND CONCLUSION

a) A review of the condition of language instruction reveals many opinions and some facts. The opinions cover the complete range from optimism to pessimism. The facts, to the extent that they are revealed by the status studies and error analyses, are almost uniformly discouraging. Error analyses of student writing by Eason, Day, Butler, Wheeler, DeBusk, Alshouse, and Swenson and Caldwell revealed high error frequency and a high persistence of error. Two comprehensive status surveys by Smith and another by Pooley and Williams documented inadequacies in curriculum and method. Gruen's status survey, somewhat different in method and less comprehensive than the others, reached similar conclusions. Lange, too, revealed the persistency of error and certain inadequacies of instruction which presumably engender poor writing.

All the studies mentioned were published between 1929 and 1948. In the absence of recent large-scale studies resembling Smith's and Pooley's, it is not possible to speak in terms of hard facts about the current situation. Clearly, however, such works as *Freedom and Discipline in English* (1965) and "The Basic Issues in Teaching of English" (1959) have revealed a widespread judgment among those long in touch with professional matters that much still requires improvement. Although the wind of change is blowing, it remains to be seen whether it is merely an ineffectual breeze or (worse) a blow too big to serve any but destructive purposes.

b) Statistical and nonexperimental studies using correlation analysis by Hoyt, Rapeer, Boraas, Asker, Segal and Barr, Catherwood, Bradford, and Robinson failed to show a significant relationship between grammatical knowledge and writing ability. Except for Wykoff's study, the experimental studies by Briggs, Symonds, Crawford and Royer, Cutright, Ash, Benfer, Clark, Warner and Guiler, Milligan, Frogner, Kraus, Smith, and Maize also failed to support the case for grammar. After a tally of procedural and other limitations, the research still overwhelmingly supports the contention that instruction in formal grammar is an ineffective and inefficient way to help students achieve proficiency in writing.

c) What linguistics can contribute to the teaching of writing is a story just now beginning to unfold. Most (not all) specialists in the field appear to prefer to avoid practical claims for linguistics and to defend linguistics on the grounds that it is worth knowing, a humanistic study, a part of general-liberal education. So far, the experimental evidence supports the view that linguistics is about as effective as traditional grammar in improving writing. De Lancey, in seeking to relate reading comprehension to a knowledge of form classes, failed to provide impressive evidence of the worth of a linguistic approach. Zais, in his study of the linguistic characteristics of punctuation symbols, could find no connection between the linguistic characteristics of a symbol and the effectiveness of the method used to teach it. In this contest of methods and philosophies, linguistics has not yet scored, but many innings remain to be played. The achievement of transformational sentence-combining appears to be less a clue to the worth of a grammatical or linguistic approach than a clue to the worth of controlled practice in composing sentences.

d) One major study by McColly and other lesser efforts by Fellows, Dressel-Schmid-Kincaid, Buxton, Heys, Burton-Arnold, and Christiansen reached the conclusion that writing does not teach writing; that is, the act of writing alone—the simple increasing of the number of writing opportunities—does not result in a statistically significant improvement in writing skill. A study by Lokke and Wykoff, which reached a contrary conclusion, appears to be too faulty to be counted on either side of the issue. Evidence supplied by McColly and Buxton suggests that less writing in conjunction with better teaching will obtain measurably superior results. Motivation, selective criticism, discussion, practical explanation, and revision are the important features of instruction. Intensive evaluation, like the mere multiplying of writing assignments, is costly in effort for everyone and fails to achieve positive results (Fellows, Heys, Burton-Arnold). The transformational sentence-combining method (mentioned in c above) may be interpreted as a controlled and limited form of the writing-to-teach-writing method.

Chapter IV

To Diagram or Not To Diagram?

1. BACKGROUND

A former president of the National Council of Teachers of English has called sentence diagraming a "Form of mental gymnastics. . .not helpful to writing nor to a real understanding of grammar."[1] The managing editor of *Charm* is reported to have said that she is "a great believer in diagraming" and that her children "learned the parts of speech and the relation of phrases to main clauses much more readily" after she had taught them diagraming.[2] These quotations illustrate sharply conflicting views on the subject of diagraming.

Sentence diagraming has a long history as a method of language instruction. Like parsing, of which it is a two-dimensional refinement, sentence diagraming had been a feature of Latin instruction. As English supplanted Latin in the schools, diagraming was taken over as a feature of English instruction.[3] According to Harry A. Greene, diagraming retained its popularity as an instructional device until the mid 1920's when, for uncertain reasons, it disappeared almost completely from elementary and secondary textbooks. Perhaps the emphasis at the time upon functional grammar contributed to the decline of diagraming. By the mid 1930's diagraming had begun to reappear and now seems to have regained a large measure of its popularity.[4]

Fluctuations in textbook writers' and teachers' devotion to diagraming seem to be unrelated to research findings, and, in fact, a "careful search" by Greene "of all available compilations of investigations" failed to locate a single study prior to 1940 which experimentally examined sentence diagraming as a means of language instruction.[5] However, between 1940 and 1945, four studies directly or indirectly related to diagraming were completed at the University of Iowa

---

[1] Lou La Brant, *We Teach English* (New York: Harcourt, Brace & Co., 1951), p. 210.
[2] Quoted in Joseph Mersand, *Attitudes toward English Teaching* (Philadelphia: Chilton Company, 1961), pp. 316–317.
[3] Louis Zahner *et al.*, *Language in General Education* (New York: Appleton-Century-Crofts, 1940), pp. 65–66.
[4] Harry A. Greene, "Direct versus Formal Methods in Elementary English," *Elementary English,* 14 (May 1947), 278.
[5] *Ibid*, pp. 278–279.

under Greene's direction. To Greene and his graduate students we owe most of such knowledge as we have about the effectiveness of sentence diagraming.

There are different kinds of sentence diagrams. The informal diagram retains the linear sentence and suggests syntactical relationships by means of arrows, circles, underlinings, etc., all of which may be used in impromptu combinations by the teacher. The formal diagram varies in detail from textbook to textbook but in general consists of a predetermined analytical scheme employing different sorts of lines in different relationships to a horizontal line called a "base line." Formal diagrams are intended for use by both teachers and students. The following illustration of a formal diagram is from a freshman handbook.[6]

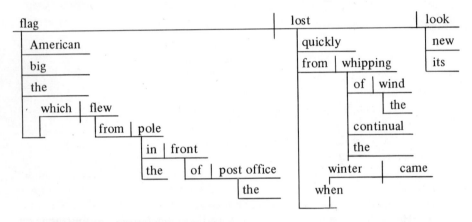

(The big American flag which flew from the pole in front of the post office quickly lost its new look, when winter came, from the continual whipping of the wind.)

The informal diagram is not, as yet, a subject of controversy because it involves no special learning by students; it is used by the teacher only incidentally, that is, as the opportunity arises, to illustrate rapidly some grammatical point; and it retains the linear form in which language naturally occurs. The effectiveness of the informal diagram is not so much a question of its being a diagram as of its being a grammatical approach to language problems. The formal diagram, however, is both a grammatical approach and a definite schematic device intended to achieve a modification of students' use of language. It is the formal diagram, then, which is the subject of disagreement and the subject of a few comparatively recent investigations.

[6] Louise E. Rorabacher, *A Concise Guide to Composition* (New York: Harper and Brothers, 1956), pp. 116–117. [Second edition, Harper & Row, 1963.] Diagram used by permission.

2. STUDIES

The inquiry into the worth of sentence diagraming began in 1940 with the appearance of Kenneth C. Barghahn's master's thesis.[7] This study sought to discover whether diagraming (1) increases students' reading comprehension, (2) increases students' ability to use the English language correctly, and (3) qualifies as functional grammar. The reference to functional grammar means only that Barghahn wished to find out whether achieving skill in diagraming is worthwhile for its own sake.

After setting up a control group of 45 students and an experimental group of 40 students, Barghahn tested each in diagraming, silent reading, and English correctness. Then, for 6 weeks he taught diagraming to the experimental group. At the end of the instructional period, Barghahn again tested both groups for the same skills and, finally, compared the changes in scores of both groups to see if diagraming had conferred any special benefits.

Barghahn concluded: (1) Instruction in diagraming improves skill in diagraming; (2) instruction in diagraming does not lead to greater reading comprehension; (3) instruction in diagraming does not lead to greater or more rapid mastery of English correctness; and (4) diagraming, when mastered, is not functional because "an increase of skill in diagraming for its own sake is of no value to the student."[8]

The limitations of Barghahn's study are numerous, and Barghahn himself listed most of them:

> The groups were not as large as they should have been. . . . The diagraming group was decidedly inferior to the undrilled group in intelligence, having a mean I.Q. 17.66 points less than that of the undrilled group. . . . Furthermore, it is possible that six weeks is not a long enough period to teach diagraming sufficiently to affect the skills measured in this study. . . . Then too it is impossible to be sure that the tests used for the study were adequate enough to measure the skills upon which this experiment was based.[9]

Greene, under whom Barghahn did his work, described the study as "preliminary,"[10] and it does seem that the study is too weak methodologically to be reliable.

Two years later, in 1942, another of Greene's students, Walter W. Barnett,[11] repeated Barghahn's study but improved the method by lengthening the instructional period from 6 to 12 weeks and by ability-pairing the students in the control and experimental groups. Barnett's conclusions agree with Barghahn's.

[7]Kenneth C. Barghahn, "The Effects of Sentence Diagraming on English Usage and Reading Comprehension" (Master's thesis, University of Iowa, 1940).

[8]*Ibid.,* pp. 35–36.

[9]*Ibid.,* p. 37.

[10]Greene, "Direct versus Formal Methods," *Elementary English,* p. 279.

[11]Walter W. Barnett, "A Study of the Effects of Sentence Diagraming on English Correctness and Silent Reading Ability" (Master's thesis, University of Iowa, 1942).

The case against diagraming rests principally upon an experiment conducted by James R. Stewart, also a student of Greene's. Stewart's purpose was to determine the "effect of sentence diagraming on capitalization, punctuation, usage and sentence structure skills, and grammar information. . . ."[12] Stewart obtained the cooperation of 20 teachers in 20 different schools. Each teacher taught two ninth grade English classes, one serving as a control and the other as an experimental class. In this way, Stewart hoped to control the "teacher variable." By means of a table of random numbers, Stewart identified which of the two classes in each school would be the control group and which the experimental group. Only classes not grouped according to ability (so-called heterogeneously grouped classes) were permitted to participate in order to increase the likelihood of the classes being of approximately equal ability. Pairs of classes were selected only from schools that had taught "little or no diagraming for the past several years."[13] Approximately 1,000 students were involved.

The instructional program for the control group consisted of writing original sentences, rewriting poor sentences, and doing some workbook-type exercises involving, for example, underlining or listing correct answers. All work in diagraming was rigorously excluded. The program for the experimental group, however, consisted of intensive study of sentence structure using only diagraming as the method of instruction. Thus, both groups received instruction in how to write effective sentences, but the control group was taught largely by the "direct" method of writing and revision whereas the experimental group was taught by the "indirect" method of diagraming. It should be noted that the emphasis upon grammar was the same for both groups; instruction in both the control and experimental classes was designed to employ identical grammatical concepts. Grammar, then, was rendered a constant, and the focus of the study remained on diagraming, the instructional variable in the two situations.

In order to regulate as closely as possible the content and methods employed in each of the two classes in the widely separated schools participating in the investigation, Stewart prepared two booklets for distribution to the teachers. The booklet for use in the control or composition classes was 52 pages long and contained 40 lessons of which 7 were review lessons. The last 5 lessons were supplementary and were provided in case some classes completed the work sooner than expected. The idea was to keep the length of time of the experimental teaching the same for all classes—8 weeks—but to permit classes to work within a margin of 5 lessons at the speed most natural to them. The booklet for use in the experimental or diagraming classes was 48 pages long and contained 33 lessons of which 7 were review and 5 supplementary. The material was taken

---

[12] James Reese Stewart, "The Effect of Diagraming on Certain Skills in English Composition," *Journal of Experimental Education,* 11 (September 1942), 2; based on Stewart's Ph.D. dissertation, same title, University of Iowa, 1941.
[13] *Ibid.,* p. 3.

in slightly modified form from a textbook,[14] which Stewart described as "returning frankly to the use of diagraming as a teaching method."[15]

Because Stewart planned to use students' ability to construct sentences as a measure of the effectiveness of sentence diagraming, it was necessary to find a test that would measure students' ability to construct good sentences and would not measure merely student's ability to recognize good sentences. Existing tests being inadequate to his needs, Stewart devised a test of his own.

> In order to insure each pupil's encountering the same situations, ideas were supplied in a series of short simple statements and the pupils asked to organize them into the most interesting and effective sentences possible. Operations necessary to combine these ideas into effective sentences constituted items in the test. . . . The reliability and indications of the validity of the test were secured. Correlations between both teachers' judgments and performance, as measured by the *Willing Composition Scale* and scores on the sentence structure test, indicated that the test possessed a high degree of validity. . . . At the same time, the within-groups correlation technique yielded a reliability coefficient of .78 for the sentence structure test.[16]

At the start of the experiment, each teacher administered the 1940 Iowa Every-Pupil Test in English Correctness (usage, capitalization, and punctuation sections only), a test of grammatical information, and Stewart's new sentence-construction test. Then, for 8 weeks, the teachers followed the courses of study detailed in the booklets Stewart had prepared. At the end of the 8-week instructional period, each teacher gave the 1939 Iowa Every-Pupil Test in English Correctness (usage, capitalization, and punctuation sections only), readministered the grammar information test, gave a second version of Stewart's sentence-construction test, and gave a diagraming test. All tests were scored under Stewart's supervision. Data for all students absent more than 10 times and for students who did not take both the initial and final tests were excluded from the computations. According to Stewart, "the data. . .were analyzed by the methods of analysis of covariance which, by the use of initial measures, secures the same increase in precision as does the matching or equating of groups."[17]

The following are Stewart's conclusions which, he said, "seem defensible":

1. The learning of capitalization, punctuation, and English usage is no more pronounced under an instructional program composed largely of diagraming exercises than it is under a plan emphasizing composition exercises.
2. The diagraming of sentences is no more effective in teaching

---

[14] Grace J. Walker, Nell F. Bartels, and Mary E. Marye, *Adventures Wise and Otherwise* (New York: Harcourt, Brace and Co., 1935).
[15] Stewart, "The Effect of Diagraming on Certain Skills," *Journal of Experimental Education*, p. 3.
[16] *Ibid.*, p. 4.
[17] *Ibid.*, p. 5.

grammar information than is exercise on certain functional aspects
of composition.
3.   Sentence structure is taught as effectively by a composition method
     as by the diagraming of sentences.[18]

To these conclusions Stewart added the following interpretation of the educational implications of his findings:

> In the opinion of the writer, sentence diagraming is a mechanical
> skill that has little or no value in itself. That is, it is of no particular
> worth to a pupil to be able to analyze and graphically portray sentences
> over and above the improvement that it might bring about in the
> ability to write effectively. Furthermore, diagraming does not lend itself
> to correlation with any other subject or project in the program of the
> school.
>   In the light of these observations and of the above stated con-
> clusions, there is considerable doubt concerning the advisability of
> employing sentence diagraming as a method of teaching language
> composition.[19]

Stewart's study has certain limitations which he recognized and enumerated.
First, the role of the teacher in an investigation of this kind is apparently impossible to control completely, and the possibility (though not the probability)
exists that the teacher may consciously or unconsciously permit a preference for
one method to influence his teaching. Second, the conclusions are based on data
derived from tests which are certainly not perfect instruments. Third, although
students did develop skill in diagraming, it may be that an 8-week instructional
period is too brief to permit students to realize the full benefits of diagraming. A
study by R. J. Harris (described in Chapter III) suggests that an experimental
period of two years will reveal changes that are not detectable even after a full
year of instruction.
    In defense of the study it can be said that the first of Stewart's limitations
is inescapable and that he established such methodological safeguards as one can
reasonably hope for. The second limitation is common to all studies using tests.
Perfection in testing, like perfection in other areas of human endeavor, is something to seek to approximate but not something which one seriously expects to
achieve. At least Stewart established the validity and reliability of his chief test.
The third limitation, that is, the brevity of the experimental period, appears to
be the most consequential in the light of Harris' results and in spite of Barnett's
inability to detect differences when he lengthened the experimental period
from 6 to 12 weeks. However, one may wonder whether the potential benefits
of diagraming could possibly be so great as to repay an investment very much
longer than the 8 weeks of concentrated work devoted to it by Stewart's
students.
    As for the strengths of the study, the first is its comfortably large group of

[18]*Ibid.*, p. 7.
[19]*Loc. cit.*

participants. The second is its provision for differences in students' initial ability. The third is its ability to measure students' skill in constructing, not recognizing, good sentences. The fourth is careful preparation of instructional material. The fifth is its provision of safeguards (for example, the use of the diagraming test to check upon "whether the instructional program had been properly carried out" by the cooperating teachers[20]). The sixth, as Greene has pointed out, is its dynamic rather than static experimental technique—by which is meant that weaker studies (like Barghahn's) measure the influence of diagraming skill on previous knowledge of usage and other English skills, whereas stronger studies (like Stewart's) "measure the improvement effect in one field upon skill in another."[21] The seventh is the inclusion of a composition test; this enabled Stewart to avoid exclusive reliance upon short answer tests which may measure mastery of isolated terms of usage but cannot directly measure ability to originate well-constructed sentences.

An investigation by Clair J. Butterfield tested whether the study of grammar improves students' ability to punctuate.[22] It is not, therefore, directly concerned with diagraming, but it does indicate something about diagraming indirectly. Diagraming is a grammatical approach to sentence structure. If the grammatical approach improves students' ability to handle punctuation, perhaps it will—through diagraming—improve sentence structure.

Butterfield's experiment, which resembles Stewart's, was based on 831 students. One group used materials adapted from a textbook which taught punctuation and grammar as though they were interrelated (indirect approach), and a second group, taught by the same teachers, used materials adapted from a textbook which taught punctuation as though it were an instrument of communication, an instrument for the clarification of meaning (direct approach).

The study, written under Greene's supervision, found that direct teaching of punctuation is more effective than indirect teaching of punctuation. In other words, grammar instruction teaches grammar better than it teaches punctuation, and, apparently, the way to learn punctuation is to study it directly as a device for the clarification of meaning. This generalization, of course, does not apply to situations in which the choice of punctuation is determined by arbitrary custom, as would be the case with, for example, the colon following the salutation in a business letter. By raising doubts about the usefulness of one indirect method of improving writing, Butterfield's study also calls into question other indirect methods of improving writing, such as diagraming.[23]

Anthony L. Tovatt's study, which appeared in 1952, seems to have provoked a stronger than usual reaction from the advocates of diagraming. The study has a plausible air, a dramatic quality, and some blunt language; also, it is almost

[20]*Ibid.*, p. 4.
[21]Greene, "Direct versus Formal Methods," *Elementary English*, p. 280.
[22]Clair J. Butterfield, "The Effect of a Knowledge of Certain Grammatical Elements on the Acquisition and Retention of Punctuation Skills" (Ph.D. dissertation, University of Iowa, 1945).
[23]Greene, "Direct versus Formal Methods," *Elementary English*, pp. 282–285.

devoid of statistical paraphernalia. Aside from the question of its merits as a study, it is a fine piece of antidiagraming propaganda.

The basic assumption underlying Tovatt's study is this: "If diagraming is a skill which is taught principally to help us write good sentences, then we, as recipients of such training, must be making use of this skill in our daily living."[24] In order to test this assumption, Tovatt asked 150 people to (1) diagram a given sentence, (2) indicate whether they visualize the parts of the sentence as they would diagram them, and (3) indicate what they think should be stressed in high school instruction in the English language. The group of participants consisted of 50 graduate students in education, 36 "Engineering English" students, and 27 undergraduates in education—all from the University of Colorado—and 37 members of a parent-teacher association. "These individuals were chosen on the assumption that they might have more occasion to 'apply' diagraming skills to written work than would an equal number of auto mechanics, hairdressers, or ranchers."[25]

The findings were described by Tovatt as "startling": (1) 144 persons, 96 percent of the total group, could not diagram the sentence; (2) 6 persons, 4 percent of the total group, were able to diagram, but of these 6 only 2 said they used diagraming when they wrote; (3) 57 persons, 38 percent of the total group, could not diagram but "still maintained that, when they wrote, they visualized sentence elements as they would diagram them"; (4) 87 persons, 58 percent of the total group, could not diagram and claimed not to visualize sentence elements as they would diagram them; and (5) 86 nondiagramers, 57 percent of the total group, believed that teachers should place greater stress on grammar and diagraming.[26]

In the light of the preceding information, Tovatt concluded that the "carry-over value of diagraming beyond the classroom to actual writing situations in life is to be seriously questioned." Tovatt also concluded that—since people who have learned diagraming in school are later unable to diagram but still think they are diagraming when they write and want more diagraming taught—"it is clear that we as English teachers are perpetuating a fiction for a fact."[27]

Throwing down the gauntlet in the peroration is all right if one does not have to throw in the towel during the rebuttal. What does this study show, if anything? The one thing it demonstrates incontrovertibly is that diagraming is not used by the overwhelming majority of people who write English. Admittedly, the study has its loose ends; for example, it does not examine how well its participants can write, and, therefore, the possibility exists that they write poorly and that their poor writing may be owing to their inability to diagram. That the participants do write passably well seems, however, to be a more reasonable

---

[24] Anthony L. Tovatt, "Diagraming: A Sterile Skill," *English Journal*, 41 (February 1952), 91.
[25] *Ibid.*, p. 92.
[26] *Ibid.*, pp. 92–93.
[27] *Ibid.*, p. 93.

assumption in view of their high average educational level. Despite any weaknesses in the study, the conclusion that diagraming is not functional among adults who write seems safe enough.

3. SOME REACTIONS

After the publication of Tovatt's study, two articles appeared which challenged Tovatt's interpretation of his findings. Neither challenged the findings themselves. The writer of one of these articles, Zelma Becker, a high school teacher, argued that diagraming is a visual aid which "presents graphically the grammar we are teaching" and that, anyway, utility is no measure of value: "Do we remember formulas we learned in chemistry. . . ? Could we repeat many of the laws of physics. . . ? Were these courses of no value?"[28]

The writer of the second article, Herman O. Makey, a former high school teacher, also made the point about diagraming being a visual aid.[29] After equating diagraming with sentence analysis, he proceeded to defend analysis "as a necessary step in getting meaning." But Makey's main thrust against Tovatt is that diagraming can help students to improve their perception of the relationship of sentence parts and, having accomplished that, has served its purpose so that it is not likely to be used after one has completed his schooling.[30]

Makey's final point would be a valid theoretical objection if Tovatt's study existed in isolation from the work of Stewart and others. Since this is not the case, the answer to Makey's objection is that Stewart's major study and other lesser studies have all cast doubt upon the efficiency and effectiveness of diagraming as an instructional device in the classroom, and Tovatt's study merely provides substance for similar doubts about the efficacy of diagraming after schooldays are over.

Perhaps the most resourceful defense of diagraming is an article by Don M. Wolfe, a professor of English and author of a textbook on the teaching of English.[31] Wolfe's article disagrees with criticisms of diagraming by J. N. Hook, Lou La Brant, and Dora V. Smith—all of whom have widely published in English education. Wolfe also objects to the studies done by Greene's students, and he endorses Becker's criticism of Tovatt's study.

The heart of Wolfe's defense of diagraming is his contention that researchers erred in examining the effectiveness of diagraming to improve students' language skills. What they should have examined, according to Wolfe, is the extent to which diagraming is useful in teaching grammar, that is, useful in recognizing transitive verbs, prepositions, predicate pronouns, etc. Because Wolfe believes that this is what researchers should have done but failed to do, he concludes that there does not exist "any substantial evidence one way or another on the ef-

[28]Zelma Becker, "Discard Diagraming?" *English Journal,* 41 (June 1952), 319.
[29]Diagraming as a visual aid is discussed in the concluding section of this chapter.
[30]Herman O. Makey, "A Means or an End?" *English Journal,* 42 (March 1953), 159–160.
[31]Don M. Wolfe, *Creative Ways to Teach English* (New York: Odyssey Press, 1958).

fectiveness of diagraming"[32] and that "teachers who prefer diagraming should trust their own classroom experience, speaking their minds and going their way undeterred by the present casual judgments of some educational theoreticians."[33]

In an incidental way, the investigations Wolfe criticizes actually did what he asserts they failed to do. They showed that the students who studied diagraming improved their ability to diagram. Since it is impossible to improve one's skill in diagraming without improving one's ability to classify words grammatically, it is certain that the students learned some grammar. Nevertheless, added grammatical knowledge did not seem to help them to outperform the nondiagramers on tests of language skill.

However, Wolfe is accurate in saying that the studies were not specifically designed to test improvement in grammar. But why the studies should test the relationship between diagraming and grammar, as Wolfe would prefer, and not test the relationship between diagraming and ability to use the language is not explained. Clearly, the researchers were interested in identifying the immediately practical value which diagraming might have. Even if diagraming had been shown to improve students' grasp of grammar, it would still be necessary to probe further to discover whether grammar improves students' use of language. Actually, evidence on this point of the influence of grammar on use had been in existence before any investigation of diagraming had begun, and this evidence indicates that a strictly grammatical approach to students' language difficulties is not fruitful in comparison with other methods.[34]

Abraham Bernstein, like Wolfe, is the author of an English methods textbook which recommends diagraming. Bernstein's sprightly discussion of diagraming contains a few very important concessions. The first is that a student "cannot diagram without prior sentence sense; all the diagraming in the world will not give sentence sense." The second is that diagraming "structures the orthodox. Where unorthodoxy sneaks in, diagraming breaks down." The third is that diagraming "works best with the student who has already seen grammatical light."[35] These concessions are important because they sharply restrict the use of diagraming to a fraction of the school population and to a segment of the language which is "orthodox" in that it contains no diagram-fracturing idioms or other locutions which do not readily fit the diagrammatic scheme. If these concessions were to be taken seriously, there would be precious little opportunity to use diagraming, even in classrooms presided over by teachers strongly committed to it.

[32]Don M. Wolfe, "Diagraming: Trust Your Experience, Not Theories," *Clearing House*, 27 (February 1953), 349.

[33]*Ibid.*, p. 353.

[34]See especially Ellen Frogner, "Grammar Approach Versus Thought Approach in Teaching Sentence Structure," *English Journal*, 28 (September 1939), 518–526.

[35]Abraham Bernstein, *Teaching English in High School* (New York: Random House, 1961), pp. 56–57.

Bernstein's case for whatever diagraming remains rests on his contention that "nothing visualizes sentence sense like diagraming,"[36] that studies critical of diagraming are inadequate, that no study has shown that diagraming and grammar study—not usage study—"fail to contribute to sentence sense and expressional improvement," that diagraming "widens our perceptions of language," and that "Grammar study *does* transfer with the better students."[37] In addition to the apparent contradiction over whether diagraming imparts "sentence sense," it would seem that most of these points are articles of faith rather than arguments based on evidence. True, diagraming "visualizes" the sentence. But how accurate or valuable is a visual representation that violates the linear nature of all language, ignores context, and cannot accommodate "unorthodox" sentences? Granted, for the sake of discussion, that grammar does transfer with the better students. But is it not more important to know how much transfer occurs and whether grammar is more transferable than something else? Rather than discuss the charge that research related to diagraming is inadequate, one may ask whether Bernstein has better evidence for his contentions. The only relevant study he cites is by Ingrid M. Strom who found a significant correlation between instruction in grammar and improvement in reading. But Strom cautioned that her results might be owing to the special nature of the instruction in grammar,[38] and, what is more, Strom is very skeptical, judging from her recent writings, about the utility of "indirect methods," including diagraming. In reviewing research for 1959-1960, Strom made the following comment about one of her own studies:

> Outlining the significant studies in grammar and usage carried out during the last fifty years, Strom[39] . . .summarized the cumulative results with the statement that the evidence from research shows clearly and overwhelmingly that direct methods of instruction, focusing on writing activities and the structuring of ideas, are more efficient in teaching sentence structure, usage, punctuation, and other related factors than are such methods as nomenclature, drill, diagraming, and rote memorization of rules.[40]

Strom repeated these comments in her review of research for the following year, 1960-1961.[41] It looks very much as though Bernstein's authority is not on his side.

It is not possible to leave the subject of research in diagraming without com-

[36] *Loc. cit.*

[37] *Ibid.*, pp. 75-76.

[38] Ingrid M. Strom, "Does Knowledge of Grammar Improve Reading?" *English Journal*, 45 (March 1956), 133.

[39] Ingrid M. Strom, "Do Grammar Drills Help Writing Skills?" *NEA Journal*, 49 (December 1960); *Research in Grammar and Usage and Its Implications for Teaching Writing, Bulletin of the School of Education of Indiana University*, 36, 5 (September 1960).

[40] Ingrid M. Strom, "Summary of Investigations Relating to the English Language Arts in Secondary Education: 1959-1960," *English Journal*, 50 (February 1961), 112-113.

[41] Ingrid M. Strom, "Summary of Investigations Relating to the English Language Arts in Secondary Education: 1960-1961," *English Journal*, 51 (February 1962), 123.

menting upon the nature of many of the articles on diagraming in the professional journals. It is easy to see how Betty MacMillan, writing in 1932, could urge teachers to diagram and could report with engaging optimism that in her classes diagraming "creates interest."[42] It is possible to understand how Everett Gillis, writing in 1941, could recommend diagraming even though his own schoolboy experiences with it were, he admits, "painful."[43] But it is harder to find a justification for the following comment, published in 1953, by two teachers at an Arkansas college:

> Being fully aware of the danger of a sentence diagram as an end in itself, we nevertheless are convinced that the diagram presents to the student the clearest picture of the syntactical structure of a sentence. The diagram is simply and ultimately a visual aid. The Reed and Kellogg system is employed because of its simplicity. . . .[44]

No rational basis for their support of diagraming is supplied by the Sisters of Notre Dame (of Notre Dame Academy in Worcester, Massachusetts), writing in 1957.[45] Nor does Thomas D. Edwards, writing in 1958, do more than assume the effectiveness of diagraming as an instructional device.[46] Also writing in 1958, Katherine B. Peavy conceded that diagraming can be "very dull"; nevertheless she convinced herself that "A little dramatization can work wonders" in making diagraming interesting.[47] The message implicit in this review of the professional literature is that the articles defending diagraming are likely to consist of experimentally unsubstantiated opinions or sincere but subjective accounts of supposedly successful lessons; and the reader, who knows his professional facts of life, would be merely prudent if he took these articles with a large grain of salt and gave his attention instead to any others he can find which argue from verifiable premises.

A more substantial contribution is Edward L. Anderson's article which was written for the Current English Committee of the National Council of Teachers of English and published in the Current English Forum section of *Elementary English*. Anderson's article draws on his familiarity with the development and psychology of language. Unfortunately, it is not documented, but at least it is liberally supplied with illustrations. Anderson's criticisms of diagraming are (1) "what appear to be sentences of quite clear and relatively simple meaning

[42] Betty MacMillan, "The Value of Diagrams in Teaching Grammar," *Volta Review,* 34 (June 1932), 277–278.
[43] Everett Gillis, "Fine Art of Diagraming," *Texas Outlook,* 25 (September 1941), 47–48.
[44] Ralph Behrens and Eugene Nolte, "Linguistics and the Sentence Diagram," *College English,* 15 (November 1953), 126.
[45] Sisters of Notre Dame, "Grammatical Analysis," *Catholic School Journal,* 57 (November 1957), 310.
[46] Thomas D. Edwards, "The Grammatical Approach," *School and Community,* 44 (April 1958), 20–21.
[47] Katherine B. Peavy, "Shall We Teach Diagraming?" *The Instructor,* 67 (February 1958), 108.

often prove to convey decidedly different meaning in different situations"; such a sentence as *He is a lady-killer* would diagram the same way regardless of the intended meaning; however, "what is more important about such a sentence—a blackboard picture of its separate words, or the possible meanings it can express?" (2) "sentences whose 'syntax' may appear very simple are sometimes analyzable in different ways, depending on what a speaker or writer intends and on what a listener or reader understands to be meant"; diagraming ignores the meaning which only context can supply; (3) "sentences of clearly different meaning and different word order may result in identical diagrams"; thus diagraming is an exercise in grammatical classification which may or may not in a given sentence be related to the meaning which the sentence was written in the first place to express; and (4) "diagraming is not consistent with the nature of language. We do not hear sentences in separate compartments, nor do we see them on slanting lines. . . . We hear our language in a time sequence, marked by variations in pitch, tone, and rhythm. We do not, in ordinary reading, see sentences arranged in these peculiar ways. It would seem better to learn to analyze *what is important to analyze* in sentences by examining them as they come to us by ear or by eye."[48]

4. IS DIAGRAMING A VISUAL AID?

A common defense of diagraming is that it is a visual aid. Behrens and Nolte, Gillis, MacMillan, Becker, Makey, Bernstein, Wolfe (all previously cited), and many others in and out of print have defended diagraming in whole or part on the grounds that it visualizes or, to use the most common expression, is a visual aid. There is no doubt about its being visual, but whether it is an aid is precisely the question at issue. To call diagraming a visual aid is to beg the question, hardly a sporting thing to do. Proponents of diagraming would be more accurate if they spoke of it as a visual device purporting to represent sentence structure and purporting to help the student to understand sentence structure and to use it more expertly. Expressed in such precise language, the allegation does not sound very strong.

Elementary logic and tautology aside, there are reasons and some further evidence for doubting the worth of diagraming as a visual aid. If the studies by Stewart and others show anything, they show that diagraming is not much of an aid, visual or any other kind. But, forsaking this point as well, one can still refer to the investigations of children's ability to read diagrams.

It so happens that there are very few studies dealing with children's ability to read diagrams, and there are no studies at all dealing with children's ability to read sentence diagrams. In fact, the confident statements about diagrams being a visual aid are themselves evidence of how poorly informed people can be about how little they know.

[48]Edward L. Anderson, "Diagramming Sentences," *Elementary English,* 30 (February 1953), 116-117.

In six studies reported in four articles, Morton S. Malter[49] found that the
"proper interpretation of conventionalized diagrammatic symbols is an acquired
skill" and that "children experience difficulty in reading diagrams."[50] He also
found that children have difficulty interpreting straight lines such as those "relating members of families."[51] Since this is similar to the way straight lines are
used in sentence diagrams, it is reasonable to suppose that Malter's finding would
have some relevancy to the present question. Another interesting finding is that
children are more successful at interpreting arrows and circles, which are symbols
typically employed in so-called informal sentence diagrams.[52] Finally, Malter's
observation that "sophisticated adults" often overlook the fact that "diagrams
consist of abstract symbols" should be carefully considered by symbol-familiar,
sophisticated teachers whose long acquaintance with sentence diagrams has
helped to convince them of its powers as a visual aid.[53]

One limitation of the Malter studies is that they do not specifically deal with
sentence diagrams, and another is that they include only students in Grades IV
to VIII. However, the grade limitation at least allows an application to most
and, possibly, all of junior high school.

Two observations about sentence diagraming come to mind in connection
with Malter's studies. First, if understanding diagrams and diagrammatic symbols
is a learned and not very easy accomplishment, then what is the wisdom of
asking students to learn a difficult symbolic system (diagraming) in order to
learn another difficult symbolic system (English)? Besides, sentence diagraming is the only instructional device which teachers insist that students master.
Second, sentence diagraming is unlike any of Malter's diagrams in that it does
not actually reproduce pictorially or representationally the matter under consideration but, rather, distorts the "picture" by giving grammatical relationships
priority over meaning so that it is difficult, sometimes impossible, to read the
original sentence from the diagram.

The only diagram which resembles the sentence diagram is the "exploded
diagram" which increases the distance between the parts in order to show their
interrelationships and the order in which they can be reassembled. Sentence
diagrams also increase the distance between the parts, or words, but they show
only grammatical patterns of modification which need not correspond to word

[49]Morton S. Malter, "The Ability of Children to Read Cross-Sections," *Journal of
Educational Psychology*, 38 (March 1947), 157-166; "The Ability of Children to Read a
Process-Diagram," *Journal of Educational Psychology*, 38 (May 1947), 290-298; "The
Ability of Children to Read Conventionalized Diagrammatic Symbols," *Journal of Educa-
tional Psychology*, 39 (January 1948), 27-34; "Children's Ability to Read Diagrammatic
Materials," *Elementary School Journal*, 49 (September 1948), 98-102.
[50]Malter, "Children's Ability to Read Diagrammatic Materials," *Elementary School
Journal*, p. 102.
[51]Malter, "Ability of Children to Read Conventionalized Diagrammatic Symbols,"
Elementary School Journal, p. 34.
[52]*Loc. cit.*
[53]*Loc. cit.*

order. Since the principal mechanism for conveying meaning in English is word order, it must follow that sentence diagrams have an inherent weakness.

5. WHAT ABOUT LINGUISTIC DIAGRAMS?

To this point the discussion has been confined to what is called the formal or traditional or Reed and Kellogg system of sentence diagraming.[54] It is these diagrams that have become familiar to generations of school children. These, also, are the diagrams which Stewart and others have studied.

The coming of structural linguistics and the subsequent appearance of other linguistic systems has produced a growing number of new ways to diagram.[55] Supporters of each system have freely urged the superiority of their system as a fuller and more accurate picture of the dynamics of the language. Although specialists are inclined to agree that linguistic grammars are superior to traditional grammar in that they provide a more satisfactory and empirically a more defensible description of the language, they do not agree as to which of the several linguistic grammars is the most satisfactory. Another disagreement concerns whether any of the "new grammars" will provide students with a better means for learning to use the language. Also, there is disagreement over whether student writers are helped any more by the "new diagrams" than they have been helped by the "old diagrams." Experimental evidence on this point is lacking.

The controversy over the worth of diagrams new and old is interesting and may, finally, be valuable if it produces able research. Meanwhile, it may be worth mentioning a few writers whose points of view are representative.

Don L. F. Nilsen attacked traditional diagraming for being inadequate in seven language situations. He urged that transformational grammar can do a better job, and he concluded that transformational grammar should become the "new model" since traditional diagraming has failed to produce "spectacular improvement in language skills" even though it has been a "basic part of our curriculum for a considerable length of time."[56] The one study which Nilsen cited to support his confidence in generative-transformational grammar is by Frank J. Zidonis (and is discussed in Chapter III, section 3).

H. A. Gleason, unlike Nilson, maintained that Reed-Kellogg (traditional) diagraming has been too severely criticized,[57] but he acknowledged that it has shortcomings.[58] Especially pertinent is Gleason's assertion that "Much of the attack and defense" of traditional diagraming "has been based on ignorance. . . .

[54] Alonzo Reed and Brainerd Kellogg, *Higher Lessons in English* (New York: Maynard, Merrill and Company, 1877). Editions also appeared in 1885, 1896, and 1906.

[55] Linguistics and the teaching of writing is discussed in Chapter III, section 3. Some illustrations of diagrams employed by linguists may be found in H. A. Gleason, Jr., *Linguistics and English Grammar* (New York: Holt, Rinehart and Winston, Inc., 1965), pp. 151 ff.

[56] Don L. F. Nilsen, "New Diagrams for Old," *English Record,* 16 (October 1965), 36.

[57] Gleason, *Linguistics and English Grammar,* p. 143.

[58] *Ibid.,* p. 151n.

The major difficulty. . .has been prevailingly bad teaching."[59] The assumption implicit in Gleason's comment is that traditional diagraming or any valid diagrammatic approach will serve as an aid to student writers if the diagrammatic system is itself well taught. Gleason did not recommend that linguistics be added to the curriculum, but he did urge that "certain basic notions" drawn from linguistics should influence instruction in the future.[60] Gleason alluded to his own successful attempts to teach by using techniques associated with linguistic analysis,[61] but neither in Gleason's book nor elsewhere is there, as yet, any verifiable evidence that a linguistic diagram is a superior way to improve students' handling of the language.

A plague on both your houses is Neil Postman's position with respect to diagrams old and diagrams new. To Postman, both old and new systems are "irrelevant" to whatever is important about language study. According to Postman, the "primary goal in language teaching is to help students increase their competence to use and understand language, especially those styles, varieties, and functions of language that most intimately affect their lives."[62] In his sharply worded article, Postman deplored any language study in the schools which is essentially concerned with categorizing or labeling words. Postman's "alternative to linguistics as grammar" is *"linguistics as the rigorous study of language situations"* (Postman's italics). A language situation is "any human event in which language is used to share meaning. A poem. . .joke. . .expression of condolence. . .editorial. . .advertisement. . .song."[63] Unlike many other commentators on the diagraming issue, Postman rested his argument on an explicitly stated philosophy of what language instruction in the present-day world should strive to achieve. He sees diagraming as a purely grammatical instrument for the clarification of syntax which exists apart from meaning and apart from the social and human context in which language is used. From this point of view, diagraming and linguistics-as-grammar are simply bad education. How accurate the linguistic grammar happens to be is irrelevant. How well diagraming helps students to manipulate structure outside the language situation or communication process is irrelevant, that is, irrelevant to the proper aims of language instruction as Postman sees them. Is the grammatical study of language which underlies the use of diagrams able to provide students with what they need to know amid the "troubles, controversies, and disasters that define what we call contemporary life"?[64] This question challenges much of current practice. To the extent that it deals with values and purposes, it cannot be answered by controlled experiments.

[59]*Ibid.*, p. 143.
[60]*Ibid.*, p. 484n.
[61]*Ibid.*, p. 485n.
[62]Neil Postman, "Linguistics and the Pursuit of Relevance," *Education Synopsis,* 12 (Winter 1966–1967), 27.
[63]*Loc. cit.*
[64]*Ibid.*, p. 29.

If it is not possible to dismiss the whole issue, as Postman has done, then it is necessary to await experiments which, hopefully, will reveal precisely what practical benefits the new diagraming can bestow upon students. Experiments with traditional diagraming, like Stewart's, will not suffice because the claim will quickly be made, rightly or wrongly, that traditional diagraming failed because its substratum of Latinate grammar is an inadequate description of English. Since there is no ready way to test this contention, it will be necessary to conduct new experiments to determine the instructional value of the new diagrams.

At this moment, it would seem that the status of the new diagrams is similar to the camel's whose nose has just parted the tent flap. Two well-known scholars have recently published a freshman handbook in which tree diagrams are included but relegated to a 25-page appendix. They do not openly claim that tree diagrams will help students to write; instead, they assert that diagraming is a "useful method of clarifying relationships of the various elements of a sentence. . . ."[65] But freshman handbooks are universally expected to serve the practical purpose of helping students to improve their writing. This handbook, by including diagraming, implies that diagraming will provide some measure of practical assistance. The need is clear for research which will help the authors to decide whether to excise the appendix or to restore its contents to full-fledged inclusion in the main portion of the book.

6. SUMMARY AND CONCLUSION

a) The reasons for changes in the popularity of formal diagraming are unknown. Previously a feature of Latin instruction, diagraming became a part of English instruction when English supplanted Latin in the schools. It retained its popularity until the mid 1920's when it declined sharply. By the mid 1930's, diagraming began to revive and now is popular once again.

b) Experimental investigation of the worth of diagraming began as late as 1940 with a "preliminary" experiment by Barghahn. Barnett, in 1942, repeated the study with certain improvements in method. The largest and methodologically most advanced study of diagraming was completed by Stewart in 1941. All three of these studies agree that, in Stewart's words, "diagraming is no more effective" in teaching language skills than other methods of instruction. In 1945, Butterfield examined direct and indirect methods of teaching punctuation and found that direct methods are more effective, thereby raising doubts about indirect methods such as diagraming. Tovatt, in 1952, found that diagraming is not used by the overwhelming majority of people when they write and that 38 percent of the participants not only could not diagram but claimed nevertheless that when they write they visualize their sentences as they would diagram them.

[65] Albert H. Marckwardt and Frederic G. Cassidy, *Scribner Handbook of English* (4th ed.; New York: Charles Scribner's Sons, 1967), pp. 481-506.

c) The reaction to these investigations of diagraming is mixed. Comments in the professional journals are, with some exceptions, likely to be favorable to diagraming and may or may not give evidence of the writer's awareness that experimental studies exist. Although some methods textbooks urge the use of diagraming, most either omit any reference to it or specifically reject it. Among the better-known scholars in English education, the strong inclination is to reject diagraming.

d) A common defense of diagraming is that it is a visual aid. Granted that it is visual, is it an aid? Experiments by Stewart and others suggest a negative answer. Six experiments by Malter dealing with children's ability to read conventionalized diagrammatic symbols suggest that understanding diagrams and diagrammatic symbols is a learned and difficult skill.

e) The research described has dealt only with diagrams known variously as the formal or traditional or Reed-Kellogg type. Other systems of diagraming devised in recent years by linguists have not, as yet, been tested experimentally. Although their value as visual representations of the so-called new grammars is not in question, it remains to be determined whether they are capable of helping students to increase their ability to use the language.

· · · · ·

It is better not to teach traditional diagraming. This conclusion is less sweeping than it may appear because it does not deny that diagraming has some utility. Not one of the experimental studies critical of diagraming claims that diagraming fails to teach anything. Instead, the studies conclude that diagraming is not a superior method of instruction (see, for example, Stewart's conclusions quoted earlier). The reason, then, for the strong opposition of Stewart and others to diagraming is that it imposes unnecessary, time-consuming, and effort-consuming tasks without conferring any special instructional advantages. Although there are many ways to skin a cat, the best way will do the job at least as neatly as any other and in the shortest time. If, then, efficiency is the criterion, diagraming does not work well enough to justify all the fuss and bother. Recommending diagraming is like advising someone to find the number of cows in a field by counting legs and dividing by four. Furthermore, diagraming perpetuates a distorted and incomplete picture of English structure because of its dependence upon Latinate grammar. In short, it is better not to teach diagraming.

Chapter V

The Promise and the Fulfillment

Back in 1934, W. S. Guiler and Emmett A. Betts observed what they called the "dearth of valid research in English teaching."[1] Similar views have been expressed before and since. For example, in 1962, Ingrid Strom noted the "dearth of rigorously controlled experimental studies."[2] It would be easy to build a plausible case for the failure of scientific experimental investigation in the field of English education and to find adherents to an antiresearch orthodoxy. Jean Hagstrum stopped just short of indicting the experimental method in his review of Braddock's *Research in Written Composition*,[3] but William R. Rosegrant, in his review of Braddock's book, was frankly pessimistic about the value of both the research of the past and the research of the future.[4] David H. Russell, writing in 1963 as president of the National Council of Teachers of English, noted the existence of one group in NCTE which opposes research and another which simply ignores research.[5]

What is interesting about the opponents and ignorers of research is not that they exist, for they have always existed, but that they have become a cause for concern. In the past, educational research was carried on almost exclusively by resolute individuals, some of whom were established scholars and many of whom were doctoral candidates. The large group in the profession, the teachers, were uninvolved, uninformed, and seemingly uninterested in the products of research or in the very idea of research. That this situation has begun to change is one of the most encouraging and salutary events to occur in many decades.

There are other hopeful signs. At last there is money available for research in the teaching of English. To those who remember well the long austerity, the present availability of funds for research in English must almost seem like a sign that the millennium is at hand. Another encouraging development is the attention which the organized profession, largely the NCTE, is giving to the problems

---

[1] Walter Scribner Guiler and Emmett Albert Betts, "A Critical Summary of Selective Research," *Elementary English Review,* 11 (March 1934), 77.

[2] Ingrid M. Strom, "Summary of Investigations Relating to the Language Arts in Secondary Education: 1960-1961," *English Journal,* 51 (February 1962), 123.

[3] Jean H. Hagstrum, "Research in Written Composition," *College English,* 25 (October 1964), 53.

[4] William R. Rosegrant, "Scientific Research Can Become Respectable?" *College Composition and Communication,* 15 (October 1964), 170.

[5] David H. Russell, "NCTE Counciletter," *English Journal,* 24 (November 1963), 639.

involved in conducting research. These problems are many, but the most important are identifying key subjects for inquiry, refining techniques for inquiry, and informing would-be researchers about how best to investigate what. Underlying all is the problem of nurturing a respect for what research can reveal and a willingness to apply research results. This matter deserves some further comment.

In general, the quality of research in the teaching of English has been, at best, spotty. Too often the research has not deserved to shape classroom practices, but, then, neither has it deserved the indifferent reception it has been accorded. When one recalls the circumstances under which the research of the past was conducted—the poverty and lack of coordination of effort—it actually seems surprising that the research is as good as it is.

It is ironic that educational research should have suffered deprecation and neglect during the very period when research in other fields enjoyed the highest regard. To most people, scientific research means research in the biological and physical sciences. The fruitfulness of research in these fields is attested to by a long list of major and minor achievements which have determined the character of much of life in our time. That the physical and biological sciences have been both life-giving and death-dealing does not in any way diminish the respect in which they are held. Even nuclear physics, which is as theoretical a field as any, has achieved an explosion to which we dare not close our ears. The reverberations proclaim, among other things, that scientific research works. No equivalent reverberations proclaim the efficacy of research in education. It is small wonder, then, that the customary attitude of people in and out of the PTA toward scientific educational research is take-it-or-leave-it.

Yet it is a distortion to compare the products of educational research with the achievement in the physical and biological sciences. From the start, the methods of science have been most successful in providing an understanding of nature and, particularly, in affording means to manipulate nature. The same techniques applied to the so-called behavioral sciences (of which education is one) have been less fruitful. Why?

Thales, according to Diogenes Laertius, thought that the most difficult of all tasks is to know oneself. According to Pope's well-known line, the proper study of mankind is man. Together these observations (the second an extension of the first) comprise a satisfactory definition of what the behavioral sciences seek to accomplish. The magnitude of the job is awesome. There have been many handicaps.

One of the handicaps to educational research is its newness. Educational research is a mere infant which, unlike research in chemistry, has not had time to live through its phlogiston period and to hammer out its own precepts and methods on the hard pragmatic anvil. Everything should be done to speed the process, but, obviously, more time will have to pass before education as a field of inquiry achieves maturity.

Perhaps the greatest handicap to educational research is that laboratory conditions are immensely hard to achieve. Under the best of circumstances it would be difficult to isolate the variables in human behavior and to identify the factors that influence behavior. But actual circumstances are not the best and cannot be the best until better ways can be found to create an experimental environment. Furthermore, it is clear that morality imposes certain limits upon what can be attempted. A class of students cannot be treated like a swarm of fruit flies. Moral limitations do not operate so strongly in research in other fields—not because the researchers are unconcerned with morality but because the moral issues are either fewer or different. The man who sends a cloud chamber aloft to obtain data about cosmic rays need not trouble himself with questions of the rightness or wrongness of what he is doing. If he sees any issue at all, it is likely to concern the uses to which his knowledge, once discovered, is put.

Nowadays, few people seem to worry about the legitimacy of scientific inquiry, the organized mining of nature's secrets. Hawthorne's point of view seems eccentric; how can the quest for knowledge be a punishable sin? In contrast, the contemporary fashion seems to be to fear ignorance and to trust to methods which have had some success in discovering what works. But there are terrors on both sides. In seeking to avoid the darkness are we to be blinded by the light?

There is nothing to return to, only the conditions that bred Bedlam and bubonic plague. All one can do is to proceed along the path already taken and to try to step more cautiously and wisely. The urgent need is for improved techniques for educational research and for all other behavioral investigations. The urgent need, too, is for a resurgence of humanistic values without which all efforts must be merely mechanical and of steadily diminishing worth.

If experimental research in education has never been given a fair shake, we have only ourselves to blame. It would be supremely illogical to conclude that what has not been performed cannot be performed or that what has seldom been performed cannot be performed more often. It is equally illogical to conclude that what has not been performed will be performed. The wise response to the present situation is to muster talent, determination, and dollars as has never been done before. For the sake of a better education and the better world to which it can minister, it is too soon to abandon as an hypothesis what Emerson knew in his heart—that intellect annuls Fate.

Bibliography

Abbott, Edwina E. "On the Analysis of the Memory Consciousness in Orthography," *Psychological Monographs,* 11 (November 1909), 127-158.

Abernethy, Ethel M. "Photographic Records of Eye Movements in Studying Spelling," *Journal of Educational Psychology,* 20 (December 1929), 695-701.

Allen, Harold B. "From Prairies to Mountains," *College English,* 26 (January 1965), 260-266.

_____. *Language, Linguistics, and School Programs.* Proceedings of the Spring Institutes, 1963, of the NCTE. Champaign, Ill.: National Council of Teachers of English, 1964. O.P.

Allen, L. H. *Some Errors in Spelling Made in Leaving Certificate Examination of 1917.* Sydney: New South Wales Teachers College, 1919.

Alshouse, H. S. "Errors in English That Survive College Training," *Pennsylvania School Journal,* 79 (February 1931), 474.

American Classical League. *The Classical Investigation, Part I, General Report.* Abridged Edition. New York: New York University, 1924.

Andersen, W. N. "Determination of a Spelling Vocabulary Based upon Written Correspondence," *University of Iowa Studies in Education,* 2, 1 (1921), 1-66.

Anderson, Edward L. "Diagraming Sentences," *Elementary English,* 30 (February 1953), 116-118.

Archer, Clifford P. "Shall We Teach Spelling by Rule?" *Elementary English Review,* 7 (March 1930), 61-63.

_____. "Transfer of Training in Spelling," *University of Iowa Studies in Education,* 5, 5 (1930), 1-63.

Arnold, Dwight L. "Spelling Lessons and Ability to Spell," *Elementary School Journal,* 42 (September 1941), 35-40.

Arnold, Lois. "Writer's Cramp and Eyestrain—Are They Paying Off?" *English Journal,* 53 (January 1964), 10-15.

Ash, I. O. "An Experimental Evaluation of the Stylistic Approach in Teaching Written Composition in the Junior High School," *Journal of Experimental Education,* 4 (September 1935), 54-62.

Asker, William. "Does Knowledge of Formal Grammar Function?" *School and Society,* 17 (January 27, 1923), 109-111.

Ayer, Fred C. "An Evaluation of High-School Spelling," *School Review,* 59 (April 1951), 233-236.

Ayres, L. P. *The Spelling Vocabularies of Personal and Business Letters.* New York: Russell Sage Foundation, 1913.

Baker, William D. "The Swimming Coach," *English Journal,* 56 (January 1957), 40-41.

Barghahn, Kenneth C. "The Effects of Sentence Diagraming on English Usage and Reading Comprehension." Master's thesis, University of Iowa, 1940.

Barnett, Walter B. "A Study of the Effects of Sentence Diagraming on English Correctness and Silent Reading Ability." Master's thesis, University of Iowa, 1942.

Barnhart, Clarence L. "General Introduction," *American College Dictionary.* New York: Random House, Inc., 1951.

Beatty, Dorothy M. "A Comparison of Two Methods of Teaching Spelling." Ph.D. dissertation, State University of Iowa, 1955; in *Dissertation Abstracts,* 15, 11 (November 1955), 2110–2111.

Becker, Zelma. "Discard Diagraming?" *English Journal,* 41 (June 1952), 319-320.

Behrens, Ralph, and Eugene Nolte. "Linguistics and the Sentence Diagram," *College English,* 15 (November 1953), 126-127.

Benfer, Mabel C. "Sentence Sense in Relation to Subject and Predicate." Master's thesis, State University of Iowa, 1935.

Bernstein, Abraham. *Teaching English in High School.* New York: Random House, Inc., 1961.

Betts, Emmett A. *Second Spelling Vocabulary Study.* New York: American Book Company, 1949.

————. *Spelling Vocabulary Study.* New York: American Book Company, 1940.

Blake, Robert W. "Linguistics and Punctuation," *English Record,* 15 (October 1964), 9-13.

Boraas, Julius. "Formal English Grammar and the Practical Mastery of English." Ph.D. dissertation, University of Minnesota, 1917.

Braddock, Richard, Richard Lloyd-Jones, and Lowell Schoer. *Research in Written Composition.* Champaign, Ill.: National Council of Teachers of English, 1963.

Bradford, Leland P. "Study of Certain Factors Affecting English Usage," *Journal of Educational Research,* 35 (October 1941), 109-118.

Breed, Frederick S. *How to Teach Spelling.* Dansville, N. Y.: F. A. Owen Publishing Company, 1930.

Briggs, Thomas H. "Formal English Grammar as a Discipline," *Teachers College Record,* 14 (September 1913), 1-93.

Brittain, Frances, and James A. Fitzgerald. "The Vocabulary and Spelling Errors of Second-Grade Children's Themes," *Elementary English Review,* 19 (February 1942), 43-50.

Brown, Corinne B. "Teaching Spelling with a Tachistoscope," *English Journal,* 40 (February 1951), 104-105.

Browning, Julia M. "Writing Vocabularies: A Study of Significant New Words in the United States Since 1926." Master's thesis, University of Texas, 1957.

Brueckner, Leo J. "Language: The Development of Ability in Oral and Written Composition," *Thirty-eighth Yearbook, Part I.* National Society for the Study of Education. Bloomington, Ill.: Public School Publishing Company, 1939.

Bryan, Fred E. "How Large Are Children's Vocabularies?" *Elementary School Journal,* 54 (December 1953), 210-216.

Buckingham, B. R., and E. W. Dolch. *A Combined Word List.* Boston: Ginn and Company, 1936.

Bunyan, M. F. "Classical Allusions in the English Reading of High School Pupils." Master's thesis, University of Wisconsin, 1922.

Burton, Dwight L., and Lois V. Arnold. *Effects of Frequency of Writing and Intensity of Evaluation upon High School Students' Performance in Written Composition.* United States Office of Education Cooperative Research Project No. 1523. Tallahassee: Florida State University, 1963.

Buswell, Guy T. *Fundamental Reading Habits: A Study of Their Development.* Supplementary Educational Monographs, No. 21. Chicago: University of Chicago Press, 1922.

Butler, David C. "Frequencies of Errors in Freshman Themes," *English Journal,* 25 (January 1936), 57-60.

Butterfield, Clair J. "The Effect of a Knowledge of Certain Grammatical Elements on the Acquisition and Retention of Punctuation Skills." Ph.D. dissertation, University of Iowa, 1945.

Buxton, Earl W. "An Experiment to Test the Effects of Writing Frequency and Guided Practice upon Students' Skill in Written Expression." Ph.D. dissertation, Stanford University, 1958; in *Dissertation Abstracts,* 19, 4 (October 1958), 709.

Calhoun, Robert T. "A Comparison of a Typical and an Intensive Method of Teaching Spelling," *Elementary School Journal,* 55 (November 1954), 154-157.

Carr, W. L. "First-Year Latin and Growth in English Vocabulary," *School and Society,* 14 (September 17, 1921), 192-198.

Carroll, Herbert A. *Generalization of Bright and Dull Children.* New York: Bureau of Publications, Teachers College, Columbia University, 1930.

Carroll, J. B. "Knowledge of English Roots and Affixes as Related to Vocabulary and Latin Study," *Journal of Educational Research,* 34 (October 1940), 102-111.

Cason, Eloise B. *Mechanical Methods for Increasing the Speed of Reading.*

New York: Bureau of Publications, Teachers College, Columbia University, 1943.

Catherwood, Catherine. "A Study of Relationships between a Knowledge of Rules and Ability to Correct Grammatical Errors and between Identification of Sentences and Knowledge of Subject and Predicate." Master's thesis, University of Minnesota, 1932.

Chancellor, W. E. "Spelling: 1000 Words," *Journal of Education* (Boston), 71 (May 5, 12, 19, 26, June 2, 1910), 488–489, 517, 522, 545–546, 573, 578, 607–608.

Chase, W. Linwood. "Subject Preferences of Fifth-grade Children," *Elementary School Journal,* 50 (December 1949), 204-211.

Christiansen, Mark A. "Tripling Writing and Omitting Readings in Freshman English: An Experiment," *College Composition and Communication,* 16 (May 1965), 122-124.

Clark, Grace W. "The Relative Ability of Latin and Non-Latin Pupils to Explain Classical References." Master's thesis, State University of Iowa, 1923.

Clark, J. D. "A Four-Year Study of Freshman English," *English Journal,* 24 (May 1935), 403-410.

Clarke, W. F. "Writing Vocabularies," *Elementary School Journal,* 21 (January 1921), 349-351.

Cole, L. E. "Latin as a Preparation for French and Spanish," *School and Society,* 19 (May 1924), 618-622.

Cook, Desmond L. "The Hawthorne Effect in Educational Research," *Phi Delta Kappan,* 44 (December 1962), 116-122.

Cook, W. A., and M. V. O'Shea. *The Child and His Spelling.* Indianapolis, Ind.: Bobbs-Merrill Company, Inc., 1914.

Cornman, Oliver P. *Spelling in the Elementary School.* Boston: Ginn and Company, 1902.

Coxe, Warren W. "The Influence of Latin on the Spelling of English Words." Ph.D. dissertation, Ohio State University, 1923.

Crawford, C. C., and Madie M. Royer. "Oral Drill versus Grammar Study," *Elementary School Journal,* 36 (October 1935), 116-119.

Cutright, Prudence. "A Comparison of Methods of Securing Correct Language Usage," *Elementary School Journal,* 34 (May 1934), 681-690.

Dallam, M. Theresa. "Is the Study of Latin Advantageous to the Study of English?" *Educational Review,* 54 (December 1917), 500-503.

Davis, Bennie Joe. "A Study of the Vocabulary Overlap between Words Written by Children and Words Written by Adults." Master's thesis, University of Texas, 1954.

Day, Margaret. "How Well Do High School Graduates Write?" *English Journal,* 32 (November 1943), 493-499.

DeBusk, Burchard W. "The Persistence of Language Errors among School Children," *University of Oregon Publication, Education Series,* 2 (May 1930), 71-91.

Delacato, Carl H. "A Comparison of Two Methods of Teaching Spelling," *Elementary English,* 29 (January 1952), 26-30.

DeLancey, Robert W. "Awareness of Form Class as a Factor in Reading Comprehension." Ph.D. dissertation, Syracuse University, 1962; in *Dissertation Abstracts,* 23, 8 (February 1963), 2975.

Dickerson, Douglas F. "Misleadings vs. Actualities in Spelling," *American School Board Journal,* 120 (February 1950), 33-34.

Diserens, Charles M. "The Experimental Psychology of Motivation," *Psychological Bulletin,* 28 (January 1931), 15-65.

Distad, H. W., and Eva M. Davis. "A Comparison of Column-Dictation and Sentence-Dictation Spelling with Respect to Acquisition of Meaning of Words," *Journal of Educational Research,* 20 (December 1929), 352-359.

Dolch, Edward W. *Better Spelling.* Champaign, Ill.: Garrard Press, 1942.

Douglass, Harl R., and Clifford Kittleson. "The Transfer of Training in High School Latin to English Grammar, Spelling, and Vocabulary," *Journal of Experimental Education,* 4 (September 1935), 26-33.

Doyle, Andrew M. "A Study of Spelling Achievement," *Catholic Educational Review,* 48 (1950), 171-174.

Dressel, Paul, John Schmid, and Gerald Kincaid. "The Effect of Writing Frequency upon Essay-type Writing Proficiency at the College Level," *Journal of Educational Research,* 46 (December 1952), 285-293.

Dupree, C. W. "A Comparative Experimental Study of the Pupil-Self-Study Method and the Modern-Systematic Method of Teaching Spelling," *Journal of Experimental Education,* 6 (September 1937), 1-6.

Eason, Joshua L. *A Diagnostic Study of Technical Incorrectness in the Writing of Graduates of Tennessee County High Schools.* Contributions to Education, No. 64. Nashville, Tenn.: George Peabody College for Teachers, 1929.

Edwards, Thomas D. "The Grammatical Approach," *School and Community,* 44 (April 1958), 18-21.

Eisman, Edward. "Individualized Spelling: Second Report," *Elementary English,* 40 (May 1963), 529-530.

Emery, Donald W. *Variant Spellings in Modern American Dictionaries.* Champaign, Ill.: National Council of Teachers of English, 1958.

Eschen, Clarence Von. "Teacher Performance on the Iowa Every-Pupil Test of Basic Skills in Reading and Language." Master's thesis, State University of Iowa, 1936.

Farmer, P., and Bernice Freeman. *The Teaching of English in Georgia.* Atlanta: Georgia Council of Teachers of English, 1952.

Fellows, John E. "The Influence of Theme-Reading and Theme-Correction on Eliminating Technical Errors in the Written Compositions of Ninth Grade Pupils," *University of Iowa Studies in Education,* 7, 1 (1932), 7-44.

Finkenbinder, E. O. "The Spelling of Homonyms: An Experimental Investigation of Teaching Them," *Pedagogical Seminary,* 30 (September 1923), 241-251.

Fitzgerald, James A. *A Basic Life Spelling Vocabulary*. Milwaukee, Wis.: Bruce Publishing Company, 1951.

_____. "Spelling Words Difficult for Children in Grades II-VI," *Elementary School Journal,* 53 (December 1952), 221-228.

_____. "The Vocabulary and Spelling Errors of Third-Grade Children's Life-Letters," *Elementary School Journal,* 38 (March 1938), 518-527.

Foerster, Norman, J. M. Steadman, Jr., and J. B. McMillan. *Writing and Thinking*. Boston: Houghton Mifflin Company, 1952.

Foster, Frederick M. "The Results of a Recent Spelling Test at the University of Iowa," *School and Society*, 5 (April 28, 1917), 506–508.

Fox, William H., and Merrill T. Eaton. "Analysis of the Spelling Proficiency of 82,833 Pupils in Grades 2 to 8 in 3,547 Teaching Units in the City Schools of Indiana," *Bulletin of the School of Education of Indiana University*, 22, 2 (1946), 9-45.

Francis, W. N. "Language and Linguistics in the English Program," *College English,* 26 (October 1964), 13-16.

_____. "New Perspectives on Teaching Language," *College English*, 23 (March 1962), 437–440.

Fries, Charles C. *The Teaching of the English Language*. New York: Thomas Nelson and Sons, 1927.

Frogner, Ellen. "A Study of the Relative Efficiency of a Grammatical and a Thought Approach to the Improvement of Sentence Structure in Grades Nine and Eleven." Ph.D. dissertation, University of Minnesota, 1938.

_____. "Grammar and Thought Approach in Improving Sentence Structure," *School Review,* 47 (November 1939), 663-675.

_____. "Grammar Approach Versus Thought Approach in Teaching Sentence Structure," *English Journal,* 28 (September 1939), 518-526.

Furness, Edna L., and Gertrude A. Boyd. "335 Real Spelling Demons for College Students," *College English,* 20 (March 1959), 292-295.

Garnett, Wilma L. "A Study of Status and Improvement of College Freshmen in Certain Skills of English Composition," *Journal of Experimental Education,* 6 (September 1937), 29-34.

Gates, Arthur I. *A List of Spelling Difficulties in 3876 Common Words.* New York: Bureau of Publications, Teachers College, Columbia University, 1937.

_____. "An Experimental Comparison of the Study-Test and Test-Study Methods in Spelling," *Journal of Educational Psychology,* 22 (January 1931), 1-19.

_____. *Generalization and Transfer in Spelling*. New York: Bureau of Publications, Teachers College, Columbia University, 1935.

Gates, Arthur I., and Frederick B. Graham. "The Value of Various Games and Activities in Teaching Spelling," *Journal of Educational Research,* 28 (September 1934), 1-9.

Gilbert, Luther C. "A Genetic Study of Growth in Perceptual Habits in Spelling," *Elementary School Journal,* 40 (January 1940), 346-357.

––––––. "An Experimental Investigation of Eye Movements in Learning to Spell Words," *Psychological Monographs,* 43, 3 (1932), 1-81.

––––––. "Effect of Reading on Spelling in the Ninth Grade," *School Review,* 42 (March 1934), 197-204.

––––––. "Experimental Investigation of a Flash-Card Method of Teaching Spelling," *Elementary School Journal,* 32 (January 1932), 337-351.

––––––. "Study of the Effect of Reading on Spelling," *Journal of Educational Research,* 28 (April 1935), 570-576.

Gilbert, Luther C., and Doris W. Gilbert. "The Improvement of Spelling through Reading," *Journal of Educational Research*, 37 (February 1944), 458–463.

––––––. "Training for Speed and Accuracy of Visual Perception in Learning to Spell." *University of California Publications in Education*, 7, 5 (1942), 351–426.

Gillis, Everett. "Fine Art of Diagraming," *Texas Outlook,* 25 (September 1941), 47-48.

Gleason, H. A., Jr. *Linguistics and English Grammar.* New York: Holt, Rinehart and Winston, Inc., 1965.

Gorrell, Robert M. "Giggles of Geese and a Pure of Meadowlarks," *College English,* 22 (May 1961), 555–561.

Goss, James E. "Analysis of Accuracy of Spelling in Written Compositions of Elementary School Children and the Effects of Proofreading Emphasis upon Accuracy." Ed.D. dissertation, University of Oklahoma, 1959; in *Dissertation Abstracts,* 20, 3 (September 1959), 967.

Gray, William S., and Eleanor Holmes. *The Development of Meaning Vocabularies in Reading: An Experimental Study.* Chicago: University of Chicago Press, 1938.

Greene, Harry, A. "Direct versus Formal Methods in Elementary English," *Elementary English,* 14 (May 1947), 273-285.

––––––. "Syllabication as a Factor in Learning to Spell," *Journal of Educational Research,* 8 (October 1923), 208-219.

––––––. *The New Iowa Spelling Scale.* Iowa City: State University of Iowa, 1954.

Greenwood, Forest O. "A Study of Spelling Difficulty on a High School Senior Level." Master's thesis, State University of Iowa, 1924.

Gruen, Ferdinand B. *English Grammar in American High Schools since 1900.* Ph.D. dissertation, Catholic University of America, 1934.

Guiler, Walter S. "Improving Ability in Spelling," *Elementary School Journal,* 30 (April 1930), 594-603.

Guiler, Walter Scribner, and Emmett Albert Betts. "A Critical Summary of Selective Research," *Elementary English Review,* 11 (March 1934), 75-118.

Guiler, W. S., and Gilbert A. Lease. "An Experimental Study of Methods of

Instruction in Spelling," *Elementary School Journal,* 43 (December 1942), 234-238.

Hackman, Roy B., and Henry W. Duel. "Do High School Students Who Study a Foreign Language Acquire Larger Vocabularies, Spell Their Words More Correctly, and Use Better English than High School Students Who Study No Foreign Language?" *Journal of the American Association of Collegiate Registrars,* 16 (January 1941), 155-162.

Hagman, Doris, and H. R. Laslett. "The Spelling Ability of High-School Pupils," *School and Society,* 73 (June 2, 1951), 347-348.

Hagstrum, Jean H. "Research in Written Composition," *College English,* 25 (October 1964), 53-56.

Hamblin, A. A. "An Investigation to Determine the Extent to Which the Effect of the Study of Latin upon a Knowledge of English Derivatives Can Be Increased by Conscious Adaptation of Content and Method to the Attainment of This Objective." Ph.D. dissertation, University of Pennsylvania, 1925.

Hanna, Paul R., Jean S. Hanna, Richard E. Hodges, and Erwin H. Rudorf. *Phoneme-Grapheme Correspondence as Cues to Spelling Improvement.* United States Office of Education Cooperative Research Project No. 1991. Washington, D. C.: U.S. Government Printing Office, 1966.

Hanna, Paul R., and James T. Moore. "Spelling—Spoken Word to Written Symbol," *Elementary School Journal,* 53 (February 1953), 329-337.

Harder, Keith C. "The Relative Efficiency of the 'Separate' and 'Together' Methods of Teaching Homonyms," *Journal of Experimental Education,* 6 (September 1937), 7-23.

Harris, Lynn Harold. "A Study in the Relation of Latin to English Composition," *School and Society,* 2 (August 14, 1915), 251–252.

Harris, Oliver E. "An Investigation of Spelling Achievement of Secondary-School Pupils," *Educational Administration and Supervision,* 34 (1948), 208-219.

Harris, Roland J. "An Experimental Inquiry into the Functions and Value of Formal Grammar in the Teaching of English, with Special Reference to the Teaching of Correct Written English to Children Aged Twelve to Fourteen." Ph.D. dissertation, University of London, 1962.

Haskell, Raymond I. "A Statistical Study of the Comparative Results Produced by Teaching Derivation in the Ninth-Grade Latin Classes and in the Ninth-Grade English Classes of Non-Latin Pupils in Four Philadelphia High Schools." Ph.D. dissertation, University of Pennsylvania, 1923.

Hauser, J. D. "An Investigation of the Writing Vocabularies of Representatives of an Economic Class," *Elementary School Journal,* 17 (1916-1917), 708-718.

Hawley, W. E., and Jackson Gallup. "The 'List' versus the 'Sentence' Method of Teaching Spelling," *Journal of Educational Research,* 5 (April 1922), 306-310.

Hays, Martha L. "The Spelling Ability of Normal Training Students in High School." Master's thesis, State University of Iowa, 1930.

Heilman, J. D. "A Study in Spelling," *Colorado State Teachers College Bulletin,* Research Bulletin No. 2, 18 (October 1918), 3-15.

Heys, Frank, Jr. "The Theme-a-Week Assumption: A Report of an Experiment," *English Journal,* 51 (May 1962), 320-322.

————. "Theme a Week?" *The English Leaflet,* 59 (Fall 1960), 28-31.

Hibler, Gladys H. "The Test-Study Method versus the Study-Test Method of Teaching Spelling in Grade Two: Study I." Master's thesis, University of Texas, 1957.

Hildreth, Gertrude. "An Evaluation of Spelling Word Lists and Vocabulary Studies," *Elementary School Journal,* 51 (January 1951), 254-265.

Hollingworth, Leta S. "The Psychological Examination of Poor Spellers," *Teachers College Record,* 20 (March 1919), 126-132.

Hollingsworth, Paul M. "Spelling Lists—Outdated?" *Elementary English,* 42 (January 1965), 151-152, 188.

Horn, Ernest. *A Basic Writing Vocabulary.* University of Iowa Monograph in Education. Iowa City: University of Iowa, 1926.

————."Spelling," *Encyclopedia of Educational Research.* New York: The Macmillan Company, 1960.

————. *Teaching Spelling.* "What Research Says to the Teacher," No. 3. Washington, D. C.: National Education Association, 1954.

————. "The Incidental Teaching of Spelling," *Elementary English Review,* 14 (January 1937), 3-5.

————. "The Influence of Past Experience upon Spelling," *Journal of Educational Research,* 19 (April 1929), 283-288.

————."The Vocabulary of Bankers' Letters," *English Journal*, 12 (June 1923), 383–397.

————. "The Vocabulary of Highly Personal Letters." Unpublished, 1922; reported by Horn in *A Basic Writing Vocabulary.*

Horn, Madeline. *A Study of the Vocabulary of Children Before Entering the First Grade.* Washington, D. C.: International Kindergarten Union, 1928.

Horn, Thomas D. "How Syllables Can Help in Spelling," *Education,* 76 (1956), 291-295.

————. "Learning to Spell as Affected by Syllabic Presentation of Words," *Elementary School Journal,* 49 (January 1949), 263-272.

————. "The Effect of Syllabic Presentation of Words upon Learning to Spell." Ph.D dissertation, State University of Iowa, 1947.

Hoyt, Franklin S. "The Place of Grammar in the Elementary Curriculum," *Teachers College Record,* 7 (November 1906), 467-498.

Humphrey, Marana O. "The Effect of a Syllabic Pronunciation of Words upon Learning to Spell." Master's thesis, University of Texas, 1954.

Hunnicutt, C. W., and William J. Iverson. *Research in the Three R's.* New York: Harper and Brothers, 1958. O.P.

Jespersen, Otto. *Growth and Structure of the English Language.* Ninth Edition. Oxford: Basil Blackwell, 1938.

Johnson, Falk S. "Structural Versus Non-structural Teaching," *College Composition and Communication,* 11 (December 1960), 214-215.

Johnson, Leslie W. "Study-Test Method Is Superior in Teaching Spelling," *Nation's Schools,* 46 (July 1950), 51-52.

Judd, Charles H., and Guy T. Buswell. *Silent Reading: A Study of Various Types.* Supplementary Educational Monographs, No. 23. Chicago: University of Chicago, 1922.

Keener, E. E. "Comparison of the Group and Individual Methods of Teaching Spelling," *Journal of Educational Method,* 6 (September 1926), 31-35.

Keyser, Margaret L. "The Incidental Learning of Spelling through Four Types of Word Presentation in Reading." Ed.D. dissertation, Boston University, 1948.

Kilzer, L. R. "The Test-Study Method Versus the Study-Test Method in Teaching Spelling," *School Review,* 34 (September 1926), 521-525.

King, Luella M. *Learning and Applying Spelling Rules in Grades 3 to 8.* New York: Bureau of Publications, Teachers College, Columbia University, 1931.

King, R. B. "Classical Allusions in Certain Newspapers and Magazines." Master's thesis, University of Wisconsin, 1922.

Kingsley, John H. "The Test-study Method Versus the Study-test Method in Spelling," *Elementary School Journal,* 24 (October 1923), 126-129.

Kirby, Thomas J. "Latin as Preparation for French," *School and Society,* 17 (November 10, 1923), 563-569.

· Kraus, Silvy. "A Comparison of Three Methods of Teaching Sentence Structure," *English Journal,* 46 (May 1957), 275-281.

———. "A Comparison of Three Methods of Teaching Sentence Structure." Ph.D. dissertation, University of Minnesota, 1956; in *Dissertation Abstracts,* 19, 11 (May 1959), 2808-2809.

La Brant, Lou. *We Teach English.* New York: Harcourt, Brace & Company, 1951. O.P.

———. "Writing Is Learned by Writing," *English Journal,* 30 (November 1953), 417-420.

Lamberts, J. J. "Basic Concepts for Teaching from Structural Linguistics," *English Journal,* 49 (March 1960), 172-176.

Lange, Phil C. "A Sampling of Composition Errors of College Freshmen in a Course Other Than English," *Journal of Educational Research,* 42 (November 1948), 191-200.

Lawler, Lillian B. "The Potential Remediability of Errors in English Spelling through the Study of High School Latin," *Classical Journal,* 21 (November 1925), 132-148.

Ledbetter, Bernice K. "The Test-Study Method versus the Study-Test Method of Teaching Spelling in Grade Two: Study III." Master's thesis, University of Texas, 1959.

Lees, Robert B. "The Promise of Transformational Grammar," *English Journal,* 52 (May 1963), 327-330, 345.

Leonard, Sterling A. *Current English Usage.* English Monograph, No. 1. Chicago: National Council of Teachers of English, 1932. O.P.

――――. *The Doctrine of Correctness in English Usage, 1700-1800.* University of Wisconsin Studies in Language and Literature, No. 25. Madison, Wis.: University of Wisconsin, 1929.

Lin, San-su C. *Pattern Practice in the Teaching of Standard English to Students with a Non-Standard Dialect.* United States Office of Education Cooperative Research Project No. 1339. New York: Bureau of Publications, Teachers College, Columbia University, 1965.

Link, Frances R., and Edgar H. Schuster. "Linguistics in High School," *Educational Leadership,* 19 (February 1962), 294-299.

Lokke, Virgil L., and George S. Wykoff. "'Double Writing' in Freshman Composition—An Experiment," *School and Society,* 68 (December 18, 1948), 437-439.

MacMillan, Betty. "The Value of Diagrams in Teaching Grammar," *Volta Review,* 34 (June 1932), 277-278.

Madsen, Joan M. "A Study of Current Practices in the Teaching of Latin in the Public High Schools of the State of Illinois, 1956-57." Ph.D. dissertation, University of Illinois, 1958; in *Dissertation Abstracts,* 19, 10 (April 1959), 2549-2550.

Maize, Ray C. "A Study of Two Methods of Teaching English Composition to Retarded College Freshmen." Ph.D. dissertation, Purdue University, 1952.

Makey, Herman O. "A Means or an End?" *English Journal,* 42 (March 1953), 159-160.

Malter, Morton S. "Children's Ability to Read Diagrammatic Materials," *Elementary School Journal,* 49 (September 1948), 98-102.

――――. "The Ability of Children to Read a Process-Diagram," *Journal of Educational Psychology,* 38 (May 1947), 290-298.

――――. "The Ability of Children to Read Conventionalized Diagrammatic Symbols," *Journal of Educational Psychology,* 39 (January 1948), 27-34.

――――. "The Ability of Children to Read Cross-Sections," *Journal of Educational Psychology,* 38 (March 1947), 157-166.

Marckwardt, Albert H., and Frederic G. Cassidy. *Scribner Handbook of English.* Fourth Edition. New York: Charles Scribner's Sons, 1967.

Masters, Harry V. "A Study of Spelling Errors," *University of Iowa Studies in Education,* 4, 4 (1927), 8-80.

Mathews, Mitford M. *A Survey of English Dictionaries.* London: Oxford University Press, 1933; New York: Russell and Russell Publishers, 1965.

McCann, Letitia M. "Writing Vocabularies: A Comparison of the Nature, Extent, and Mobility of Child and Adult Writing Needs." Master's thesis, University of Texas, 1955.

McColly, William. *Comparative Effectiveness of Composition Skills Learning Activities in the Secondary School.* United States Office of Education Cooperative Research Project No. 1528. Madison: University of Wisconsin, 1963.

McKee, Paul. "Teaching and Testing Spelling by Column and Context Forms." Ph.D. dissertation, State University of Iowa, 1924.

_____. "Teaching Spelling by Column and Context Forms," *Journal of Educational Research,* 15 (April and May 1927), 246-255 and 339-348.

Mearns, Hughes. "A Report on a Specific Spelling Situation," *Teachers College Record,* 26 (November 1924), 220-229.

Meckel, Henry C. "Research on Teaching Composition and Literature," in N. L. Gage, *Handbook of Research on Teaching.* American Educational Research Association of the National Education Association. Chicago: Rand McNally and Company, 1963.

Mellon, John C. *Transformational Sentence-Combining: A Method for Enhancing the Development of Syntactic Fluency in English Composition.* United States Office of Education Cooperative Research Project No. 5-8418. Cambridge, Mass.: Graduate School of Education, Harvard University, 1967.

Mendenhall, James E. *An Analysis of Spelling Errors.* New York: Bureau of Publications, Teachers College, Columbia University, 1930.

Mersand, Joseph. *Attitudes toward English Teaching.* Philadelphia: Chilton Company, 1961.

_____. "What Has Happened to Written Composition?" *English Journal,* 50 (April 1961), 231-237.

Miller, Frances. "Structural Plotting for Understanding," *English Journal,* 51 (December 1962), 632-639.

Miller, George R., Jr., and Thomas H. Briggs. "The Effect of Latin Translations on English," *School Review,* 31 (December 1923), 756-762.

Milligan, John P. "An Evaluation of Two Methods of Teaching Written Sentence Structure," *Elementary English Review,* 16 (March 1939), 91-92, 106.

Montgomery, Margaret A. "The Test-Study Method versus the Study-Test Method of Teaching Spelling in Grade Two: Study II." Master's thesis, University of Texas, 1957.

Moore, James T. "Phonetic Elements in a Three-thousand Word Spelling Vocabulary." Ed.D. dissertation, Leland Stanford Junior University, 1951.

Morrison, Ida E., and Ida F. Perry. "Spelling and Reading Relationships with Incidence of Retardation and Acceleration," *Journal of Educational Research,* 52 (February 1959), 222-227.

Morse, William C. "A Comparison of the Eye-Movements of Average Fifth- and Seventh-Grade Pupils Reading Materials of Corresponding Difficulty," *Studies in the Psychology of Reading.* University of Michigan Monograph in Education. Ann Arbor: University of Michigan Press, 1951.

Morton, Myrtle. "A Study of the Preparation of Normal Training Students for Teaching Certain Basic Skills." Master's thesis, State University of Iowa, 1936.

Newcomb, Edith I. "A Comparison of the Latin and Non-Latin Groups in High School," *Teachers College Record,* 23 (November 1922), 412-422.

Ney, James W. "Applied Linguistics in the Seventh Grade," *English Journal,* 55 (October 1966), 895-897, 902.

Nicholson, Anne. *A Speller for Use of the Teachers of California.* Sacramento: California State Printing Office, 1914.

Nilsen, Don L. F. "New Diagrams for Old," *English Record,* 16 (October 1965), 20-23, 34-36.

O'Donnell, Roy C. *The Correlation of Awareness of Structural Relationships in English and Ability in Written Composition.* United States Office of Education Cooperative Research Project No. 1524. Mount Olive, N. C.: Mount Olive College, 1963.

Olson, Willard C. "Reading Is a Function of the Total Growth of the Child," in W. S. Gray, ed., *Reading and Pupil Development,* Proceedings of the Conference in Reading at the University of Chicago. Supplementary Educational Monographs, No. 51. Chicago: University of Chicago Press, 1940.

Orleans, Jacob S. "Possible Transfer Value of the Study of Latin to English Vocabulary," *School and Society,* 16 (November 11, 1922), 559-560.

Osburn, Worth J. "Teaching Spelling by Teaching Syllables and Root Words," *Elementary School Journal,* 55 (September 1954), 32–41.

Otis, Alvah Talbot. "The Relation of Latin Study to Ability in English Vocabulary and Composition," *School Review,* 30 (January 1922), 45–50.

Otterman, Lois M. "The Value of Teaching Prefixes and Word-Roots," *Journal of Educational Research,* 48 (April 1955), 611–616.

Peake, Nellie L. "Relation between Spelling Ability and Reading Ability," *Journal of Experimental Education,* 9 (December 1940), 192–193.

Pearson, Henry C. "The Scientific Study of the Teaching of Spelling," *Journal of Educational Psychology,* 2 (May 1911), 241–252.

Peavy, Katherine B. "Shall We Teach Diagraming?" *The Instructor,* 67 (February 1958), 108-109.

Petty, Walter T. "An Analysis of Certain Phonetic Elements in a Selected List of Persistently Difficult Spelling Words." Ph.D. dissertation, University of Iowa, 1955; in *Dissertation Abstracts,* 15, 8 (February 1955), 1359-1360.

Pollock, Thomas C. "Spelling Report," *College English,* 16 (November 1954), 102–109.

Pond, Frederick L. "Influence of the Study of Latin on Word Knowledge," *School Review,* 46 (October 1938), 611-618.

Pooley, Robert C. "Looking Ahead in Grammar," *Bulletin of the National Association of Secondary School Principals,* 39 (September 1955), 56-61.

_____. "The English Teacher's Preparation in Speech," *English Journal,* 45 (April 1956), 181-187, 200.

Pooley, Robert C., and Robert D. Williams. *The Teaching of English in Wisconsin.* Madison, Wis.: University of Wisconsin Press, 1948.

Postman, Neil. "Linguistics and the Pursuit of Relevance," *Education Synopsis,* 12 (Winter 1966-1967), 25-30.

Potter, Simeon. *Modern Linguistics.* New York: W. W. Norton and Company, 1964.

Rapeer, Louis W. "The Problem of Formal Grammar in Elementary Education," *Journal of Educational Psychology,* 4 (March 1913), 125-137.

Raub, Donna Kay. "The Audio-Lingual Drill Technique." Master's thesis, George Peabody College for Teachers, 1966.

Reed, Alonzo, and Brainerd Kellogg. *Higher Lessons in English.* New York: Maynard, Merrill and Company, 1877. O.P.

Reid, Hale C., and A. N. Hieronymus. *An Evaluation of Five Methods of Teaching Spelling in the Second and Third Grades.* United States Office of Education Cooperative Research Project No. 1869, 1963.

Rice, J. M. "The Futility of the Spelling Grind," *Forum,* 23 (April and June 1897), 163–173, 409–419.

Richardson, Eva A. "An Examination of the Spelling Ability of County Normal Students in Ohio." Master's thesis, State University of Iowa, 1925.

Rinsland, Henry D. *A Basic Vocabulary of Elementary School Children.* New York: The Macmillan Company, 1945.

Rivlin, Harry N. "English Grammar as Preparation for the Study of a Modern Foreign Language," *English Journal,* 23 (March 1934), 202-207.

Roberts, Paul. "Linguistics and the Teaching of Composition," *English Journal,* 52 (May 1963), 331-335.

_____."The Relation of Linguistics to the Teaching of English," *College English,* 22 (October 1960), 1-9.

Robertson, Stuart, and Frederic G. Cassidy. *The Development of Modern English.* Second Edition. New York: Prentice-Hall, Inc., 1954.

Robinson, Nora. "The Relation between Knowledge of English Grammar and Ability in English Composition." M.Ed. thesis, University of Manchester, 1959; in *British Journal of Educational Psychology,* Part II, 30 (June 1960), 184-186.

Rogness, Alton S. "Grouping Spelling Words According to the Rule." Ed.D. dissertation, Colorado State College of Education, 1953.

Rohan, Ben J. "An Experiment in Spelling," *Journal of Educational Method,* 2 (June 1923), 412-414.

Rorabacher, Louise E. *A Concise Guide to Composition.* New York: Harper and Brothers, 1958. [Second Edition, Harper and Row, Publishers, 1963.]

Rosegrant, William R. "Scientific Research Can Become Respectable?" *College Composition and Communication,* 15 (October 1964), 170.

Rusk, R. R. "Analysis of Spelling Errors of Adults," *Journal of Experimental Education,* 2 (June 1913), 119-122.

Russell, David H. "NCTE Counciletter," *English Journal,* 24 (November 1963), 639-642.

_____. "Spelling Ability in Relation to Reading and Vocabulary Achievements," *Elementary English Review,* 23 (January 1946), 32-37.

Sand, Harold J. "An Evaluation of the Effects of Marks as Incentives to Pupil Growth in Spelling Ability and of the Comparative Values of Equated Scales and Informal Tests as Measures of the Progress," *Journal of Educational Research,* 31 (May 1938), 678-682.

Sartorius, Ina C. *Generalization in Spelling.* New York: Bureau of Publications, Teachers College, Columbia University, 1931.

Schiller, Andrew. "The Coming Revolution in Teaching English," *Harper's Magazine,* 229 (October 1964), 82-92.

Schoephoerster, Hugh. "Research into Variations of the Test-Study Plan of Teaching Spelling," *Elementary English,* 39 (May 1962), 460-462.

Scott, F. N., and J. V. Denney. *Elementary English Composition.* Boston: Allyn & Bacon, Inc., 1900.

Schuster, Edgar H. "How Good Is the New Grammar?" *English Journal,* 50 (September 1961), 392-397.

Segal, David, and Nora R. Barr. "Relation of Achievement in Formal Grammar to Achievement in Applied Grammar," *Journal of Educational Research,* 14 (December 1926), 401-402.

Senour, A. D. "An Investigation of the Effectiveness of the Test-Teach-Test Method of Instruction in Spelling," *Elementary School Journal,* 30 (May 1930), 700-706.

Sherwood, John C. "Dr. Kinsey and Professor Fries," *College English,* 21 (February 1960), 275-280.

Shubik, Helen M. "An Experimental Comparison of the Test-Study Methods of Teaching Spelling in the Third Grade." Master's thesis, Fordham University, 1951.

Sifert, E. R. "A Comparative Study of the Abilities of 8th Grade Children to Spell Studied and Unstudied Words." Master's thesis, State University of Iowa, 1926.

Sister Evangelist Marie. "A Study of Teaching Rules in Spelling," *Elementary English,* 40 (October 1963), 602-604, 647.

Sister M. Gervase Blanchard. "An Experimental Comparison of the Test-Study and Study-Test Methods of Teaching Spelling in the Eighth Grade." Master's thesis, Fordham University, 1944.

Sisters of Notre Dame. "Grammatical Analysis," *Catholic School Journal,* 57 (November 1957), 310.

Sledd, James, and Wilma R. Ebbitt. *Dictionaries and THAT Dictionary.* Glenview, Ill.: Scott, Foresman and Company, 1962.

Smith, Dora V. *Evaluating Instruction in Secondary School English.* A Report of a Division of the New York Regents Inquiry into the Character and Cost of Public Education in New York State. English Monograph, No. 11. Chicago: National Council of Teachers of English, 1941. O.P.

_____. *Instruction in English.* United States Office of Education Monographs, No. 20. Washington, D.C.: United States Governement Printing Office, 1933.

Smith, Henry Lester, and Merrill T. Eaton. "A Study of the English Usage Spelling, and Vocabulary of 251 Graduate Students at Indiana University," *Bulletin of the School of Education of Indiana University*, 16, 5 (1940), 7-68.

Smith, Rosemary A. "Practice in Writing Versus Drill in Mechanics." Master's thesis, University of Colorado, 1948.

Spache, George. "A Minimum Reading-Spelling Vocabulary for Remedial Work," *Journal of Educational Research,* 33 (November 1939), 171-174.

Sparrow, Julia L. "A Study of the Relationship between Spelling Ability and Reading Ability," Ph.D. dissertation, State University of Iowa, 1951.

Stewart, James Reese. "The Effect of Diagraming on Certain Skills in English Composition," *Journal of Experimental Education,* 11 (September 1942), 1-8.

Stone, George Winchester, Jr., ed. *Issues, Problems, and Approaches in the Teaching of English.* New York: Holt, Rinehart and Winston, Inc., 1961.

Strom, Ingrid M. "Do Grammar Drills Help Writing Skills?" *NEA Journal,* 49 (December 1960), 25.

_____. "Does Knowledge of Grammar Improve Reading?" *English Journal,* 45 (March 1956), 129-133.

_____. Research in Grammar and Usage and Its Implications for Teaching Writing. Bulletin of the School of Education of Indiana University, 36, 5 (September 1960).

_____. "Summary of Investigations Relating to the English Language Arts in Secondary Education: 1959–1960," *English Journal,* 50 (February 1961), 111-125.

_____. "Summary of Investigations Relating to the English Language Arts in Secondary Education: 1960-1961, *"English Journal,* 51 (February 1962), 123-140.

Suggs, Lena R. "Structural Grammar Versus Traditional Grammar in Influencing Writing," *English Journal,* 50 (March 1961), 174-178.

Swenson, Esther J., and Charles G. Caldwell. "The Process of Communication in Children's Letters," *Elementary School Journal,* 49 (October 1948) 79-88.

Symonds, Percival M. "Practice Versus Grammar in the Learning of Correct English Usage," *Journal of Educational Psychology,* 22 (February 1931) 81-95.

Symonds, Percival M., and Edith M. Penney. "The Increasing of English Vocabulary in the English Class," *Journal of Educational Research,* 15 (February 1927), 93-103.

Templin, Mildred C. "Phonic Knowledge and Its Relation to the Spelling and Reading Achievement of Fourth Grade Pupils," *Journal of Educational Research,* 7 (February 1954), 441-454.

Third Yearbook of the Department of Superintendence. 1925.

Thompson, Robert S. *The Effectiveness of Modern Spelling Instruction.* New York: Bureau of Publications, Teachers College, Columbia University, 1930.

Thorndike, E. L. "The Gains Made in Ability in English by Pupils Who Study Latin and by Pupils Who Do Not," *School and Society,* 18 (December 8, 1923), 690.

Thorndike, Edward L., and Irving Lorge. *The Teacher's Word Book of 30,000 Words.* New York: Teachers College, Columbia University, 1944.

Thorndike, E. L., and G. J. Ruger. "The Effect of First-year Latin upon Knowledge of English Words of Latin Derivation," *School and Society,* 18 (September 1, 1923), 260-270.

Tidyman, W. F. "A Critical Study of Rice's Investigation of Spelling Efficiency," *Pedagogical Seminary,* 22 (September 1915), 391-400.

Tidyman, W. F., and Edith Johnson. "Value of Grouping Words According to Similar Difficulties in Spelling," *Journal of Educational Research,* 10 (November 1924), 297-301.

Tinker, Miles A. "Eye Movements in Reading," *Journal of Educational Research,* 30 (December 1936), 241-277.

_____. "The Study of Eye Movements in Reading," *Psychological Bulletin,* 43 (March 1946), 93-120.

Tireman, Loyd S. "The Determination of the Ability of a Group of Sixth, Seventh, and Eighth Grade Pupils to Proofread Their Written Work for Errors in Spelling." Master's thesis, State University of Iowa, 1924.

_____. "Value of Marking Hard Spots in Spelling," *University of Iowa Studies in Education,* 5, 4 (1930), 1-48.

Tone, Robert L. "The Value of Rules for Teaching Derived Forms in Spelling." Master's thesis, State University of Iowa, 1924.

Tovatt, Anthony L. "Diagraming: A Sterile Skill," *English Journal,* 41February 1952), 91-93.

Tovatt, Anthony, and Arno Jewett. "This World of English," *English Journal,* 49 (March 1960), 192-196.

Townsend, Agatha. "An Investigation of Certain Relationships of Spelling with Reading and Academic Aptitude," *Journal of Educational Research,* 40 (February 1947), 465-471.

Wagner, C. A. "Experimental Study of Grouping by Similarity as a factor in the Teaching of Spelling." Ph.D. dissertation, University of Pennsylvania, 1912.

Walker, Louisa V. "Latin in Current Periodicals and Newspapers." Ph.D. dissertation, University of Wisconsin, 1923.

Wallin, J. E. W. *Spelling Efficiency in Relation to Age, Grade, and Sex and the Question of Transfer.* Baltimore: Warwick and York, 1911.

Warner, Paul G., and Walter S. Guiler. "Individual *vs.* Group Instruction in Grammatical Usage," *Journal of Educational Psychology,* 24 (February, 1933), 140-151.

Watson, Alice F. *Experimental Studies in the Psychology and Pedagogy of Spelling.* New York: Bureau of Publications, Teachers College, Columbia University, 1935.

Weinfeld, Frederic D. "A Factor Analytic Approach to the Measurement of Differential Effects of Training: An Evaluation of Three Methods of Teaching Composition." Ed.D. dissertation, Graduate School of Education, Harvard University, 1959.

Westover, Frederick L. *Controlled Eye Movements versus Practice Exercises in Reading.* New York: Bureau of Publications, Teachers College, Columbia University, 1946.

Wheat, Leonard B. "Four Spelling Rules," *Elementary School Journal,* 32 (May 1932), 697-706.

Wheeler, Arville. "A Study to Determine the Errors That Appear in Written Work of Rural and Urban Pupils in Certain School Systems in Kentucky," *Journal of Experimental Education,* 8 (June 1940), 385-398.

Wilcox, Myron J. "The Use of a Rule in Teaching Spelling." Master's thesis, State University of Iowa, 1917.

Williams, Robert D. "Linguistics and Grammar," *English Journal,* 48 (October 1959), 388-392.

Wilson, Louis A. "Children's Spelling Needs and Their Implications for Classroom Procedure," *Elementary School Journal,* 47 (October 1946), 98-102.

Winch, W. H. "Additional Researches on Learning to Spell: The Question of 'Transfer' and of 'Direct' versus 'Indirect' Methods," *Journal of Educational Psychology,* 7 (February 1916), 93-110.

_____. "Experimental Researches on Learning to Spell," *Journal of Educational Psychology,* 4 (November 1913), 524-537.

Wise, Carl T. "Selection and Gradation of Words in Spelling," *Elementary School Journal,* 34 (June 1934), 754-766.

Withers, A. M. "Professors of English on the Latin Question," *Educational Forum,* 13 (January 1949), 219-225.

_____. "What It Takes to Get English," *Word Study,* 26 (October 1959), 1-4.

Wolfe, Don M. *Creative Ways to Teach English.* Second Edition. New York: Odyssey Press, 1966.

_____. "Diagraming: Trust Your Experience, Not Theories," *Clearing House,* 27 (February 1953), 349-353.

Wolfe, H. Alena, and F. S. Breed. "An Experimental Study of Syllabication in Spelling," *School and Society,* 15 (June 3, 1922), 616-622.

Woodring, Maxie N. *A Study of the Quality of English in Latin Translations.* New York: Bureau of Publications, Columbia University, 1925.

Wykoff, George S. "The Relation of a Knowledge of Grammar and Punctuation to Writing," *Educational Administration and Supervision,* 31 (October 1945), 385-393.

Zahner, Louis, and others. *Language in General Education.* New York: Appleton-Century-Crofts, 1940.

Zais, Robert S. "The Linguistic Characteristics of Punctuation Symbols and the Teaching of Punctuation Skills," *English Journal,* 52 (December 1963), 677-681.

Zedler, Empress Y. "Effect of Phonic Training on Speech Sound Discrimination and Spelling Performance," *Journal of Speech and Hearing Disorders,* 21 (June 1956), 245-250.

Zidonis, Frank J. "Generative Grammar: A Report of Research," *English Journal,* 54 (May 1965), 405-409.